D0481690

WHAT WAS
LIBERALISM?

WHAT WAS LIBERALISM?

THE PAST, PRESENT, AND PROMISE OF A NOBLE IDEA

JAMES TRAUB

BASIC BOOKS
New York

Basic Books
Hachette Book Group
1290 Avenue of the Americas, New York, NY 10104
www.basicbooks.com

Printed in the United States of America
First Edition: September 2019
Published by Basic Books, an imprint of Perseus Books, LLC, a subsidiary of Hachette Book Group, Inc. The Basic Books name and logo is a trademark of the Hachette Book Group.

The Hachette Speakers Bureau provides a wide range of authors for speaking events. To find out more, go to www.hachettespeakersbureau.com or call (866) 376-6591.

The publisher is not responsible for websites (or their content) that are not owned by the publisher.

Print book interior design by Linda Mark.

The Library of Congress has cataloged the hardcover edition as follows:

Names: Traub, James, author.
Title: What was liberalism? : the past, present and promise of a noble idea / James Traub.
Description: First edition. | New York : Basic Books, 2019. | Includes bibliographical references and index. |
Identifiers: LCCN 2019011714 (print) | LCCN 2019016345 (ebook) | ISBN 9781541616844 (ebook) | ISBN 9781541616851 (hardcover)
Subjects: LCSH: Liberalism—History. | Liberty—History.
Classification: LCC JC574 (ebook) | LCC JC574 .T73 2019 (print) | DDC 320.51—dc23
LC record available at https://lccn.loc.gov/2019011714
ISBNs: 978-1-541-61685-1 (hardcover), 978-1-541-61684-4 (ebook)

LSC-C

10 9 8 7 6 5 4 3 2 1

To my mother

Contents

Why Liberalism Matters

WHEN I WAS BORN, IN 1954, AMERICANS USED THE WORD *liberal* to describe almost everything they liked about themselves. "The American assumes liberalism as one of the presuppositions of life," the historian Arthur Schlesinger Jr. wrote at the time. "He is, by nature, a gradualist; he sees few problems which cannot be solved by reason and debate; and he is confident that nearly all problems can be solved." Liberalism meant optimism, rationalism, pragmatism, secularism. It was not so much a political platform as a national disposition. In his 1955 book *The Liberal Tradition in America*, Louis Hartz, another celebrated Harvard historian, observed that America had never had a national Liberal Party because it would have been superfluous; America, he wrote, echoing Alexis de Tocqueville, had been born liberal. At the time, of course, the president, Dwight Eisenhower, was a Republican, but his election had only confirmed the liberal consensus, for the 1952 Republican platform had accepted for the first time the programs of the New Deal, including Social Security. For all their very real disagreements, the two parties professed a broad faith in free markets, a modest commitment to deploying the state to protect vulnerable citizens and promote public goods, and a bedrock respect for individual rights.[1]

In the America of my boyhood, everything and everyone seemed to be liberal. My father voted Republican—but liberal Republican. My mother was an actual card-carrying member of New York's thoroughly marginal Liberal Party. The only really bad people in our household politics were the crackpots who joined the far-right John Birch Society, founded by candy manufacturer Robert Welch. We were not allowed to eat Sugar Babies because he made them. The only time we saw what we considered the lunatic fringe advance anywhere near the middle of American society was in 1964, when the Republicans nominated for president Barry Goldwater, the Arizona senator who seemed to be prepared to fight World War III in order to defeat Communism. "Extremism in defense of liberty is no vice," Goldwater said. But Communism didn't threaten our liberty; extremism did. At Rosh Hashanah services at my temple in suburban New York, a few weeks before the election, the rabbi, who never spoke about politics on the High Holy Days, implored the congregants to vote for President Lyndon Johnson. They did, of course, and the rout Goldwater suffered felt like a decisive response to anti-liberalism.

In fact, the story was much more complicated than that. Goldwater joined a rabid Cold War conservatism to a tradition of anti-statist free-market liberalism that could be traced back to Adam Smith, or even to John Locke. In 1980, Ronald Reagan, once Goldwater's most effective proxy, became president. Throughout my adult life, these right-liberals, who called themselves conservatives, traded power with left-liberals, who generally called themselves progressives. When Francis Fukuyama famously argued in 1989 that history had come to an end because liberalism had defeated all its ideological rivals, he had in mind this broader, older understanding of the word. Democrats and Republicans were much further apart in 1989 than they had been in 1954, but both were recognizably heirs of the liberal tradition.

Yet that familiar left-right world now seems almost as archaic as the postwar consensus. We—not just Americans but citizens of the West—live in a world where liberalism, however understood, is under dire threat from illiberalism. For all the vast differences between them, George W. Bush and Barack Obama have more in common with each other than they do with Donald Trump—or with Viktor Orbán or Jarosław Kaczyński, the autocratic populists who dominate the politics of, respectively, Hungary and Poland. Though in 2016 he sought and won the nomination of the institutional party of conservatism, the party of free markets and small government, Trump openly mocked the alleged benefits of free trade and promised to protect Social Security and Medicare. He gleefully flouted elements of the liberal consensus that conservatives in the past had only clandestinely transgressed. This plutocratic populist trafficked in fear rather than hope; luridly evoked the dangers that people of color, especially immigrants, allegedly posed to his white audience; encouraged acts of violence against protesters; invented whatever facts suited his purpose. If voters had wanted a conservative, they could have chosen one from among his seventeen rivals for the GOP nomination; yet Trump dispatched them with ease. He has ruled precisely as he campaigned. And he remains, as of this writing, the darling of his own party.

The rise of illiberalism is the greatest shock of my political life. And it's precisely because I grew up in a world of consensual liberalism that Trump's election seemed to come out of the blue. I thought political life was confined to the oscillations between left and right, as, I think, did most people of my generation, and for that matter most politicians. Liberals and conservatives thought that the greatest threat to the American future was one another. They were wrong. The greatest threat is that we will normalize violence and hatred; that we will abandon science, facts, and reason itself; that we will marginalize and persecute minorities. The twentieth century shows us how very short the path is from populism to authoritarianism.

Now that we know that a world exists beyond the confines of liberalism, we must think about what is precious in that legacy and what we are in danger of losing. That means, first, recognizing what liberalism is and isn't. We are in the habit of using the expression "liberal democracy" as if it were redundant—as if liberalism were intrinsically democratic and democracy inherently liberal. Yet liberalism first arose as a corrective to systems of majority rule. James Madison famously warned of the dangers of the "tyranny of the majority," an expression one finds echoed in the works of Alexis de Tocqueville and John Stuart Mill, the great liberal thinkers of the middle of the nineteenth century. There is no inherent reason why the unlimited right of free speech, or the right to do as you wish so long as it doesn't harm others, should enjoy majority support. Some core liberal principles, such as protecting the rights of political minorities, or of any kind of minorities, are countermajoritarian.

Some early liberals were deeply skeptical that individual freedom could be reconciled with majority rule at all. Others, including of course the Founders, believed that liberty could be made compatible with equality. Many of the mechanisms that we associate with democracy itself, such as the separation of powers, serve to limit the reach of the democratic state and thus protect each of us from all of us. But formal structures are not the whole story. Mill and Tocqueville both would have said that what matters most, in the end, are not explicit rules but values and habits, or what we would now call "norms": freedom of speech, for example, will survive only so long as people are prepared to defend it. This was the great lesson of the rise of totalitarianism in the middle of the twentieth century. Though Weimar Germany was formally liberal and democratic, the German people ultimately acquiesced to the surrender of their liberties in the name of an immense collective purpose. From the terrifying experience of totalitarianism the great midcentury liberals, above all Isaiah Berlin, saw how monstrous leaders could lead a whole people into tyranny. Liberalism was far more fragile than it looked; under sufficient pressure, people could abandon what appeared to be settled beliefs.

Liberalism and majoritarianism act as restraints upon one another. They function, or should function, as one another's conscience. A liberalism that simply defers to the majority will is scarcely worth defending. At the same time, liberalism presupposes a respect for the individual and for her capacity to choose her own path. Liberalism without democratic support dwindles into elitism: liberals are left bemoaning mass ignorance while the ordinary citizen responds with a sense of resentment that cynical leaders know very well how to exploit. That is more or less the quandary in which liberals find themselves today.

I chose to write this book as the history of an idea, rather than as a diagnosis of a sudden illness, because we cannot make sense of the crisis we now find ourselves in unless we understand what liberalism is and how it developed. How did liberalism gain the consensual status it enjoyed in much of the twentieth century? What happened to erode that support? Did the material circumstances that had made liberalism into a majoritarian faith disappear? Did conservatives undermine liberalism? Did liberals themselves lose their way? Mine is hardly the first history of liberalism. But even so recent a work as Edmund Fawcett's erudite *Liberalism: The Life of an Idea*, published in 2014, was written from the safe perch of dueling liberalisms. We look differently at the idea now that we see that it is in danger of disappearing. Understanding liberalism's development will help us redeem the idea both from the contempt with which conservatives disfigured it and from the triumphant vacuity that obscured its meaning during the Cold War era.

The problem of vacuity, of liberalism as all good things, is not easily dismissed, for liberalism suffers from conceptual indistinctness. As an idea, it has less internal coherence than a codified orthodoxy like communism, though more than a mere mood, like Romanticism. Like its twin, conservatism, liberalism is a word that has proved to be so compelling that it has remained in use even as the context in which it is used has changed drastically, to the point that people of radically different views regard themselves as the true heirs of the liberal tradition. But if liberalism doesn't have a fully coherent inner logic, it does have a taxonomy, a set of species relationships to which a common ancestor contributed the original genes.

Liberalism begins with the idea of limited government. Sovereignty rests with the body of the people, as Locke said; they make a limited grant of that power to their rulers. (Many liberals nevertheless reject Locke's metaphor of a contract, as well as his belief in natural law.) All forms of absolute power violate that premise. The only secure protections against absolutism are rules and institutions limiting the power of the state—the separation of powers, an elected legislature dedicated to open and public debate, an independent judiciary. What distinguishes *constitutional liberalism* from this broader idea of limited government is the recognition that absolute power can no more be vested in "the people" than it can in an executive. The legislative supremacy of the French Revolution was as dangerous to liberty as the absolute monarchy that it replaced. The state must be designed in such a way as to protect individuals from all forms of arbitrary power, an axiom made explicit in the Bill of Rights of the US Constitution. Such a state need not be democratic in the sense that power is determined through regular elections among the whole body of citizens. It need not even be republican: Louis Philippe I accepted the French throne in 1830 under a liberal constitutional design.

If constitutional liberalism is concerned with the relationship between the state and the individual, *personal liberalism* defines the sphere of inviolate personal rights. Personal liberalism depends on a modern understanding of the self. The Founders, imbued as they were with a Roman sense of patriotism and citizenship, saw individuals as public beings endowed not just with rights but also with civic obligations. Only when this neoclassical sensibility gave way to the Romanticism of the nineteenth century did individuals come to be seen rather as subjective beings dedicated to their own development. The first political thinker to found a liberal vision on this modern sense of personhood, and then to systematically define the contents of the protected sphere of the individual, was John Stuart Mill. In his 1861 essay *On Liberty*, Mill defended an almost unlimited freedom of expression but also of behavior—what he called "experiments of living." The threat that preoccupied him was not the state but "society," which seeks to compel conformity. Modern liberals share Mill's sense that no one way of being is intrinsically right, that society profits from a diversity of ideas and even lifestyles, that to submit to the dictation of society is to restrict what is most precious—your individual, particular self. Isaiah Berlin would use the expression "negative liberty" to describe Mill's concept of the right to speak, think, and act as you wish.

The foundation of *economic liberalism* is Locke's claim that people form commonwealths in order to protect their property. Self-interest is not a Christian sin; it is the law of nature. A century later, Adam Smith added the idea that the most effective means of promoting this natural wish for gain is through the self-regulating mechanism of the marketplace, guided by an "invisible hand" that makes self-interest the instrument of collective good. Much of nineteenth-century English thinking was shaped by this association of liberty with economic self-interest. In the twentieth century the idea was taken up by Austrian thinkers like Friedrich Hayek, who argued that even the modest inroads on liberty imposed by the democratic regimes of the 1920s and '30s had paved the way for fascism. Free-market liberalism was then popularized by American neo-conservatives and installed as a governing principle by Ronald Reagan and Margaret Thatcher. Nothing has introduced as much terminological confusion into liberalism as the free-market doctrine, both because latter-day liberals hold a much more expansive view of the state than do the legatees of Hayek, whom they thus regard as conservative, and because many free-market liberals do, in fact, hold classically conservative views of social policy as well as foreign affairs.

Finally, *political liberalism*, which fuses liberalism in all its diverse meanings, constituted not just the governing doctrine but the civic religion of the world in which I was raised. This was Schlesinger's "vital center," to use the title of his 1949 liberal apologia—a secular, pragmatic, rational, optimistic middle point between the dire absolutisms of left and right. This distinctively American formulation of liberalism traces its roots to the years around World War I, when self-described progressives, who had come to view economic liberalism as a flimsy ideological mask over the brutal social Darwinism of the lords of business and industry, made common cause with the liberal supporters of Woodrow Wilson, each to some extent converting the other. Political liberalism accepts the power of free markets to produce mass prosperity but also uses the state to temper its excesses and to provide crucial public goods—education and health care, old-age and unemployment insurance, railways and roads. These two streams found their supreme point of convergence in FDR. Internationally, the post–World War II order shaped and dominated by American power rested on American liberal principles—a belief in the rule of law rather than raw power and in institutions rather than men, a faith in the free flow of ideas and goods, a deep distrust of collectivism and the overweening state.

The house of liberalism does not simply have many rooms; it has warring factions. Liberals of the left regard free-market liberals as hand-maidens to plutocracy; those of a libertarian bent regard liberal Democrats as socialists in disguise. Both have good reason to believe that the other has abandoned central aspects of the liberal faith. Yet the overlap between them is real. All liberals start with the belief that individuals have an intrinsic right to have their personal choices respected, and thus that the state must honor those choices whether or not they enjoy majority support. Liberals are skeptical about transcendent goods, at least in the public realm; they put their faith in debate and political conflict rather than in revelation or all-encompassing doctrines. Because liberals believe that a person's nature is not fixed and thus that individuals can improve their own conditions, they are broadly optimistic about human prospects. People who do not share these views, or that temperament, should not be called liberals. Some are socialists or communists; some are conservatives; some are totalitarians; and some are illiberal democrats.

One could not say, without doing violence to history, that the West evolved toward ever-greater degrees of liberalism. First, that development was far smoother in the Anglo-American world than on the Continent. Second, large parts of Europe revolted against more or less liberal rule and fell under the trance of fascism. (Communism, the total-itarianism of the left, took root in the deeply illiberal soil of Russia.) Yet Fukuyama's claim, at least when he made it, captured the sense that after an epoch of crisis, liberalism had triumphed over its chief rivals. First fascism disappeared, and then communism. Liberalism reasserted itself in places where it had gone into eclipse and began to emerge in new places—South Korea and Taiwan, India and Turkey.

The history that I recount chronicles the rise, adaptation, and prolif-eration of an idea. In the second half of the twentieth century liberalism became the national faith of the most powerful country in the world.

The American Cold War liberals combined the anti-totalitarianism of Isaiah Berlin, Karl Popper, and others with the activist liberalism inherited from FDR. The wish to extend the benefits of the liberal state to those who had been excluded led the Democratic Party to take up the mantle of civil rights. Liberalism, at its high noon, came to mean civil rights and President Johnson's War on Poverty. By 1964 the United States appeared to have achieved the liberal dream of protecting liberty while advancing equality.

Then liberalism lost its grip on the broad American public. This failure poses piercing questions for our own time. Were white Americans simply unwilling to grant full equality to blacks? That is, had the liberal consensus rested on a tacit whites-only understanding? Or did liberals lose sight of their faith in individuals and their skepticism about the state? Did Americans recoil against liberal social engineering? The pendulum now swung in the opposite direction: the 1970s and '80s saw the rise of a new doctrine that regarded the state as a parasite devouring individual initiative and economic freedom as the key to both personal fulfillment and national renewal. The United States entered a phase in which left-liberalism and right-liberalism fought for supremacy; the fact that left-liberals adopted much of the vocabulary, and some of the policies, of the apostles of the free market argued that right-liberals won the war even when they lost some of the battles.

In retrospect, the triumph of marketplace ideology may have set the stage for our present woes. Free-market policies accelerated global forces that were already increasing economic inequality. Economic growth and social mobility had once made inequality tolerable, but that escalator had slowed to a halt. The drastic recession of 2008 hit at a moment when Americans had already begun to question whether the system would work for them as it had for their parents. Modern liberalism depended on the expectation of an ever-brighter future; the economic and psychological foundation of the faith had just crumbled.

It was also during this period that Republicans released the germ of illiberalism into the national political bloodstream. The party actively courted conservative evangelical voters who did not accept the secular state and did not defer to secular reasoning. These voters soon became the core of the Republican Party. Their absolutism predisposed them to think of the other party as not simply wrong but illegitimate. Such voters were prepared to accept virtually any means that attained the end of partisan victory; even secular Republicans were happy to exploit that radical mood.

Illiberalism was like an underground fire that burned out of sight until, all at once, it exploded into view. I explore the rise of this angry spirit in both Europe and the United States. The causes overlap, though they are not the same. Indeed, the liberal crisis played out differently in Eastern and Western Europe. Liberalism did not sink deep roots in Eastern Europe, and citizens alienated by the secular, rationalist, and polyglot culture of the West looked backward toward a real or imagined period of national glory, and toward the religious and national pillars of that old order. In Western Europe, meanwhile, the combined effect of industrial decline and the cultural dislocation of large-scale immigration, above all from the Islamic world, shook liberal rule. As race split American society, so, in recent years, has immigration and the refugee flight become Europe's cultural wound.

Americans elected their first illiberal president in 2016. Donald Trump has a rare gift for populist demagoguery, but he also found an intensely receptive audience. As in Europe, economic anger turned voters against the system, while a sense of dispossession fostered a nationalist backlash against immigrants, refugees, domestic minorities, foreigners, and liberals who seemed to take the side of these outsiders against (white) Americans. Finally, Trump was uniquely positioned to exploit the collapse of faith in fact, science, and reason. Trump's brazen indifference to truth would have exposed him to ridicule a generation earlier; in 2016, he found an audience avid for his alternate realities.

I wonder now how I, and so many others, could have remained so blithe as resentment of liberalism itself was reaching a fever pitch. In retrospect, I recognize in myself a symptom of liberal remove. For many years, as a journalist, I wrote about national politics, urban policy, education reform—the endless pitched battles between left and right. Starting about two decades ago, I began to focus on foreign policy and international affairs, which had itself become an arena of moral drama with the rise of doctrines like "humanitarian intervention." Ten years ago, I began teaching at New York University's campus in Abu Dhabi, a central node in what the university describes as a "global network university." I moved lightly across the world like other members of the cosmopolitan class. I thought and wrote a good deal about America's aspiration to shape a world in its own image by exporting its liberal, democratic ideals. I wondered whether that was even possible, but I did not wonder whether Americans continued to believe in those ideals.

I did not see that cosmopolitanism itself—the value system of the globalized world—had become a source of deep rancor. I nodded along when candidate Barack Obama said that working-class voters "cling to guns or religion or antipathy to people who aren't like them or anti-immigrant sentiment or anti-trade sentiment as a way to explain their frustrations." Hostility to liberalism was a pathology, not a worldview. Cosmopolitan liberals have been the beneficiaries of free trade, heightened immigration, the frictionless movement of ideas and people—in short, of globalization. That same system has left millions behind.[2]

In the final part of this book I ask how we can apply the lessons of liberalism's past in order to salvage its future. Liberalism has persisted through adaptation; how does it need to adapt to a globalized, postindustrial—and, it seems, post-truth—world? I argue that liberals cannot succeed simply by marshaling their half of the country against the half that voted for Donald Trump. Liberals must respond to Trump's populist nationalism with an affirmative nationalism that speaks to Americans collectively. That will require serious self-reflection, for the same globalized forces that most liberals embrace have brought real harm to many Americans—who in turn resent liberals for their privileged positions. Liberals will have to decide between the insistent demand of marginalized groups for recognition of their special identities and the need to address the American people as a whole. Liberal nationalism sounds like a contradiction in terms—but only if one flattens liberalism into pure, heedless individualism. Modern liberalism has sought to strike a balance between our individual rights and our obligations to the community. That is the heritage of this great doctrine, and its future as well.

CHAPTER ONE

Protecting the People
from Themselves

*You must first enable the government to control the governed,
and in the next place oblige it to control itself.*

—JAMES MADISON

IN THE FALL OF 1787 ALEXANDER HAMILTON ASKED JAMES
Madison (as well as John Jay) to join him in writing the series of essays
that would come to be known as *The Federalist Papers*. Hamilton's goal was
to defend the United States Constitution, which had just been drafted and
signed, from critics who regarded a strong central government as an invitation to a new tyranny almost equal to that under which the colonies had
once labored. Madison had done more to frame the Constitution than any
other man, and he fully shared Hamilton's belief that the national government must exercise supremacy over the states, a view known as federalism.
Yet he was far more zealous about individual liberty than Hamilton. The
New York financial wizard envisioned a powerful centralized state that
someday would compete on an equal footing with the principalities of
Europe. Madison, by contrast, had come to the paradoxical conclusion
that only a robust national authority could control the conflicting interests inherent in a large and rapidly spreading nation, and thus protect the
elemental right of citizens to speak and think as they wished.

In *Federalist* 51, Madison observed that the separation of governmental powers into legislative, executive, and judicial departments, as well as the sharing of authority between federal and state jurisdictions, prevented the government from encroaching on the liberties of citizens. This was unobjectionable: both arch-Federalists, like Hamilton and John Adams, and advocates of a minimal state, like Thomas Jefferson, regarded the doctrine of the separation of powers as holy writ. Madison, however, went on to make a claim at odds with patriotic pieties: in a republic, he wrote, it is not enough "to guard the society against the oppression of its rulers"; it is equally necessary "to guard one part of the society against the injustice of the other part." Since "different interests necessarily exist in different classes of citizens," a majority, united by a common interest, might come to threaten the rights of the minority.[1]

Because liberalism has no codified body of ideas, one can begin its story in any of several places, depending on how one understands its essence. Some begin with the republican thinkers of ancient Rome; some with John Locke or even Thomas Hobbes, both of whom understood sovereignty as inhering in ordinary men rather than in their rulers; some with the French Enlightenment thinkers, including Jean-Jacques Rousseau and the Marquis de Condorcet, who championed the rights of men in the face of absolutism. None of the American Founders thought of themselves as "liberal"; all, however, were committed both to the doctrine of popular sovereignty and to the sanctity of individual liberty. Among them, none thought more deeply than Madison did about the tension between those two principles, and about the mechanisms needed to reconcile equality with liberty.

How, Madison asked in *Federalist* 51, can the people be protected from themselves? He noted that authority could be vested in some outside body or figure with the power to override the will of the majority, but then the people would have yielded up their sovereignty. The alternative solution lay inside the operation of "free government": so long as the state was large enough and various enough, the sheer multiplicity of interests, when allowed free rein, would prevent the rise of an overweening majority. The natural impulse of self-aggrandizement could serve democratic purposes: "Ambition," Madison wrote, "must be made to counter-act ambition."[2]

Madison's polemical purpose—the job Hamilton had signed him up for—was to demonstrate that a robust state in the heart of a large, unified republic not only did not threaten liberty but safeguarded it. The Federalists won that fight for all time; no one argues today, as the French thinker Montesquieu had in the generation before the Founders, that a republic needs to be compact and homogeneous. Now we read *Federalist* 51 as an early expression of the inherent tension between the obligation to respect democratic majorities and the imperative to protect individual liberties and minority rights. Madison's own answer is no longer entirely persuasive, for we see that wealth and power can create unfair advantage in the political marketplace, as they do in the economic marketplace, allowing the "ambitions" of a few to outweigh those of the many. But the tension Madison identified has remained central to liberal thought. His very modern embrace of the clash of interests set him apart from his peers, who imagined a state guided by a single, knowable public good.

We do not regard Madison today as a colossus like Washington, Jefferson, Adams, or Hamilton. At five feet four, he was small even for his time. Madison was terribly shy when young and even as an adult spoke so softly in front of an audience as to be almost inaudible. Though he spent his entire professional life as a politician, he hated campaigning. Yet Madison had a gift for friendship; great warmth suffuses his letters. He bound himself to mentors like Washington and Jefferson, but also to peers, including the turbulent Hamilton. His mastery of complex material, his equanimity, and his willingness to let others shine made him the indispensable man of the Constitutional Convention. "He is a gentleman of great modesty," said a fellow delegate, William Pierce of Georgia, "with a remarkable sweet temper." Both Jefferson and Washington depended on Madison for his fine judgment of men, of issues, and of the prevailing winds of politics. Few men, then or now, combine profound erudition with acute political instincts as Madison did.[3]

Madison was a rationalist through and through. New Englanders like John Adams and his son John Quincy combined the Enlightenment commitment to rationality with a deep Calvinist conviction of fallenness and sin. Revolutionary leaders in Tidewater Virginia, living in a kind of pastoral Athens made possible by slave labor, tended to be freethinkers. Madison, who was born in 1751 into a wealthy plantation family near the Blue Ridge Mountains of Virginia, had few, if any, religious convictions. He appears, in his early letters, to be an amused spectator of life's follies. One subject, however, infuriated him: "that diabolical, hell-conceived principle" of religious persecution, as he wrote to his dear friend and fellow Princeton graduate William Bradford in 1774. The Anglican clergy had gotten several Baptist ministers clapped in jail for heresy. "Religious bondage shackles and debilitates the mind," he wrote to Bradford, "and unfits it for every noble enterprise, every expanded prospect."[4]

Even after Madison joined the revolutionary cause, he remained preoccupied by the debate over freedom of conscience. He served as a precocious aide to George Mason, who drew up the Virginia Declaration of Rights at the same moment Thomas Jefferson composed the Declaration of Independence. Madison strengthened Mason's call for religious toleration by adding the phrase, "All men are entitled to the full and free exercise" of their religious views. Apparently that was too much for the delegates to swallow, for the language had to be softened to read, "All men are entitled to . . . the free exercise of religion, according to the dictates of their conscience." A decade later, Madison would cite these lines in a petition inveighing against a plan by the Virginia Assembly to subsidize religious instruction. If the legislature has the power to override so fundamental a liberty, Madison wrote, then we must concede that "they may controul the freedom of the press, may abolish the trial by jury, may swallow up the Executive and Judiciary powers of the State." The hyperbolic language alerts us to the intensity of Madison's commitment to individual liberty.[5]

Like Jefferson, Madison was an endlessly curious polymath. In 1785 he wrote to Jefferson with a list of books he was hoping the latter could find for him in Paris, where he then served as a diplomat for the new nation: "treatises on the ancient or modern Federal Republics"—to help him frame the argument for federalism—"on the Law of Nations, and the History, natural and political, of the new World. . . . Pascal's provincial letters, Don Ulloa"—an eighteenth-century Spanish scientist and New World traveler—"in the original; Linnaeus' best edition," and a French account of travels in China, which "must be very entertaining." Yet the casts of the two men's minds were very different. Jefferson was an Olympian, an abstracted being only occasionally troubled by the discrepancy between the world of his fancies and the world before him; Madison was a pragmatist, a close observer of the world before his eyes. When, later that year, Jefferson wrote from his Parisian aerie with the startling suggestion that all debts be canceled and all laws rewritten every thirty-four years, since one generation ought not bind another, Madison graciously acknowledged the "sublime truths" that his friend's speculative reasoning had disclosed while offering to examine them with "the naked eye of the ordinary politician." In fact, he pointed out, the persistence of rules over time, of which Jefferson complained, constituted a source of legitimacy. "Tacit assent . . . may be inferred where no positive dissent appears." Justice must arise from lived experience rather than abstract philosophy.[6]

Madison understood that one could be committed to the cause of liberty without falling prey to blind faith in it. The revolution had been partly fueled by a simple-minded belief in liberty as against power. Among patriots drawn to the "paranoiac mistrust of power" of England's radical Whigs, as the historian Gordon Wood wrote in *The Creation of the American Republic, 1776–1787*, "every accumulation of political power, however tiny and piecemeal, was seen as frighteningly tyrannical." Man was natural; the state, artificial—a thing not of men but against them. As Thomas Paine wrote in *Common Sense*, the pamphlet that helped kindle the flame of revolution, "Government, like dress, is the badge of lost innocence; the palaces of kings are built on the ruins of the bowers of paradise."[7]

That was a fine motto to fuel an insurrection against an imperial power, but it scarcely served as a guide for self-rule. The experience of the years following the revolution, including Shays' Rebellion, a violent insurrection against state governments and state courts by farmers burdened with ruinous levels of debt in 1786–1787, demonstrated to many of the Founders that democracy posed dangers of its own to liberty, including the right to property. Madison was particularly clear-eyed on this score. As he wrote in another one of his extraordinary letters to Jefferson, "In our Governments the real power lies in the majority of the community, and the invasion of private rights is *chiefly* to be apprehended, not from acts of Government contrary to the sense of its constituents, but from acts in which the Government is the mere instrument of the major number of the Constituents." Madison was describing what today we would call populism.[8]

Madison understood that "the people" were, in the end, people—not a virtuous abstraction but a collection of individuals with interests of their own. Yet unlike Hamilton, who took a dim view of the ordinary man, or Adams, who so feared "the mob" that in his *Discourses on Davila* he advocated an executive who would embody the "monarchical principle" of authority, Madison instinctively sided with the citizen against oppressive authority. The differences among them became painfully manifest in 1791 when, in the aftermath of the French Revolution, Thomas Paine wrote *The Rights of Man*, a blazing manifesto that endorsed revolutionary mob violence and asserted that "the nation" has "at all times an inherent, indefeasible right to abolish any form of government it finds inconvenient." Jefferson, thrilled both by the Revolution and by Paine's call to arms, offered a kind of blurb for the American edition expressing the hope that the essay would refute "the political heresies that have sprung among us"—a transparent reference to Vice President Adams's alleged softness on monarchy. John Quincy Adams then leaped to his father's defense with a series of essays so horror-struck by revolutionary upheaval that they could have sprung from the pen of conservative philosopher Edmund Burke. The breach between Jefferson and Adams would not be healed for decades. Madison sided with Jefferson and Paine. He was thrilled to be made an honorary citizen of France in 1793, though by that time the guillotine had become the chief instrument of the popular will. Madison seems to have been far more alive to the dangers posed by "the people" in the United States than in France.[9]

During the American Revolution Madison was commissioned as a colonel in the Virginia military, which allowed him to keep that cherished honorific later in life, though he never saw military action. In 1779 he was elected to the revolutionary Congress of the Confederation, where he served until 1783, and then won election to the Virginia House of Delegates. He returned to Congress in 1786 and then served on Virginia's delegation to the Constitutional Convention in Philadelphia. In short, he was a politician, as he had said to Jefferson—conscientious, difference splitting, immune to utopian schemes. In 1785, Madison received a letter from a Kentuckian, John Brown, who asked whether the state's constitution, then being drafted, should limit the franchise to property holders or allow universal (white male) suffrage. Madison suggested a "middle way," though not a very practical one: limit the ballot for the Senate to the propertied but allow a broader franchise for the House. It was true, he wrote, that men of property would seek to impose their interests on the poor; yet both had valid claims to the protection of the state. A democratic politics had to contain, and neutralize, that conflict. Interest could be made to counteract interest.

By that time Madison had become convinced that the national passion for liberty had produced a hopelessly enfeebled central government. He and Hamilton worked together to convene a constitutional convention to replace the Articles of Confederation. We need not linger on Madison's role there, or on the debates in Philadelphia over how powers were to be apportioned among the branches of government and between the federal and state authorities. All of the men who signed the Constitution—as well as figures like John Adams and Jefferson, who were abroad in 1787—accepted the core principles of federalism and the separation of powers. All broadly accepted the balance the Constitution struck between liberty and power. They did, however, differ strongly on whether the document was finished. Those who still feared the depredations of a strong state, like George Mason, insisted that the Constitution could not be ratified absent a Bill of Rights stipulating those liberties that no government could infringe on.

Madison's standing in our national pantheon owes a great deal to his almost sole authorship of the Bill of Rights. Yet his role obscures essential elements of his own thinking. Madison considered a Bill of Rights unnecessary; whatever powers the Constitution did not confer on government, he thought, plainly remained with the people. He agreed to draft the amendments only in order to mollify figures like Mason or Jefferson who otherwise might have joined the Anti-Federalist opposition. In a 1788 letter to the latter, Madison explained that he had supported the addendum "only because it might be of use" and then dilated on the concerns he had about the prospect of a public debate over precious individual rights. "I am sure," Madison wrote, "that the rights of conscience, in particular, if submitted to a public definition, will be narrowed much more than they would be likely ever to be by an assumed power"—that is, by some benevolent external authority. Indeed, he added, "repeated violations of these parchment barriers have been committed by overbearing majorities in every State." He was thinking of, among other things, the debate over religious funding on which he had advised the Virginia Assembly. "Should a Rebellion or insurrection alarm the people as well as the Government, and a suspension of the Habeas Corpus be dictated by the alarm, no written prohibitions on earth would prevent the measure."[10]

Madison was hardly alone in fearing that liberties would not be safe with democratic majorities. What was distinctive was his pragmatic skepticism of "parchment barriers." Madison understood that republican government could survive only if citizens believed in the formal rules codified in constitutions—thus his observation to Jefferson about the value of "tacit assent." Madison's greatest hope for the Bill of Rights, he said, was that eventually it would "become incorporated with the national sentiment."[11]

Madison had always been more attracted to political power than to intellectual reputation; rather than publishing tracts, like Jefferson or Adams, he had been content to pour his fine intellect into public documents, whether the Virginia Declaration of Rights or the Virginia Plan, which served as a first draft for the Constitution, or the Constitution itself. But when Hamilton invited him to join the journalistic project to vindicate the Constitution, Madison decanted a decade's worth of reflection into forty-odd essays—the great literary achievement of his life. In his first contribution, *Federalist* 10, he laid out his one truly original contribution to political doctrine: that, despite Montesquieu's famous claim that republics can flourish only in small states, it is the multiplicity of conflicting interests arising in large, various states that best protects republican values. It is, Madison argued, through "the enlargement of the orbit within which such systems are to revolve," whether by increasing the size of the nation or by compounding many states into one—as the Constitution proposed to do—that republics secure their prosperity and stability.[12]

Madison did not think, as a modern advocate of laissez-faire would, that the free play of selfish interests in itself secures the public good. Quite the contrary; private goods are the enemy of the public good. Madison defined a faction as "a number of citizens . . . united and actuated by some common impulse of passion, or interest, adverse to the rights of other citizens, or to the permanent and aggregate interest of the community." When the Founders railed at England's "corruption," they meant that power had been captured by interest. Yet Madison accepted that faction is intrinsic to society, and above all to free society. People naturally differ in abilities and preferences. This "diversity in the faculties of men," he wrote in *Federalist* 10, leads to diversity of economic position and thus of interest. Some wish the government to protect debtors, and some, creditors. Some want to impose tariffs, and some don't. Madison described the protection of these diverse faculties as "the first object of government." He appears to mean that government must safeguard our ability to make the personal choices that shape our lives.[13]

Almost all of Madison's contemporaries abhorred parties and bemoaned them once they arose. In his Farewell Address, George Washington described faction as "a frightful despotism" that so disordered society that men turned to actual despotism in order to escape its effects. Only a steady recourse to civic virtue could prevent the spirit of party from arising in America as it had elsewhere. Madison, by contrast, put his trust in multiplicity and the competition it fostered. In *Federalist* 50, he wrote that the unitary, party-less society celebrated by so many of his peers "ought to be neither presumed nor desired; because an extinction of parties necessarily implies either a universal alarm for the public safety, or an absolute extinction of liberty." It is scarcely a coincidence that Madison, along with Jefferson, founded America's first political party, the Democratic-Republicans.[14]

Madison had at least an implicit theory of human nature, and it was neither the Enlightenment rationalism of Jefferson nor the Calvinist darkness of the New England Puritans. His views were closer to our own. In *Federalist* 51, after suggesting that government be so designed that ambitions check one another, Madison asserted,

> It may be a reflection on human nature that such devices should be necessary to control the abuses of government. But what is government itself but the greatest of all reflections on human nature? If men were angels, no government would be necessary. If angels were to govern men, neither external nor internal controls on government would be necessary. In framing a government which is to be administered by men over men, the great difficulty lies in this: you must first enable the government to control the governed, and in the next place oblige it to control itself.[15]

The word *liberal* would not enter the vocabulary of politics and political philosophy until the nineteenth century. Nevertheless, not just Madison but all the Founders stand as precursors to the liberals of a later generation. They were all heirs of John Locke, the seventeenth-century champion of the sovereignty of the people. In his *Second Treatise of Government*, Locke argues that men are born into a state of liberty; that they voluntarily choose to surrender some of that liberty, retaining the rest, in the formation of a state; and that they act not out of a moral or religious impulse but rather out of the secular, self-regarding wish to ensure "the preservation of their property." It is from this premise that Jefferson derived his ringing assertion that all men have an "inalienable right" to "life, liberty, and the pursuit of happiness." The balance that the Framers struck in the Constitution between liberty and power constitutes the first explicit working out of those Lockean principles. That is why the historian Louis Hartz wrote in 1955 that Americans were born liberal.[16]

Among that first generation, however, Madison comes closest to our own understanding of liberalism. Hamilton was far more nonchalant than were any of his colleagues about the dangers that a strong state posed to individual liberties. Jefferson, by contrast, was nonchalant about the dangers that the mass of individuals posed to the liberty of each. That tension lay at the heart of Madison's thinking. In a letter to fellow Virginian James Monroe in 1786, he wrote, "There is no maxim, in my opinion, which is more liable to be misapplied than the current one, that the interest of the majority is the standard of right and wrong." A majority might well choose "to despoil and enslave the minority of individuals." Yet the solution to the problem of the tyranny of the majority lay inside, not outside, of democracy—in the "internal architecture" of government, though ultimately in the minds of citizens. The utopian wish for a society of one mind was a formula for despotism; variety offered a far more secure bulwark of liberty.[17]

We see in Madison's combination of pragmatism and idealism, skepticism and optimism, rationalism and political realism, a forerunner of the liberal temperament. Yet in one fundamental respect both Madison and all of his peers belonged to a species of pre-liberals. For all the primacy in their minds of individual liberty, they did not think of individuals, and thus of liberty, as we do or as the thinkers of an ensuing generation would. A self, for them, was not a private, autonomous being, free to pursue a particular path in life, but a citizen, a member of a blessed community. "Every man in a republic is public property," as the Philadelphia patriot Benjamin Rush once put it. A republic depends upon virtue, as George Washington said in his Farewell Address. Citizens must be counted on to curb their wishes—their interests—for the good of the republic, for all men knew that it was self-dealing that corrupted republics, England very much included. The Founders had all drunk deeply from the history of the Roman republic, and they kept before their eyes the examples of the heroes and martyrs of that world, above all Cicero and Cato. John and Abigail Adams addressed one another in their letters as "Brutus" and "Portia" (Brutus's wife and Cato's daughter).[18]

Hamilton, the voice of enlightened self-interest, came closest to our own understanding of the relationship of the individual to society when he compared contemporary Americans to ancient Greeks in *Federalist* 8: "The industrious habits of the people of the present day, absorbed in the pursuits of gain and devoted to the improvements of agriculture and commerce, are incompatible with the condition of a nation of soldiers, which was the true condition of the people of those republics." The liberty to which virtually all his peers, Madison very much included, devoted themselves was public or civil liberty, not private freedom of action. It would take another, and very different, revolution to demonstrate the need for a politics of the private self.[19]

In 1795, Benjamin Constant, a young Frenchman who had been raised in Switzerland, felt safe enough to travel to France. The eighteen-month spasm of violence and anarchy known as the Terror had exhausted itself and given way to the relatively calm, if feckless, regime known as the Directory. Like many young men across Europe—he was born in 1767—Constant had been thrilled by the overthrow of the aristocratic and clerical order, and the rise of republican government, after 1789. Like many others, he had been horrified by the collapse of the Revolution into what felt like madness. He could not accept that the Terror was the logical and inevitable denouement of the Revolution. Like Russian Mensheviks in 1917 and Iranian secular reformers in 1980, he felt called to defend a middle place between revolution and tyranny. In 1797 he published an essay, *Des réactions politiques* (*Of Political Reactions*), in which he sought to define that space, which he called "liberal." He noted that when Gracchus Babeuf, a veteran of the Terror who had called for violent insurrection against the Directory, was given a proper trial before being swept off to the guillotine, many people wondered why Babeuf had enjoyed the protection of legal processes that he would have denied his enemies. It is, Constant wrote, "precisely because they wouldn't have observed them that you must do so. It is this that distinguishes you; it is this, uniquely this, that gives you the right to punish them; it is this that makes them anarchists, and you the friends of order."[20]

Both in *Of Political Reactions* and in his later work, until his death in 1830, Constant championed many of the same principles that the American Founders had: limited government, the separation of powers, freedom of speech and of conscience, a secular public space, social as well as political equality. The Founders would have been quick to agree with Constant's assertion that a just state must respect the rule of law even when prosecuting those who hold such principles in contempt. It was not, however, a problem that preoccupied them, at least once their own revolution was over, because they no longer faced the threat of arbitrary power. Constant did, and it was the difference between the French and the American revolutions that shaped his thoughts in a direction much closer to modern liberalism. The yoke under which the colonies suffered had been imposed by what was then regarded as the world's most enlightened power; what the American patriots were pleased to call tyranny amounted to the denial of the political representation that they deserved as citizens of the British Crown. The French revolted against their own despotic and aristocratic social order. And that revolt, as Constant put it in *Of Political Reactions*, "surpassed its limits" and became a kind of ideological monster. The imperative to counter that ideology with the original motivating principles of 1789—as he understood them—made Constant the first anti-totalitarian philosopher. Twentieth-century liberals like Isaiah Berlin would turn back to Constant to counter the all-encompassing claims of fascism and communism.[21]

Constant's language tends toward the sinuous and the paradoxical—"Bloody-minded men seize on the indignation that arises against bloody-minded men." Constant was laboring to turn familiar arguments inside out. His target was not the radicals who prosecuted the Terror—they had all fallen beneath the blade by that time—but rather the reactionaries who found in the excesses of the Revolution the pretext to reverse the gains of 1789: the end of the feudal system and of the monarchy, the abolition of the church tithe, the issuance of the Declaration of the Rights of Man.[22]

In a chapter added to a later edition, Constant focused his fire on authoritarians who actually celebrated the Terror as the tonic France needed to restore order and discipline after the rambunctious freedom of the republic. He argued that crimes committed in the name of principle must not be allowed to discredit principle. And he looked to the republican constitution of 1791 as the incarnation of the very idea of principle, of rules that transcend the moment and the particular figures who govern. The only alternative to principles, he wrote, is *arbitraire*—arbitrary rule. That is why, Constant insisted, both the radicals and the reactionaries who scorned the order established by the constitution would plunge France into anarchy. Strikingly, he classed Edmund Burke's famous critique of the Revolution in the name of tradition and decorum—"the decent drapery of life"—as a form of *arbitraire*, for the conservative thinker was prepared to abdicate principle in favor of "considerations, preconceptions, memories, weaknesses."[23]

Constant used the word *liberal* casually. He spoke of "liberal" ideas and admonished writers who, though "eminently liberal in their abstract principles," proved to be "illiberal in their personal enmities." He seemed to intend the word in its self-evidently positive sense of "generous" or "open-handed." The abstract principles in whose name the Revolution was waged—liberty, equality, fraternity—are liberal ones. The alternative to those liberal principles was not only the arbitrary denial of principle itself but the extremism of both sides. The abolition of nobility was "salutary," Constant wrote, but not the "execrable" oppression of individual nobles. As a result of this excess, he wrote, the nobility was being reinstated under the Directory. The same was true of the excesses of the spirit of atheism that led to the destruction of churches and the murder of priests. A radicalism of the left provoked a radicalism of the right. In the vanished center lay not simply a humane moderation but a body of constitutional principles that gave society its permanent orienting points. That was the liberalism of *Des réactions politiques*. The American revolutionaries had not lived in an ideological era and so had had little need to think about a middle path between extremes; Constant was the first to seek to define the space that later liberals would inhabit.[24]

Constant was an outsider by both birth and temperament. He was a Protestant; his ancestors had moved from France to escape persecution. Born into a well-to-do family, he had been educated in Brussels, Holland, Germany, and Scotland, and after completing his schooling he had taken a position in the court of the Duke of Brunswick. Only at the age of thirty had he moved to France. Though he thought of himself as deeply French, his adversaries attacked him as a foreigner. He had, in any case, made a virtue of his marginal position. Constant was a skeptic, not so much philosophically as personally; zeal of any kind made him uneasy. He once wrote, "I have very little talent for admiring myself when I feel righteous indignation."[25]

The Constant of the late 1790s occupied a position comparable to that of the Founders in the 1780s, seeking to articulate an argument for an effective state that would be consistent with the commitment to individual liberty. He wrote in *Des réactions* that a weak government, as the Directory then self-evidently was, created a vacuum of authority that citizens were inclined to fill with unauthorized acts of enforcement, potentially leading to civil war. Thanks to his reputation as a principled advocate of strong government firmly anchored in constitutional principles, in 1799 Constant was appointed by the Senate to the Tribunat, a body of sages that advised the legislature on the merits of proposed legislation. Napoleon had just been appointed First Consul, and the Senate may have hoped that Constant would defend its powers from the ambitious young military leader. In his first speech, Constant criticized "the regime of servitude and silence" that he said Bonaparte was then devising. Constant did, indeed, take the role of leader of the opposition. By 1802, Napoleon had had his fill of criticism and relieved Constant of his post. The philosopher returned to the safety of Switzerland, where he would remain until the Bourbon Restoration put Louis XVIII on the throne in 1814.[26]

During his period of enforced exile, Constant wrote two enormous manifestos on government. The fact that he did not allow either to be published in his lifetime, perhaps recognizing that his opinions would not be welcome in Napoleonic France, helps account for the modest scale of his posthumous reputation. Constant kept a diary, later published as

Journaux intimes, wrote autobiographical works and a novel, and produced a five-volume history of religion. He was best known at the time as the companion of Madame de Staël, a woman of letters, political intriguer, and avowed enemy of Napoleon. She, too, returned to France with the fall of Napoleon. When Bonaparte made his astonishing return to Paris in April 1815, he made the remarkable gesture of inviting Constant to help him write a new, republican constitution. Constant must have somehow convinced himself that the emperor was sincere, for he joined him for the hundred days of his final tenure. Napoleon's defeat sent Constant packing yet again, this time to London. By 1816, he was back in France, where he would remain for the rest of his life. He served as a deputy in the National Assembly from 1819 to 1822, and again from 1824 until his death in 1830.

The vicissitudes of this public life did not make Constant reconsider his commitment to republican and constitutional principles. If anything, the experience of Napoleon's charismatic authoritarianism added to Constant's sense of the frailty of individual liberty. But what did "liberty" mean in the new era of the total state? It was here that Constant made his most original and important contribution to liberal thought. In a famous 1819 lecture, "De la liberté des anciens comparée à celle des modernes" ("The Liberty of Ancients Compared with That of Moderns"), Constant observed that in the classical world, liberty was understood in civic terms as the full participation of each citizen in the political life of the state. For that very reason, he went on, "they admitted as compatible with this collective freedom the complete subjection of the individual to the authority of the community." Freedom to choose one's own religion, for example, would have been counted "a crime and a sacrilege" in Athens or Rome. Individual liberty had to give way before the just claims of the state.[27]

But Constant, like Hamilton, recognized that the personal liberty sought by modern men was incompatible with the ancient demands of citizenship. "The aim of the moderns is the enjoyment of security in private pleasures," he observed, "and they call liberty the guarantees accorded by institutions to those pleasures." Modern liberty essentially meant the right to be left alone. The thought would have scandalized

John Adams and his son, both of whom almost courted opportunities to surrender their lives for their country. But unlike the Adamses, Constant saw that the same state that demanded patriotic sacrifice was capable of gross violations of personal liberty. In the name of "useless experiments," he wrote, the revolutionaries tried to compel France to "enjoy the good she did not want, and denied her the good which she did want."[28]

Constant's openness to human complexity made him reluctant to reduce his own arguments to cut-and-dried formulations. He admitted that he sympathized with the impulse to deny men personal liberty in the name of civic liberty. "One could not read the beautiful pages of antiquity," he wrote, "one could not recall the actions of its great men, without feeling an indefinable and special emotion, which nothing modern can possibly arouse. . . . Once we abandon ourselves to this regret, it is impossible not to wish to imitate what we regret." The sense of emulation was so much the stronger, and thus more excusable, under the vicious government of Louis XVI.[29]

Yet the willingness to sacrifice personal wishes in the name of a great cause had prepared the French for a new despotism. Constant did not blame the ancients so much as their Enlightenment heirs, including the Abbé de Mably, the renowned Jesuit thinker. For the Abbé, Constant wrote, "any means seemed good if it extended the area of authority over that recalcitrant part of human nature whose independence he deplored." Yet it is precisely in the recalcitrant part of human nature, the part that acts simply according to one's wishes, that true liberty lies. The more that natural impulse arises, the more the votaries of the general will are determined to crush it. But France was not to be reduced to the condition of Sparta.[30]

There is an echo in the essay of the economic liberalism of Adam Smith and Jean-Baptiste Say, Constant's contemporary and the father of what came to be called neoclassical economics. Constant celebrated the rise of commerce, which, by transforming physical property into the immaterial form of currency, had foiled the state's effort to control private affairs, for the government no longer knew quite what to seize. Not only does commerce "emancipate individuals," Constant observed, "but, by creating credit, it places authority itself in a position of dependence." The state has to look to private citizens for credit, thus reversing the usual relationship between the two. Yet Constant appears to have been uneasy at the reduction of liberty to economic self-gratification. He did not lose sight of the republican ideals of his youth. Liberty, he asserted, must reach beyond the freedom to act as one wishes in order to encompass "the right to exercise some influence on the administration of the government." The state as Constant envisioned it could not demand civic engagement, for he had seen the horrors that lay in that direction, but the individual in a republic would naturally aspire to be a citizen as well as a consumer.[31]

The unending political turbulence of his time turned Constant against any ideology that proposed to aggrandize power for allegedly higher purposes. He opened one of his major works, *Principles of Politics Applicable to All Governments*, written during his exile from Napoleon's France though published only in 1980, with a striking attack on Rousseau, the philosophical hero of the Revolution. Rousseau had championed the idea of the "general will," a collective public good transcending all private interests, in whose name individuals would surrender their own sovereignty to a just ruler. In reality, Constant observed, dictators will justify their rule as the necessary instrument of the public good. "These representatives of the general will," Constant wrote, "will have powers all the more formidable in that they call themselves pliant instruments of this alleged will and possess the means of enforcement necessary to ensure that it is manifested in that which suits them." This astute observation anticipates the anti-totalitarian liberalism of the mid-twentieth century.[32]

The issue between Constant and Rousseau was not sovereignty, for both accepted that it lodged in the people themselves. The people delegated sovereignty to their representatives. But, Constant went on, in the language of Locke, that delegation must be limited. "There is," he wrote, "a part of human existence which remains individual and independent, and by right beyond all political jurisdiction. . . . If society crosses this boundary, it becomes as guilty of tyranny as the despot whose only claim to office is the murderous sword." Personal liberty must be shielded from the claims not only of tyranny but of virtue. Even if governments only seek to protect and promote virtue, Constant wrote, "I would still hold that virtue would be better off independent." He suggested that we leave the encouragement of virtue to society.[33]

This spirited defense of the sanctity of private choice makes Constant distinctively modern. So, too, does his skepticism of the application of abstract principles to political life. Constant saw intrinsic value in variety and for that reason argued, like Madison, that large states can make better republics than small ones. Rulers must resist the temptation to "impose uniformity on heterogeneous populations" and thus sacrifice the "host of sentiments, memories, local tastes" that constitute individual happiness. A just state is one that permits these myriad wishes and purposes to flourish and that determines the public good through an open contest among them. The state itself must remain neutral. Constant was deeply committed to parliamentarianism because he conceived of legislatures as the sites of compromise and debate. "What is the general interest," he wrote, in a rebuke to Rousseau, "except the compromise that takes place between particular interests?"[34]

There may be no country in Europe today where the word *liberal* has so pejorative a meaning as France; on the left, the word is used to describe a heartless devotee of laissez-faire (though some have grudgingly accommodated themselves to the classically liberal president Emmanuel Macron). Yet in the first half of the nineteenth century no country contributed as much to the development of liberal thought as France. Political upheaval is a tonic to serious political thinking. In the span of sixty years, France experienced revolution, terror, imperial republicanism, royal restoration, popular insurrection, constitutional monarchy, a yet greater insurrection, and the return of monarchy. These convulsions taught many of the thinkers who lived through them to distrust utopian visions and to see that tyranny could take innumerable forms. What mattered, in the end, was less the outward form than the inner nature of the regime. Indeed, François Guizot, the foremost political thinker of the generation immediately following Constant, observed that in modern states, elements of democracy, aristocracy, theocracy, and the like exist alongside one another. This heterogeneity, he wrote, serves as a check on absolutism, for "the essence of liberty is the simultaneous manifestation and action of all interests, all rights, all social elements and forces."[35]

Constant had sought to strike a balance between the egalitarian ideals of the Revolution and its excesses—between radicalism and reaction. Thinkers who had not lived through the Revolution did not share that sense of dashed idealism and regarded that period as an object lesson in the violence of the mass public. Though a passionate defender of limited government and, above all, of the central role of parliaments, Guizot was neither a democrat nor even a republican: he believed that political rights should be limited to those few with the "capacity" to govern and considered monarchy an essential principle of government. Guizot's father had been sent to the guillotine; his fear of the masses was bone deep. "The aim of representative government," he said, "is to oppose a barrier at once to tyranny and to confusion."[36]

One of the brilliant young men who attended Guizot's celebrated Paris lectures on the history of government was Alexis de Tocqueville, who would advance liberal thinking into the ensuing generation. Tocqueville burst on the scene of European letters with the publication in 1835 of the first volume of *Democracy in America*. Most of us read Tocqueville today as an early social anthropologist, the first outsider to study *Homo americanus* in his natural habitat. Tocqueville *was* that; his subject, however, was not America but democracy. Tocqueville used the word *democracy* to describe, not a set of political institutions, but the social fact of equality and all that resulted from it. America was the most democratic of nations because it was the most equal. In this regard it was a harbinger, for Tocqueville believed that equality of condition was on the rise in France and across Europe. The overthrow of Charles X in 1830 and the subsequent installation of constitutional monarchy demonstrated that the democratic spirit could not be stemmed. "The spell of royalty is broken," Tocqueville wrote, "but it has not been succeeded by the majesty of the laws." An aristocrat of ancient lineage with a deep love of French tradition and history, Tocqueville regarded demo-

cratic equality with far greater trepidation than Constant had, though at
the same time he recognized the dynamic of his times as Guizot did not.
Since the spirit of egalitarianism could not be wished away, it would have
to be tamed. The great goal of statesmen, he wrote, must be "to educate
democracy; to reawaken, if possible, its religious beliefs; to purify its
morals; to mold its actions."[37]

Tocqueville did not regard democracy as inherently friendly to liberty.
"When I see that the right and the means of absolute control are conferred on any power whatever," he wrote, "be it called a people or a king,
an aristocracy or a democracy, a monarchy or a republic, I say there is the
germ of tyranny." In certain respects he found in the United States the
living proof that democracy could imperil liberty. "I know of no country
in which there is so little independence of mind and real freedom of discussion as in America," he wrote. As soon as the majority pronounces its
opinions, he went on, "everyone is silent, and the friends as well as the
opponents of the measure unite in assenting to its propriety."[38]

Yet the spirit of equality had not destroyed liberty in the United
States. In his travels across the country Tocqueville found the innumerable mechanisms—political and social, legal and informal—that made the
people democratic in spirit as well as in fact. America's laws, its constitution, its federal system, had persuaded each citizen that he was the equal
of every other and offered him a chance to play a part in the system of
governance. Democracy was thus a political reality experienced by every
American. Tocqueville was enormously impressed by the gravity with
which American citizens accepted the obligation to serve as sheriff or
alderman, or to take their place on a jury. One cannot read these passages
today without a sense of wistfulness for a largely vanished era when democracy was more of a daily exercise than it is today.

Tocqueville remarked that, as important as the system of law was,
American social institutions served as the greatest bulwark of all. Freedom of worship turned religion into a spur to liberty rather than a system
of authority; public education created an enlightened people, if few men
of learning. Perhaps the single most important insight of *Democracy in
America* is that it is the *habits* of free men that secure democracy. "Too

much importance is attributed to legislation," Tocqueville concluded, "too little to custom." It is "the customs of the American people . . . which render them the only one of the American nations that is able to support a democratic government." He understood, as Madison had, that it was not "parchment barriers" but daily habits that sustained liberal society.[39]

In 1839 Tocqueville became a deputy in the French Assembly. He saw firsthand the growing venality of Louis Philippe and called on those around him to institute reforms, lest the people rise up once again to overthrow a despised king. Yet when the revolution that he foresaw actually arrived in 1848, Tocqueville was appalled by the violence in the streets and called for swift police action. He went on to serve as foreign minister to the autocratic Louis Napoleon. Though the popular forces that briefly ruled France showed far more signs of anarchy than of tyranny, Tocqueville concluded that the people would be prepared to follow a tyrant who promised to sweep away aristocratic privilege. "The French," he wrote mordantly, "decided that it would be better to live as equals under a master than to be unequal with liberty."

In *The Old Régime and the Revolution*, written in his last years—he would die from tuberculosis in 1859, at the age of fifty-four—Tocqueville accepted that the absolutism of the last century deserved to perish but bitterly lamented the rise of a vulgar and grasping mass culture. Equality has not produced tyranny, but its leveling force has flattened all that was rare and fine. Money has become the sole measure of value; people are "withdrawing into a narrow individualism where all public virtues are smothered." Real liberty—"ordered liberty," in Tocqueville's tart phrase—offers the opportunity to aspire to those "public virtues." Perhaps Constant would say that in the end Tocqueville chose ancient over modern liberty. Whatever may have been the case in America, in the traditional and unequal society of Europe, one had to choose between liberty and equality. Tocqueville knew very well where he stood. "I passionately love freedom, legality, the respect for rights," he wrote in 1841, "but not democracy."[40]

The struggle between liberty and equality, and between aristocratic and democratic values, preoccupied both liberals and conservatives in the nineteenth century. We will see it recur in the works of John Stuart Mill, who ultimately did not regard the tension between these values as irreconcilable. The rise of liberal democracy in the twentieth century would vindicate Mill's faith more than Tocqueville's pessimism. Yet Tocqueville's ardor for liberty, as well as his profound literary gifts, ensured his continuing relevance. He would become a source of inspiration in the 1970s and '80s for French anti-Communist liberals and for Eastern European intellectuals defying Soviet oppression.

CHAPTER TWO

John Stuart Mill and
the Defense of Liberty

There is a circle around every individual human being
which no government . . . ought to be permitted to overstep.

—JOHN STUART MILL

IN THE OPENING PAGES OF *ON LIBERTY*, JOHN STUART MILL
observed that representative government does not, by itself, guarantee
the protection of individual liberty. By 1859, when the essay was published, that assertion had become almost a truism: "In political speculations," Mill wrote, "'the tyranny of the majority'"—the phrase Madison
had used in *Federalist* 10—"is now generally included among the evils
against which society requires to be on its guard." Both the American
Framers and French liberals like Constant had been acutely sensitive to
the threats that even an apparently benevolent state posed to the freedom of conscience or expression. Mill, however, intended to point to a
threat to liberty that had never, he thought, been fully recognized: what
he called "society," the informal consensus that operates in every community, democratic or not. Mill wrote,

There needs protection also against the tyranny of the prevailing feeling and opinion; against the tendency of society to impose, by means

its own ideas and practices as rules of con-
from them; to fetter the development and,
nation, of any individuality not in harmony
ll characters to fashion themselves upon the

Tocqueville had, of course, said as much, and Mill had deeply admired
and brilliantly reviewed each volume of *Democracy in America*. Mill was
building on a liberal tradition that he knew very well. But he was adding
something that lay at the very heart of his thinking: the association of
liberty with individuality, with subjectivity, with the formation of a self
according to one's own model. The tyranny of opinion, he wrote, was
pernicious even though society exacted a lesser penalty than the state,
because it penetrated "more deeply into the details of life . . . enslaving
the soul itself." The limited state, the separation of powers, the respect for
constitutional principle—the great liberal developments of the previous
two centuries—could not by themselves preserve the jewel of selfhood.
There was something in life itself and, above all, in the dawning modernity of Mill's age that would strap the unwary into the Procrustean bed
of conformity. The argument that Mill would go on to formulate for the
right of the individual to stand apart from society as well as the state,
to develop according to his or her own lights, made him the founder of
modern liberalism.

But it wasn't only a more modern conception of the self that separated
Mill from liberals like Guizot or Tocqueville, or from the free-market
liberals who had come to play a prominent role in English thinking and
politics. Mill instinctively sided with citizens who demanded political
rights from autocratic leaders—including during the tumultuous year of
1848. He championed the cause of the marginalized and stood with the
few women prepared to demand the full rights of citizenship. He was a
utilitarian—it was Mill who coined the term—who held society to the
standard of the greatest good for the greatest number. Mill championed
liberty *and* equality. He did not accept a liberalism that valued the one at
the expense of the other. Yet he could not fully resolve the tension be-

tween these two supreme goods. He could not reconcile them as modern liberals would, for Mill did not regard the state with the same respect that they do.

Mill arrived at his mature views only after long years of reflection and great personal turmoil. He had to fully become the self of which he wrote, and that becoming is part of the story of liberalism. Mill was raised to be an analytical machine. In his *Autobiography*, he famously described the experiment in human development of which he was the unwitting subject. His father, James Mill, set him to learning Greek at three and Latin at seven. The goal was never simply to get the works by heart but to understand them; the elder Mill would quiz his son on long walks, explaining whatever he didn't understand. James Mill was not only trying to produce a prodigy; he wished to vindicate a theory of human nature, first propounded by Locke, that held that people come into the world as blank slates, without moral sentiments—or indeed any sentiments—inscribed in their breasts. Individuals consist of what they are exposed to—or what is poured into them. The precocious logical powers that he developed in his son seemed to prove this early version of behaviorism. "The first intellectual operation in which I arrived at any proficiency," Mill wrote, "was dissecting a bad argument, and finding in what part the fallacy lay." He was about twelve at the time.[2]

James Mill was the leading disciple of the philosopher Jeremy Bentham, who shared his mechanistic understanding of human nature. The very first words of Bentham's *An Introduction to the Principles of Morals and Legislation*, published in 1789, read, "Nature has placed mankind under the governance of two sovereign masters, *pain* and *pleasure*. It is for them alone to point out what we ought to do, as well as to determine what we *shall* do." Bentham was himself an extraordinary analytical machine, slicing to ribbons such cherished concepts as conscience and natural law, which he called "nonsense on stilts." So, too, with church, community, even state—all were "fictitious bodies" men had endowed with spurious life, and all should be dismantled if they harmed the collective good. In place of conventional moral categories Bentham proposed a "felicific calculus" to measure the "utility" of any given action, which is to say the extent to which it increased pleasure or diminished pain. The individual, in Bentham's scheme, was little more than a unit of measurement.[3]

In 1811 James Mill asked Bentham, then the most celebrated thinker in England, to serve as the guardian of his five-year-old son. Nothing in Mill's strange, lopsided upbringing made him recoil at Bentham's impoverished conception of human nature. Indeed, Mill was struck as if by lightning when he first read *An Introduction* at age fifteen. It provided this secular and unsentimental young man "a religion," as he later put it, "the inculcation and diffusion of which could be made the principal outward purpose of a life." Mill became the chief contributor to the *Westminster Review*, which inveighed against aristocratic privilege and called for fully representative government, complete freedom of speech, and expansion of the franchise. He hoped to spend his life as a Benthamite warrior.[4]

Then, at age twenty, the powerful but very brittle instrument that was John Stuart Mill cracked: he suffered a debilitating nervous breakdown. Mill felt not only despondent but bewildered, for nothing in Bentham's categories could explain his state of mind. If people were made as Bentham and James Mill thought they were, then he had no reason to be unhappy. Indeed, his father had told him that the goal of education was to create an association between salutary feelings and matters of the general good, so that doing right made one happy. He accepted the principle, "but to know that a feeling would make me happy if I had it," as he wrote, "did not give me the feeling." Mill found himself wondering whether he would actually feel profound happiness if the Benthamite radicals magically achieved their goal of expanding the franchise and curbing the authority of Church and Crown. He knew at once that the answer was no. Then what? He could scarcely discuss these painful insights with his unforgiving father or with his silent, cowed mother. As Mill later reflected, "I . . . grew up in the absence of love and the presence of fear; and many and indelible are the effects of this bringing up, in the stunting of my moral growth."[5]

Mill claimed in the *Autobiography* that his depression lifted when he found himself weeping at a passage in a French memoir about a young man who vows, after his father's death, to dedicate himself to supporting his mother and his siblings. That has the ring of melodrama. During this time he felt deeply touched by the poetry of Wordsworth. The poet's great subject was not pleasure or pain but joy, and the source of that joy was inside each of us, and thus open to all, whatever the material conditions of their life. Wordsworth supplied an answer to the terrible question Mill had asked himself, for his poems showed "what would be the perennial source of happiness, when all the greater evils of life shall have been removed." The answer lay in the realm of sentiment rather than logic.[6]

Mill turned to the works of Thomas Carlyle and Samuel Taylor Coleridge, Romantics who believed, with Wordsworth, that people had within themselves the spark of the divine. He distrusted their faith in intuition, yet he was increasingly prepared to surrender his own dogmas. "If I am asked," he wrote, "what system of political philosophy I substituted for that which, as a philosophy, I had abandoned, I answer, no system: only a conviction, that the true system was something much more complex and many-sided than I had previously had any idea of." Mill picked up the idea of "many-sidedness" from the German Romantic Goethe. That the world cannot be reduced to logical terms is an insight from poetry rather than philosophy. Mill was embracing a wider and deeper understanding of humanity, and of himself.[7]

Mill did not surrender his radical critique of the old order of privilege and hierarchy, nor did he ever forsake Bentham's utilitarian premise that the test of any policy was whether or not it offered the greatest good for the greatest number. In his first truly ambitious essay, *The Spirit of the Age*, written in 1831, Mill predicted that "the nineteenth century will be known to posterity as the era of one of the greatest revolutions of which history has preserved the remembrance." Old doctrines and old ways of thinking had lost their power to compel acquiescence: the poor no longer deferred to the rich, nor the young to the old; new men must be governed in new ways. He had been visiting Paris during the popular uprising that forced the hated Charles X from the throne, and he'd written to his father of the extraordinary selflessness, modesty, and seriousness of the ordinary French people he'd met. Mill lived to regret his views of 1830 when the new ruler, Louis Philippe, turned out to be not only illiberal but corrupt.

Yet Mill welcomed the convulsion of 1848. Unlike Tocqueville, whom he immensely admired, Mill viewed the insurrection as a legitimate expression of the people's right to overthrow a tyrant. "No government can now expect to be permanent," he wrote in "Vindication of the French Revolution of 1848," "unless it guarantees progress as well as order; nor can it really continue to secure order, unless it promotes progress." Mill sided instinctively with the downtrodden.[8]

In "Civilization," an essay published in 1836, Mill observed that power in society was passing from the individual to the mass—to the mass of people as well as to institutions of mass opinion, such as unions and newspapers. The dynamic of "combination," as Mill called it, had unleashed world-transforming energies. An aroused people had demanded political power commensurate to their economic might. The Reform Act of 1832, which expanded the franchise, if modestly, would come to be seen as the first stage of a great drama. Yet Mill, like Tocqueville, feared progress even as he welcomed it. In long reviews of the two volumes of *Democracy in America*, Mill celebrated Tocqueville's assertion that the experience of governance at the local level had given ordinary Americans a genuine understanding of democratic processes. But he also noted approvingly that Tocqueville was immune to "that species of democratic radicalism that would admit at once to the highest of political franchises, untaught masses that have yet not been experimentally proved fit even for the lowest." He shared Tocqueville's fear that democracy, which was steadily forging the "mass society" of the industrial age, will shatter the delicate fabric of life, and he quoted Tocqueville's eloquent summation of the difference between aristocratic and democratic culture: "The general character of old society was diversity; unity and uniformity were nowhere to be met with. In modern society, all things threaten to become so much alike, that the peculiar characteristics of each individual will be entirely lost in the uniformity of the general aspect." Carlyle or Coleridge could scarcely have put the problem more succinctly.[9]

Modern society had begun to dwarf modern man. "The individual becomes so lost in the crowd," as Mill wrote in "Civilization," "that though he depends more and more upon opinion, he is apt to depend less and less upon well-grounded opinion; upon the opinion of those who know him." People are ever more prey to the "quackery" of advertising and publicity. Literature itself is corrupted by the marketplace. When there is so much to read, who will take the time required to read a book of quality?[10]

Mill was one of the very first writers to recognize and explore the contradictions of modernism, the threatened subordination of all values save those of the marketplace and the mass man. At times his wish to sustain the kinds of traditional values promoted by venerable institutions makes Mill sound more like Burke than Bentham. In an 1840 essay on Coleridge, Mill declared that the philosophes of the Enlightenment had undermined not only the rule of corrupt autocrats but the very idea of legitimate authority, thinking that "they could not better employ themselves than in . . . discrediting all that still remained of restraining discipline, because it rested on the ancient and decayed creeds against which they made war." People needed to believe in something beyond the self— some "fixed point . . . which men agreed in holding sacred."[11]

Is there a contradiction here? Mill's vocabulary is drawn from the rhetoric of conservatives like Carlyle who cherished the aristocratic order, which tied the present to the past and offered to each person a place in an ancient hierarchy. Mill was certainly more conservative, and more deeply under the spell of the Romantics, at age thirty than he would be at fifty. But he would never fully resolve the tension between his progressive faith in the forces of history, which were annihilating both the hateful and the beautiful, and his belief that the individual cannot flourish in a moral and cultural vacuum. Indeed, he anticipated what was to become a fundamental critique of liberal individualism: freedom, by itself, cannot create a world worth cherishing. The individual liberated from the constraints of state and society is a monad, an atom, a self-contained entity with no access to the communities, whether of faith or of affiliation, that stand between the individual and the state. Both cultural conservatives, like Burke and Tocqueville, and Catholic conservatives, like the French monarchist Joseph de Maistre, deplored the cult of the secular individual. Mill's own answer was to look to society to fashion the institutions within which individuals could flourish.

M ill spent much of the 1840s writing his two most extensive works, *A System of Logic, Ratiocinative and Inductive* and *The Principles of Political Economy*. In the latter, Mill attempted both to sum up existing understandings of economics and to devise a form of political economy suitable to the democratic world then coming into being. Mill did not accept Marx's view that class conflict was the engine of human history. But he was just as decisively opposed to the feudalistic view of the Tories, which presupposed a hereditary owning class that would take responsibility for farm laborers and industrial workers. This doctrine, he observed sardonically, dictated "affectionate tutelage on the one side, respectful and grateful deference on the other." This was the exact opposite of the democratic education that he favored. For this reason, Mill opposed benevolence, whether private or state directed, as a solution to the problems of the poor. In the face of the terrible Irish potato famine, Mill argued against direct payments to the poor and even against the regulation of working conditions, both of which smacked to him of paternalism. Why not, he suggested, make wasteland available to the poor, so that they might instead support themselves?[12]

Mill shared many of the views of the economic liberals inspired by the work of Adam Smith, who had described the hidden dynamics by which self-seeking economic behavior produced general prosperity. Since Mill is widely seen as the fountainhead of liberalism, free-market liberals like Friedrich Hayek—whom we will encounter later—have long sought to claim him, or at least the Mill of the 1830s and '40s, as one of their own. It is true that, like Constant, Mill believed that the state should be kept out of private economic transactions. More than that, he thought of the state in almost purely negative terms, regarding as meddlesome paternalism virtually any form of state assistance to the needy. But Mill did not believe that the economic life of man lay at the core of his being. (Nor, to be sure, did Adam Smith.) In *On Liberty*, he vindicated unrestrained economic activity on the grounds of efficiency, but he also pointedly noted that "the principle of individual liberty is not involved in the doctrine of Free Trade."[13]

Nineteenth-century economic liberals understood labor as the means by which individuals not only sustained themselves but realized their highest nature. We work, and improve the earth, and in this lies our nobility. To buy cheap and to sell dear, declared Richard Cobden, the pamphleteer and political activist who led the agitation to overturn England's protective Corn Laws in the 1840s, was to give to humanity "the means of enjoying the fullest abundance of earth's goods, and in doing so carrying out to the fullest extent the Christian doctrine of 'Doing to all men as ye would they should do unto you.'" This view was anathema to Mill, who regarded economic freedom not as an end in itself but as a means for individuals to free themselves from the fetters of dependency and want. In *The Principles of Political Economy*, he wrote that he would be prepared to accept a no-growth economy if the alternative were the ceaseless struggle for wealth. In virtually everything he had written over the two previous decades, Mill had described the unchecked acquisitive impulse as one of the chief corrosive forces wearing away at civilization. He was, in effect, too conservative to be a liberal in this regard.[14]

What's more, Mill viewed the existing distribution of economic power as a grotesque injustice that undermined the claims of free-market theory. In *The Principles*, he made the startling claim that if he had to choose between communism, meaning the abolition of private property, and "the present state of society with all its sufferings and injustices," he would take the former. The hardest-working men earned the least while the idle gentry gathered rents. Private property itself, and not just marketplace restraints, had become a means for the perpetuation of the wealth and station of a tiny elite. Mill did want the state to reform the legal framework of property rights: he argued for an end to primogeniture, the taxation of inheritances, and other means to diffuse wealth. Beyond that, he thought it was up to private actors, rather than the state, to make the kind of drastic changes in economic life that would free men from the bondage of drudgery and serfdom. The idea was chimerical even then, because the primitive economy of Adam Smith's time, in which individuals contracted with one another, had already been replaced in the mid-nineteenth century by an economy of large private firms and semiorganized factory workers. There was no point appealing to the conscience of a company. Mill's largely negative view of the state as an obstacle to liberty left him with no convincing answer to the economic injustices he saw. Mill never satisfactorily addressed the conflict between liberty and social justice. That work was left to later thinkers.[15]

Mill was a handsome young man with rich auburn hair over a great, pale forehead. He unspooled vast paragraphs in slow, measured cadences. He never raised his voice. He was rarely harsh, though personal warmth was almost unnatural to him. His life changed decisively in 1830, when he met and promptly fell hopelessly in love with Harriet Taylor, a beautiful, sensitive, highly intelligent, and, unfortunately, married woman two years his junior. Harriet would not destroy her life by running away with Mill, nor did he wish to lose all caste by doing so. By 1832, Harriet had persuaded her complaisant husband, John Taylor, to accept her love for Mill so long as the two did nothing to embarrass him, or themselves, in society.

The high-minded Mill had never before experienced even infatuation, much less passionate love. He had fully expected solitude to be his lot. His most intimate vision of domestic life, drawn from his own household, was terribly grim. Mill's love for Harriet gave him something precious to protect for the first time—even more, something jeopardized by social conventions, which, until now, he had criticized in the abstract without ever even remotely transgressing. His family and many of his friends disapproved of his union with Harriet. When Taylor died, in 1849, Mill and Harriet were finally able to marry; the only witnesses were Harriet's children. Mill felt isolated and persecuted because of the one great act of emotional courage and openness of his life. The combination of beleaguerment and heroic resistance confirmed Mill's growing sense that the Romantic ideal of self-realization was the great good that needed protection both from the reactionary forces of tradition and from the new dynamic of conformism that came with mass society. It showed him as well that the freedom worth cherishing was not simply intellectual but personal—the freedom not just to say, but to be. And it fully displaced Bentham's human unit from the heart of his philosophy in favor of the thinking and feeling self.

Harriet died of tuberculosis in 1858. "The spring of my life is broken," Mill wrote a friend. When *On Liberty* was published the following year, Mill prefixed a dedication to Harriet of extraordinary tenderness. "Were I but capable of interpreting to the world one half the great insights and noble feelings which are buried in her grave," he wrote, "I should be the medium of a greater benefit to it, than is ever likely to arise from anything that I can write, unprompted and unassisted by her all but unrivalled wisdom."[16]

Mill said that he first thought of writing an essay on liberty while climbing the steps of Capitoline Hill in Rome—a moment that echoed, presumably consciously, Gibbon's inspiration in the same place to write a history of the Roman Empire. The subject had its own urgency, Mill wrote to Harriet, for "opinion tends to encroach more & more on liberty, and almost all the projects of social reformers of these days are really *liberticide*." Mill was an extremely methodical thinker, and by this time he had spent years dwelling on the right of the individual to stand apart from society and the state in order to fully realize his own capacities. In *The Principles of Political Economy* he had asserted that "there is a circle around every individual being, which no government, be it that of a few, or of the many, ought to be permitted to overstep." That circle "ought to include all that part which includes only the life, whether inward or outward, of the individual, and does not affect the interests of others."[17]

Tocqueville had written that liberty could not survive the modern passion for social and economic equality; the liberal chooses liberty over equality. That was not the way Mill thought. Mill embraced the cause of the common man, advocated an expansion of the franchise, proposed reforms to diminish economic inequality. He had long abandoned the crude psychology of utilitarianism, but he still believed devoutly that the just society was one dedicated to the public good. In 1861 he would publish a lengthy essay both explaining and justifying his more refined understanding of utilitarianism. Throughout *On Liberty*, Mill insisted that the protection of individual freedoms serves the collective good. No aspect of this magisterial essay is less convincing; Isaiah Berlin would later write that Mill believed more ardently in liberty than in utility. Yet Mill was too deeply committed both to the cause of liberty and to the cause of the public good to accept that the one intrinsically contradicted the other.

Mill began *On Liberty* by making the case for a virtually unlimited freedom of expression. This was hardly unfamiliar territory; Milton had framed such an argument in his *Areopagitica*. But Mill set out to shock the reader with what sounds like an impossibly hyperbolic claim for this liberty: "If all mankind minus one, were of one opinion, and only one person were of the contrary opinion, mankind would be no more justified in silencing that opinion, than he, if he had the power, would be justified in silencing mankind." The idea sounds absurd, at least according to utilitarian principles. Mill proceeded to explain:

> But the peculiar evil of silencing the expression of an opinion is, that it is robbing the human race; posterity as well as the existing generation; those who dissent from the opinion, still more than those who hold it. If the opinion is right, they are deprived of the opportunity of exchanging error for truth: if wrong, they lose, what is almost as great a benefit, the clearer perception and livelier impression of truth, produced by its collision with error.[18]

Mill is not making a claim here about the truth. He is not saying, and indeed did not say, that the truth will naturally emerge from competition in the marketplace of ideas. (Justice Oliver Wendell Holmes coined that phrase.) He had little expectation of reaching finality. In the study of man, rather than of mathematics, Mill wrote, truth rarely lies all on one side, but rather "depends on a balance to be struck between two sets of conflicting reasons." Mill's subject, then, is truth *seeking*. "He who knows only his own side of the case," he wrote, "knows little of that." Until they have "thrown themselves into the mental position of those who think differently from them," critics are in no position to refute the wrong and thus defend the right. The rare man whose judgment deserves our confidence is the one who "has kept his mind open to criticism of his opinions and conduct." Surely there is a strong element of autobiography here, for Mill had had the courage to break with radicalism, to listen to thinkers deemed anathema by the devotees of his former faith, to live without a single fixed doctrine.[19]

Mill's view of truth converges here with his view of human nature. He did not, of course, view men as rational mechanisms, as Bentham and the Enlightenment thinkers did. Neither had he glimpsed the depths of brutality that would be disclosed in the twentieth century. Like a moralist of the previous century, a Voltaire or a Samuel Johnson, Mill cocked a sardonic eyebrow at human vanity. "While everyone knows himself to be fallible," he wrote archly, "few think it necessary to take any precautions against their own fallibility." The more important the proposition, the more likely are people to be led astray by prejudice, self-interest, or simple delusion. The results have all too often been catastrophic. Was Socrates not put to death by the leaders of one of the most elevated societies mankind has ever known? Was it not Marcus Aurelius, wisest of the Romans, who authorized the persecution of Christians? "No Christian more firmly believes that Atheism is false, and tends to the dissolution of society, than Marcus Aurelius believed the same things of Christianity." If we may punish the man we "know" is wrong, how will the truth ever flourish? The axiom that truth always triumphs over persecution is, Mill wrote, "one of those pleasant falsehoods which men repeat after one another till they pass into commonplaces, but which all experience refutes." There is a brutal honesty here that challenges the reader, then and now, to examine his or her own habits of thought.[20]

Mill tells us that we will do vastly more harm to ourselves by limiting freedom of expression than by permitting it. That, he said, is the lesson of history. Only in eras when "the dread of heterodox speculation was for a time suspended" has intellectual life flourished—and society with it. Mill adduced as examples Reformation Europe, the Enlightenment, and the Germany of Goethe. "The impulse given at these three periods,"

Mill argued, "has made Europe what it is now." It is in the interest of society to zealously protect freedom of thought, freedom of speech, and freedom of conscience because no society worth caring about can be established without them. Yet Mill also believed that most people would happily prohibit speech they find objectionable. A society ruled by democratic will would scarcely defend Socrates; one can hardly think of a clearer instance of the tyranny of the majority. The only way that Mill could square this circle was to say that most people don't understand what will make them happy. The solution to that problem, as Mill said elsewhere, is education.[21]

Mill now turned from the familiar subject of freedom of expression to the quite novel terrain of freedom of behavior. Mill wished to champion what he called, in an expression far better suited to our own time than to his, "experiments of living." People must be free, not only to speak, but to be. And this is true because of what humans are. "Human nature is not a machine to be built after a model," he wrote, "but a tree, which requires to grow and develop itself on all sides, according to the tendency of the inward forces which make it a living thing." Here, in vivid metaphorical form, is Mill's repudiation of the Benthamite view of human nature and his embrace of the Romantic one. Mill cited the German scientist and philosopher Wilhelm von Humboldt, who wrote that "the end of man is the highest and most harmonious development of his powers to a complete and consistent whole." The prerequisites for full human flourishing, Humboldt said, are "freedom, and variety of situations."[22]

Mill was not making a case for the freedom of each individual to attain an imagined ideal state—to become one of Plato's guardians. Quite the contrary: he was making a novel argument for individuality, idiosyncrasy, refractoriness. He launched a passionate attack on the Christianizing spirit of improvement of early Victorian England: "Much has actually been effected in the way of increased regularity of conduct, and discouragement of excesses. . . . These tendencies of the time cause the public to be more disposed than at most former periods to prescribe general rules of conduct, and to make everyone conform to the approved standard. And that standard, express or tacit, is to desire nothing strongly. Its ideal of character is to be without any marked character; to maim by compression, like a Chinese lady's foot, every part of human nature which stands out prominently."[23]

The living tree has been squeezed into the crippled form of the Chinese lady's foot. The reader cannot miss the intensity of Mill's disgust. It in no way reduces the force of his argument to suggest that Mill himself experienced the maiming effect of society's demand for social conformity—from his own family and friends and from a larger censorious world—and came to recognize that liberty must encompass not only the thinking mind but the acting self. Mill had encountered philosophical claims for spontaneity, originality, eccentricity in Goethe and in the English Romantics, but then life struck those abstractions like a tuning fork and made them ring.

The dread forces of conformity, Mill goes on, come in many guises: the "Calvinistic theory" that holds that an individual's will must be brought to heel, the leveling impulse that brings down the mighty and raises up the humble, the Christian reform movement that would curb unruly appetites. Against this stands only the individual who insists upon his or her individuality. And that, Mill said, is everything. It is only by cultivating individuality, he wrote, "that human beings become a noble and beautiful object of contemplation." And as the work bears the impress of the man, it is such figures who make life itself "rich, diversified, and animating," binding people to one another and "making the race infinitely better worth belonging to."[24]

Here, again, Mill runs up against the tension between his belief in the sacred sphere of the individual and the good of the majority. Mill did not share our modern democratic respect for the average person; he did not believe that most people aspire to genuine self-realization any more than they do to unfettered self-expression. "The general average of mankind are not only moderate in intellect," he wrote, "but also moderate in inclinations: they have no tastes or wishes strong enough to incline them to do anything unusual." Why, then, should they defend the right of the few to their "experiments in living"? "These developed human beings are of some use to the undeveloped," he insisted: by offering a model to others, they refresh tired ideas and show ordinary people that they do not have to bend their knees before the great god of convention.[25]

The phrase "some use" may express Mill's own misgivings about the argument. Yet because Mill does not regard human nature as fixed, he really does have an expectation that people can become more than they are at a given moment. Unlike his father or Bentham, who saw human nature in static terms, Mill's view of utility was "grounded on the permanent interests of man as a progressive being." People are not marionettes whose strings are pulled by pleasure and pain, but beings with ideals, imagination, and a conscience, who seek, or at least who are capable of seeking, their own truest selves. A greatest good, in effect, lies within each of us. As Mill famously wrote in *Utilitarianism*, "It is better to be . . . Socrates dissatisfied than a fool satisfied."[26]

Mill recognized that at times the exercise of unlimited liberty will in fact harm the collective good. He explored that boundary in the fourth section of *On Liberty*. Mill asked, "How much of human life should be assigned to individuality, and how much to society?" And he delivered an unequivocal answer: "As soon as any part of a person's conduct affects prejudicially the interests of others, society has jurisdiction over it. . . . But there is no room for entertaining any such question when a person's conduct affects the interests of no persons besides himself." Critics of Mill have argued almost from the moment *On Liberty* was published that he has drawn a sharp line where none exists, that even the most self-regarding behavior has consequences for others. The criticism may be just, but it's clear that Mill's goal was to expand as far as possible the circle of free behavior. He was perhaps the first thinker to advance the essential principle of modern liberal society: people should be allowed to do anything they want so long as it doesn't hurt others. Mill wouldn't have called that our "right," as we would, but he seemed to regard it that way.[27]

Mill asked why society should not prevent people from engaging in behaviors it considers morally wrong, such as gambling or indulging in drunkenness or idleness, whether they harm others or not. Of course, he wrote, society should not hesitate to show its disapproval of idleness, to encourage the idle to get up and work. But it should not prohibit such behavior because doing so is almost bound to cause more harm than good. Just as Mill argued earlier in *On Liberty* that society rises up in self-destructive fashion to suppress whatever truths it finds intolerable, so, he argued here, "to extend the bounds of what may be called the moral police, until it encroaches on the most unquestionably legitimate liberty of the individual, is one of the most universal of all human propensities." Society takes offense when its conventional standards are violated: the moral police may start with gamblers, but it will quickly move on to the nonconforming.[28]

This insistence on countenancing antisocial behavior in the name of liberty is perhaps the most radical and forward-looking passage of Mill's essay. We may read it today with a shrug because Mill's fight has long since been waged and won, at least in the West. Few ideas enjoy such consensual support as that our private behavior is no one's business but our own. But in advancing this claim, Mill also directed us to scrutinize our unexamined convictions. He asked readers to imagine themselves the victims of someone else's deeply held views. Muslims, he noted, view the eating of pork as a gross transgression of God's will. What if Muslims gained a majority in a given country and voted to prohibit the eating of pork even by non-Muslims? "Would it be a legitimate exercise of the moral authority of public opinion?" Mill asked. "And if not, why not?" Only because "with the personal tastes and self-regarding concerns of individuals the public has no business to interfere." The prospect of a moral police loses its appeal once we imagine ourselves the victims of it. Unless, he observed pointedly, we are prepared to assert that "we may persecute others because we are right, and that they must not persecute us because they are wrong," we must adopt a general prohibition against the legal enforcement of personal tastes, even those that we view as divinely ordained.[29]

This is a genuinely subversive line of thought, since, after all, many of Mill's readers would have taken it for granted that Christians have the right to enforce behavior upon Muslims, and not the other way around, because Christianity is true and Islam false. Throughout *On Liberty*, Mill asked readers inclined to circumscribe the liberty of others to scrutinize their own convictions, whether about speech or about conduct, and ask whether they might be rooted in convention, or self-interest, or unexamined bias, or vanity, rather than in reason. And if we start from a position of self-scrutiny and openness to others, as Mill himself always sought to do, will we not see that each of us is best served by guaranteeing others maximum personal liberty?

In the final passage of *On Liberty*, titled "Applications," Mills sought to explain what it would mean in ordinary life to apply the standards he has suggested. For example, in the case of poisons with legitimate purposes, he suggested that the state has the right to require the manufacturer to affix a warning label, since "the buyer cannot wish not to know that the thing he possesses has poisonous qualities." The state cannot, however, require the buyer to procure a doctor's certificate, since that would unduly hinder a legitimate purchase. Liquor stores should not be banned, but they can be regulated and specially taxed. Gambling should be permitted; but what about gambling dens? "There are arguments on both sides," Mill conceded. If gambling should be legal, so should it be legal to make a living from it; but society may still balk at openly permitting the solicitation of behavior it agrees to be bad. This is liberalism in practice: making fine distinctions about hard issues with a bias toward individual liberty.[30]

Mill begins to sound like a modern libertarian when he speaks about situations in which the state interferes, not to restrain individuals, but to help them. He has already proposed something that will startle modern readers. The state, he asserted, has the right to require universal education and the obligation to defray the costs for the poor, but once parents know that they must send their children to school, they may seek one wherever they wish. A society dedicated to fostering diversity of ideas and of conduct should be no less dedicated to diversity of education, since "a general State education is a mere contrivance for moulding people to be exactly like one another." Education should be a private function. The state can assure quality by mandating universal examinations from an early age. Mill would apparently be very much at home in today's charter school movement.[31]

In 1859, the government impinged very little on the lives of ordinary British citizens. Mill did not regard the state as a leviathan, because England's constitution had long since brought absolute power to heel. Neither, however, did Mill regard the state as an instrument of public benevolence. The European welfare state had not yet come into being. Mill regarded the state essentially as an encumbrance. As a general rule, he wrote, individual effort should be preferred to state action because individuals are more effective, because personal initiative should be encouraged, and, most of all, because the state must not be allowed to become pervasive. Mill even opposed the idea of a highly professional civil service because, if the nation's ablest men went to work for the government, "all the enlarged culture and practised intelligence in the country, except the purely speculative, would be concentrated in a numerous bureaucracy, to whom alone the rest of the community would look for all things."[32]

The state, in short, may no more encroach on the circle of autonomy to help men than it may do so to restrain them, for, as Mill noted in closing, "a state which dwarfs its men, in order that they may be more docile instruments in its hands even for beneficial purposes—will find that with small men no great thing can really be accomplished."[33]

In 1865, Mill was asked to run for Parliament on the ticket of the Liberals, a party that had emerged from the Whigs, who had favored limits on the power of the Crown and the Church as well as a modest expansion of suffrage to enfranchise the growing middle class and upper working class. The Reform Act of 1832, which had done just that, brought new men and new causes to the Whigs. Over time these new, middle-class men, known as liberals, turned the Whig Party into the instrument of their views. They were very incremental reformers. They continued to insist that only propertied men could exercise the franchise. Trade-union leaders in their ranks favored an increase in wages but opposed anything that smacked of class warfare, revolution, or insurrection; mobs on the Continent might take to the barricades, but England had won its fight with the king two centuries earlier and ridden out a series of lesser convulsions thereafter. Liberalism looked to the gradual evolution in England of a society of equals such as existed in the United States.

Liberals viewed the national government as a tool of the entitled. Taxation went to maintaining the idle rich and the schemes of empire; real national power, as Liberal leader Richard Cobden argued, came from the energies of working men and merchants. The Liberals consistently opposed government expenditure; between 1861 and 1865, when William Gladstone, the party leader, served as chancellor of the exchequer, national expenditure dropped from £72 million to £66 million and income tax fell sharply. In the liberal view of political economy, taxation reduced profit, which in turn forced the employer to reduce wages. The art of good government, as one liberal journal put it, consisted of "the lowest possible interference with the people." Nineteenth-century English liberalism was avowedly anti-statist.[34]

Mill shared the Liberals' distrust of government, their wish to expand the franchise, their defense of trade unions. At the same time, he found the new party far too wan for his taste. He was disgusted by its generally tepid response to the American Civil War, which Mill saw as a mighty contest between the forces of progress and the genuinely evil, and reactionary, society of slaveholders. Mill had been asked to run before and had declined. But given his immense prestige, Mill had reason to hope that he could help push the Liberals in a more radical direction. He refused to campaign and vowed that if elected, he would pay no attention to local interests. Nevertheless, or perhaps for that very reason, he won.

Mill soon found that he had a great deal in common with Gladstone, an evangelical Christian and indefatigable pamphleteer as high-minded as Mill himself. Once in Parliament, Mill supported Gladstone's Reform Bill, which would further extend voting rights. Gladstone, in turn, personally committed himself to Mill's most radical cause, expanding the rights of women, including giving them the right to vote. Gladstone memorably dubbed Mill "the Saint of Rationalism." But Mill was more than that. During his brief tenure in the House of Commons, Mill made himself the voice of the oppressed. He opposed the execution of Irish rebels against England (though he favored capital punishment) and the suspension of habeas corpus in Ireland. At mass reform meetings during the height of the debate over the Reform Bill in 1866–1867, men cheered the names of Mill and Gladstone, who had, they felt, championed the moral character of the working class—though both harbored deep reservations about whether that class deserved full political rights.

The Principles of Political Economy had made Mill the great political economist of his day, and virtually all debate on the question of marketplace intervention took the form of confirming or taking exception to his views. Mill himself took the iconoclastic view that land in Ireland must be nationalized in order to provide for the peasantry. Attacked for contradicting his own expressed free-market principles, Mill replied that economics did not stipulate a "set of maxims and rules, to be applied without regard to times, places and circumstances." Acting justly must at times take precedence over acting consistently.[35]

Mill was defeated in his bid for reelection in 1868. By this time, the Liberals had the wind in their sails. They had become the party of the working class, and Gladstone their undisputed leader. That year he began the first of four terms as prime minister. The last would end in 1894, when he was eighty-five. The Liberals remained committed to the principle that individual autonomy and self-respect required freedom, rather than assistance, from the state. Workingmen demanded the unfettered right to obtain insurance and other social benefits through their own voluntary societies rather than through public funds. Working-class radicals opposed any form of poor relief that would increase the dependence of the poor on the government. The state, they insisted, with Mill, should "educate rather than relieve the masses." Even there the state trod lightly: national education legislation introduced in 1870 stipulated that new government schools would, as Mill himself had suggested, supplement rather than replace existing voluntary and denominational ones. The liberal demand for an expanded franchise was intimately linked to the liberal rejection of the philanthropic state, for men who had the right to vote should also have the right to fashion their own lives. The spirit of Cobden was strong: working-class activists often professed faith in laissez-faire economics more zealously than did businessmen.[36]

This was the era of Dickensian work conditions in factories and mines, of child labor and the pitiless sweatshop. Modest regulation of English factories had been adopted starting in the early years of the nineteenth century. Yet the liberalism of the Liberal Party precluded most interventions on behalf of the poor. The Tories, with their aristocratic paternalism, proved far more willing to act. It was Tory prime minister Benjamin Disraeli who was chiefly responsible for the Factory and Workshop Act of 1878, which prohibited the employment of children under ten and instead required them to be in school, limited the female workweek to fifty-six hours, and extended existing restrictions on work conditions to all trades.

Despite its appeal to the workingman, the Liberal Party was immune to the new Marxian rhetoric of class conflict. When, in 1871, Gladstone's government introduced a bill to permit trade unions to organize, labor activists were quick to agree that any form of union coercion, such as the strike, must be harshly punished by law. Demands for improvements to working conditions were typically formulated as a matter of basic Christian morality: How could a man be free to go down into an unsafe mine where he was likely to be buried alive? Indeed, so central was the language of liberty that even factory reforms had to be presented as enhancements to freedom: activists claimed that since a man's life and health were his property, laws protecting worker safety did not impinge on basic liberties but, in fact, protected them.[37]

The contradiction between the ideal of autonomy and the dreadful facts of late nineteenth-century industrial life could not last long. The gross disproportion of economic power between owner and worker made a mockery of the quaint idea of free labor. At the same time, the expansion of the franchise in 1867 and again in 1885 was changing the balance of political power, amplifying calls for reform inside the Liberal Party. The allegiance of the working class to small government and laissez-faire policies could not survive democratic politics: workers increasingly demanded state protection. The ancient Liberal leader could not adapt to the new spirit. Gladstone refused to incorporate the eight-hour day into the Liberal platform ahead of the 1892 election, complaining that "the labouring classes begin to be corrupted by the semblance of power." Gladstone, one of his biographers observes, "was not an anti-reformer; but he felt that the ultimate purpose of all social and political action was to raise the moral stature of the individual and this could not be done by redressing his material grievances."[38]

A political party based on the small-government liberalism of Mill and Gladstone could not continue to attract mass working-class support. In 1900, representatives of trade unions gathered in London to establish what would become the Labour Party. Liberalism would have to adapt in order to remain a blueprint for governance in the modern world.

John Stuart Mill was the rare example of a man who grew more radical as he got older. He wrote less and less in the Coleridgean vein about the need to mend the tattered fabric of the past, and more and more about the need to explode the myths that allowed some people to dominate others. In 1869, he published *The Subjection of Women*, a tract considered so radical that even many of his friends rejected its conclusions. Mill made at length the argument for the political and legal equality of women that he had advanced in Parliament. That is remarkable enough for an era in which women were only beginning to organize and had very few male sympathizers. What is yet more impressive is how deeply Mill sought to imagine his way into the position of the oppressed. "It is only a man here and there who has any tolerable knowledge of the character even of the women of his own family," he wrote. "I mean their actually existing thoughts and feelings." Indeed, he asserted, the structure of power between men and women has robbed women of their own identity. Since men wish women to dote on them, and since women cannot exist in society save under the protection of a man, "it would be a miracle if the object of being attractive to men had not become the polar star of feminine education and formation of character."[39]

Perhaps Mill was thinking of the sad tale of his own mother when he wrote those words. What's more, Harriet's example had shown Mill the absurdity of imagining women as unequal partners to men. The tone of real outrage that suffuses the essay may owe some of its force to Mill's resentment that Harriet never had the chance to take her merited place in society. But Mill's target is not only prejudice against women but prejudice itself, and the way in which systematic mistreatment comes to seem natural merely by being customary. "Was there ever any domination that did not seem natural to those who possessed it?" he asked. Slavery appeared natural until it came to be seen as intolerable; so did absolute monarchy. And while those practices benefited only a few, the subjection of women—Mill did not hesitate to compare the system to slavery—benefits half of mankind. So, how can it not be wreathed in plausible-sounding justifications? Mill obliterated them one by one, stripping away the rationales that serve as bulwarks to male privilege. He would turn out to be a century or so ahead of his time.[40]

Mill died of erysipelas, an acute bacterial infection, on May 7, 1873. He was buried next to Harriet in Avignon. It is fair to say, almost a century and a half later, that his world is not ours; the quandaries that vexed him are not ours. He offered solutions to problems, like rigid conformism in matters of private behavior, that most people in the West no longer have to trouble themselves over. He had no convincing answers to problems that concern us very much, like the role of the state in counteracting the malign effects of the market. But liberalism is not simply, or even chiefly, a matter of finding solutions to problems. Liberalism is a temperament. The liberal temperament is respectful of individuals and individual ends; tolerant of differences both of opinion and of background; secular in its orientation toward truth; optimistic about humanity's prospects yet wary of all utopian faiths. Liberalism is not so much a text as a score, and it is John Stuart Mill who wrote that music.

CHAPTER THREE

The *New Republic* and the Refounding of American Liberalism

*What can the State do? What can we do to make the
wrong right for the people of our mills and our factories?*

—WALTER WEYL

IN EARLY 1912, WALTER WEYL, AN ECONOMIST, JOURNALIST, and labor activist, went to Lawrence, Massachusetts, to cover a strike by over ten thousand textile workers, almost all of them immigrants and most of them women. The workers had put down their tools after mill owners, known as "the wool trust," had cut their salaries in response to a law passed by the state legislature reducing maximum weekly hours from fifty-six to fifty-four. Weyl told the readers of *Outlook*, a magazine associated with former president Theodore Roosevelt, the great champion of progressivism, that the millworkers' wages, while no worse than he had found elsewhere, "were far lower than the cost of living and the demands of our American civilization imperatively require." The average salary at the mills was $8.76 a week, or about sixteen cents an hour—about half of what would have been a living wage at the time. The average life expectancy among Lawrence workers was thirty-nine; the mortality rate among the city's children before the age of six was 50 percent. The wool trust refused to increase hourly pay; a mill owner paid off a local man to plant dynamite around town and blame it on the strikers. The mayor of Lawrence sent an armed militia into the streets. Nevertheless, the strikers, who spoke twenty different languages, somehow held together, remained peaceful, and persisted through a freezing winter. "I went to Lawrence prejudiced in favor of the strikers," Weyl candidly wrote. "But I come from it more than ever imbued with the greatness of their cause."[1]

In Lawrence, Weyl saw not simply the rights of workers but the future of industrial capitalism hanging in the balance. The International Workers of the World, a union, had raced to Lawrence to support and organize the workers. Weyl knew these men and women well; their leader, Bill Haywood, was, he wrote, more "European revolutionary syndicalist" than trade union chief. Haywood hoped to stoke the fires of class warfare. "There is no dynamite in the world so utterly destructive as the blind faith that seeks to move mountains," Weyl warned. And yet was it not "ruthless capitalism" itself that had produced men like Haywood? The workers wanted bread, not bloodshed. But how long would they, and their ilk, resist the call to violent revolution? The great question, Weyl wrote in conclusion, was, "What can the State do? What can we do to make the wrong right for the people of our mills and our factories?"[2]

What can the state do? As little as possible, John Stuart Mill had said; and so, too, had said William Gladstone and the first generation of English liberals. People flourish in an atmosphere of liberty. The control of property by a hereditary class was a grotesque injustice that needed to be tamed by law, but the nineteenth-century English liberals believed that the state should only minimally intervene in relations between employer and employed. For Mill and the early liberals, "the economy" meant coal mines and small-scale factories. The power of the employer over the worker, though vastly greater than it had been in the time of Adam Smith, still seemed susceptible both to appeals to conscience by reformers and to negotiation of terms by workers. But the economy of the United States in 1912 consisted of giant institutions. The individual owner had disappeared, or had vanished into an unreachable empyrean. The firm had metamorphosed into the trust; almost every major industry was dominated by a single firm. Men and women went by the thousands through the gates of factory and mill, and while most lived better than their parents had done, others—millions of others—were crushed in the cogs of the industrial machine.

Laissez-faire liberalism now looked like a cynical anachronism. Indeed, the Liberal Party in England, returning to power in 1906 after a spell of Conservative rule, no longer accepted the old principle that the dignity of the workingman lay in his self-reliance. The "new Liberals," as they were called, insisted that men enduring squalid conditions could not live as full citizens, whatever their formal political rights. The party introduced reforms in health insurance, unemployment insurance, and pensions. The Liberal government's 1909 budget imposed substantially increased taxes on the rich in order to fund the new welfare programs for the poor and working class. A "liberal" state was no longer one that stood to the side but rather one that raised the level of the poor so that they could come into full possession of their liberty.

Walter Weyl had wrestled with this problem for years. By the time he got to Lawrence, Weyl had handed to his book publisher the manuscript for what would turn out to be his chief work, *The New Democracy*, which was published several months later to great acclaim. In it he confronted at length the problem he touched on in *Outlook*: How could America forge in its industrial life the principles of citizenship that were universally accepted, if not always practiced, in its political culture? The book secured Weyl's status as a major figure in the Progressive reform movement. Two years later, in 1914, he became—along with Herbert Croly and Walter Lippmann, public intellectuals like himself—a founding editor of the *New Republic*, the magazine that would define liberalism for several generations of Americans.

In 1912, none of these men would have called themselves liberals. They would have used that word derisively to describe Woodrow Wilson, the Democratic candidate for president and heir of the Democratic, and specifically southern, tradition of small government and states' rights. Weyl, Croly, and Lippmann considered themselves progressives. All three worked actively for Teddy Roosevelt, who hoped to regain the presidency by wresting the Republican nomination from the incumbent, William H. Taft. Failing, TR established a new party, the Progressives. Wilson, of course, won the three-cornered contest, and as president adopted much of the Progressive platform, merging one tradition with another and rendering "liberal" a term of honor among progressives. The advent of World War I in 1914 largely ended Wilson's domestic ambitions. But the Great Depression fifteen years later gave a new urgency to the agenda of economic reform. FDR proudly donned the mantle of liberalism, giving that term the meaning that it still has today, at least in the English-speaking world, as a doctrine dedicated to shaping the forces of the marketplace in order to serve the ends of social and economic justice.

The social conditions that shaped John Stuart Mill's liberalism had never existed in the United States. Tradition and history, which the English radicals had wished to shed, the conservatives to sustain, and Mill to reform as a source of vitality, had never had the weight in the United States that they did in England. America's ruling class was fluid, and it was new; the dinosaurs of Boston society might wish to cramp individuality like the bound foot of a Chinese lady, but few Americans perceived this impulse as an inescapable threat to self-realization. The fierce individuality that Tocqueville had observed made Americans genetically liberal, at least in Mill's sense.

Americans had little to fear from society and still less from their feeble government. The constitutionalism of Constant or Guizot felt no more urgent to men like Weyl than did Mill's individualism. It was the marketplace that increasingly hemmed Americans in and defined the limits of their autonomy. The conditions that Walter Weyl described in Lawrence had become widespread in the United States within a quarter century after the Civil War. Rapid industrialization had begun to urbanize what had long been a nation of small-scale farmers. By 1890, a third of the nation's 65 million citizens lived in cities and towns. Ever more men and women went to work in factories. No more than about 15 percent of them earned an income equal to what Weyl would call the demands of contemporary civilization. The Panic of 1893 led to mass destitution; the following year, "Coxey's Army," a rabble of unemployed men led by Ohio businessman Jacob Coxey, marched on Washington, demanding food and jobs. Their number eventually swelled to six thousand. Violent strikes spread across the country.

At the same time, the ownership class had swelled enormously in size and in wealth. The top 1 percent of the country earned more in wages than the bottom 50 percent and held more in property than the rest of the country combined. Yet the ripening sense of anger at the rich had no obvious political outlet. The national government, which consisted largely of the postal service and the twenty-five-thousand-man standing army, had neither the will nor the capacity to regulate business practices. The Supreme Court, in the grip of a social Darwinist ideology that equated laissez-faire with the competitive order of nature, was equally disinclined to place impediments in the path of business interests; in 1895, the court exempted manufacturing firms from the terms of the Sherman Antitrust Act, rendering the law virtually a dead letter.

The combination of drastic economic change and weak political institutions provoked two different reform movements: populism and progressivism. Populism spread like a prairie fire among farmers and townsfolk whose lives had been disrupted by industrialization, and who deeply resented the railroads that charged them to carry their produce and the northern banks that granted them credit—or didn't. A sharp drop in crop prices in the late 1880s had pushed millions of farmers into tenancy and debt. A coalition called the Farmers' Alliance channeled this spontaneous uprising into electoral politics in 1890. In 1892 the new Populist Party nominated a presidential candidate.

Like previous third parties in American history, the Populists quickly burned out as a national political force, but populism survived as an expression of rural grievance and a radical protest against the dominant ideology of the free market. The Populists spoke the native language of American democracy, defending the self-reliant individual against massed power. In the platform of their 1892 convention, the leaders of the new party wrote, "The fruits of the toil of millions are boldly stolen to build up colossal fortunes for a few, unprecedented in the history of mankind; and the possessors of those, in turn, despise the republic and endanger liberty. From the same prolific womb of governmental injustice we bred the two great classes—tramps and millionaires." Populists called on the government to nationalize the railroads and provide cheap credit to farmers. The Populists also sought to empower ordinary citizens through such political reform as the direct election of senators, the referendum, and the initiative. They called for a more democratic economy and a more democratic democracy.[3]

The Populists' vision of an economy divided between virtuous "producers" and parasitic traders and financiers had already been anachronistic when Andrew Jackson had formulated it in 1832. They sensed, as one historian wrote, "that something fundamental was happening with their lives, something they had not willed and did not want, and they responded by striking out at whatever enemies their view of the world allowed them to see." Their enemies included British bankers, "Jewish gold," immigrants, Wall Street. This fusion of bewilderment and fury would return a century later, as Americans were making the painful transition from an industrial to a postindustrial, service-oriented economy. They would find their tribune in Donald Trump.

One may think of populism and progressivism as different faiths held by different people confronting different aspects of the same problem— the disorienting effects of economic and social upheaval. Progressivism was a diffuse phenomenon: a movement of moral reform among Christians whose "social gospel" committed them to aid the disadvantaged, as well as temperance workers who wanted to purify society of the vice of drinking; a program of urban reform that sought to ameliorate the dreadful conditions of the factories and the slums into which immigrants were flooding; an administrative agenda that sought to apply new species of expertise to government and to social affairs; and a political critique of a wasteful, cruel, selfish society that seemed to know no better rule than "Help yourself."

The reform agenda of most progressives overlapped substantially with that of the populists—direct election of senators, income and inheritance taxes, public control or regulation of utilities and of the giant trusts. But the high-minded and generally highborn progressive leaders regarded the populists as an anarchic mob. Teddy Roosevelt suggested, only half-jokingly, lining up the leading populists in front of a firing squad. The besetting sin of progressivism was its elitism, its discomfort with the "unenlightened," its preference for bureaucracy and impersonal expertise over the clamor of politics. In the progressive imagination, as one scholar of the movement put it, "government would be simultaneously returned to the people and placed beyond them, in the hands of the experts." If populism formulated a response to the crisis of the time that was democratic but illiberal, progressives tended to be liberal but not very democratic.[4]

Walter Weyl was a member of the new, upwardly mobile urban class that filled the progressive ranks. A first-generation German Jew, he was raised in Philadelphia in the bookish, cultured environment of his mother's well-to-do family. More than that, he was a credentialed member of the emerging professoriat: after graduating from the Wharton School, Weyl studied economics at the University of Halle in Germany, traveling around Europe and familiarizing himself with social conditions and government reforms. He returned to the University of Pennsylvania and received his PhD in 1897.[5]

Weyl might have enjoyed a comfortable life as an academic, but he was constitutionally restless, curious, changeable. When coal workers went on strike in 1902, he went to eastern Pennsylvania to offer his services to John Mitchell, the president of the United Mine Workers. Then he decided to devote himself full-time to the vagabond life of the freelance journalist. Like other progressive champions, including Lincoln Steffens and Ida Wells, Weyl wrote about strikes and the urban poor and the lives of new immigrants. Yet he was more thinker and moralist than muckraker. Weyl made extensive notes for *The Visionary*, a novel he planned to write about the life of Christ. His Christ, like D. H. Lawrence's in *The Man Who Died*, would return to the world as a man, not a god. This was the Christ who evicted the money changers from the temple, an inspired leader who would "excoriate and denounce militarism, the police, the jails." *The Visionary*, however, never advanced beyond the stage of notes. Weyl also spent years mulling a book on class conflict. This was to be the book of all books, on the subject of all subjects. He compiled hundreds of pages of notes, but the book remained unwritten at his death. Weyl planned to write a play about "some popular economic or political problem which vitally affects the people in a direct and personal way"—"Women in Industry," "The Negro Problem," "The Jail." Weyl suffered from a kind of crippling objectivity: he could see the shortcomings of everything he wrote; nothing quite matched the majesty of his own conceptions. For all his moral passion, he was a man with more questions than answers. As his friend and *New Republic* colleague Walter Lippmann put it, Weyl "was of the company of Socrates, rather than Isaiah."[6]

The one major work Weyl brought to fruition was *The New Democracy: An Essay on Certain Political and Economic Tendencies in the United States.* Weyl's object was to reconceptualize the American past in order to lay the groundwork for a new vision of its future. *The New Democracy* opens with a headlong account of the conquest of the frontier. Weyl's central theme is the absence of any force willing or able to govern the mad energies unleashed by an open continent. America was in thrall to the cult of the heroic individual. Pioneers pitted themselves against nature, and subdued nature. This was all in the true spirit of the nation; that was the world Tocqueville had seen. But then, Weyl went on, a vast force rose up behind the individual. While pioneers had taken what they could, "the gigantic railroad, with a thousand fold greater power, had done but the same." The railroads and the land companies had bought up the land—"preempted" and "appropriated" it from people with axes and picks. Over time the pioneer gave way to the promoter and the financier, but always in the guise of American individualism, to which no exception could be taken. Nature was preempted, and then, with the rise of the giant corporation and its political handmaiden, the party boss, the city was preempted. Yet people remained blind to the forces shaping their lives. "The very qualities bred into him by the conquest made it impossible for the individualist—so long as he remained an individualist—to solve, or even see, his economic problems."[7]

Individuals had thus surrendered their autonomy to the brutal power of what Weyl called "the plutocracy." The modern American was governed not by the state but by the trust. The trusts had left intact the formal mechanisms of democracy and even the political liberties stipulated in the Bill of Rights. But they had come to exercise a ruthless and utterly undemocratic dominion over economic life, the very core of a person's being in the modern industrial world. The political language of liberty, as applied to the economy, had become a fraud. The plutocracy, Weyl wrote, "had always interpreted the phrase 'economic freedom' in the good, old, simple juridical sense, according to which a poor Roumanian, consumptive widow, half-supporting her children by sewing, is a 'free agent' enjoying 'economic freedom.'" The economic liberalism of the nineteenth century had thus become a cynical pretext for exploitation.[8]

Weyl's sympathies, like those of the populists, lay with the little guy against the forces of power. But Weyl was an economist, and he accepted the argument, then very much in vogue, that large, highly organized corporations had come to dominate the economy because they were more efficient than the small-scale firms they had replaced. In his version of nineteenth-century economic history, the recklessly wasteful rush to exploit the continent had inevitably given way to planning and organization. In the case of utilities, like the railroad or the telegraph or the streetcar, the state had no real choice save to grant monopoly control. In heavy industry, the need for standardization drove out small players. Populists like William Jennings Bryan who imagined that the trusts could be broken up in order to return the economy to its old human scale had surrendered to an economic quixotism. More than that, the romantic cult of the individual played into the hands of the lords of laissez-faire. The future belonged to national-scale bureaucratic organizations; the great question was how to turn these mighty machines to social rather than merely individual purposes.

As Weyl repudiated Jeffersonian nostalgia, so he rejected Marxian revolution: thus the middle path he recommended in his article on the Lawrence strike. Weyl believed in no religion and no sweeping ideology. He was, by temperament and belief, a meliorist. He put his faith in facts. And the facts showed that Marx's prediction of the inevitable impoverishment of the proletariat under modern industrial conditions was simply wrong. For all the gross disparities of wealth and glaring injustices that Weyl had himself seen, the truth was, he wrote, that "wages during the last half century have risen faster than prices, hours of labor have been reduced, and factory conditions have been improved." Workers were not, in fact, powerless in the face of capital: trade unions had allowed them to act collectively to improve pay and working conditions while the extension of the franchise to those without property had given them the capacity to elect sympathetic representatives.[9]

Weyl was writing at a moment when the productive power of industrial capitalism inspired awe, and that power, for him, offered the key to social transformation. Surplus, he wrote, is "a new factor in man's career" that "renders ignorance, poverty and minority rule anachronistic." Until only yesterday, society was clamped in the iron laws of Malthus, struggling to produce as much as it consumed. Hunger made men fatalistic, abject—fit subjects for tyranny. When the Industrial Revolution began to raise production above the level of consumption, people finally understood that their destiny was not in the hands of nature but in those of their fellow men. They "began to question the morality and social efficiency of all historic distributions of wealth." In Weyl's materialist worldview, it was surplus that turned subjects into citizens and that held out the possibility of revitalizing American individualism. Industrial profit, wisely administered by the "socialized democracy" Weyl envisioned, makes social change possible without revolution. The poor man can be raised up "without breaking into the rich man's granary." Paradoxically, the giant scale made possible by the Industrial Revolution is the necessary precondition for the liberation of the individual.[10]

Weyl argued in the closing chapters of *The New Democracy* that the nation needs to adopt the principles of industrial democracy. The idea of popular sovereignty and collective good must be extended from the polity to the economy: workers need rights just as citizens do. Only the state can draft and enforce those rights. America needs a national government as up-to-date as its corporations—rational, transparent, organized. Weyl called for a government that, in addition to regulating and at times controlling industries, provides national health insurance and universal free schooling. He proposed rules governing both minimum and maximum hours, child labor laws, housing laws, and a campaign to improve public health. He called for a guaranteed vote for African Americans at a time when few could exercise the franchise. This vast mobilization of the state would have been anathema to Mill and the nineteenth-century liberals. But the progressives believed that the big state, like the big corporation, would not contract the sphere of individual liberty but expand it.

The New Democracy received glowing reviews in the United States and England. Weyl found, to his immense gratification, that he had become a sought-after speaker and author. His freelance rate shot up. The American Political Science Association asked Weyl to deliver the keynote speech at its annual meeting. This did much to assuage the lingering shame Weyl felt at having abandoned academia. He received fulsome letters from Winston Churchill and the eminent historian Charles Beard. Theodore Roosevelt himself took note, calling *The New Democracy* and Herbert Croly's *The Promise of American Life* "the true books of the movement."[11]

Weyl was an economist, and he captured the material forces that had, he believed, subverted the American promise. Croly, a perpetual Harvard graduate student and itinerant journalist, had studied political philosophy; the failures he captured in his 1909 *The Promise of American Life* are political and ideological. The argument for political minimalism and maximal individualism advanced by Jefferson and then by Andrew Jackson won the battle for the American soul. The nationalism of Hamilton and John Adams never escaped the fatal taint of elitism. As a result, Croly wrote, "the democratic political system was considered tantamount in practice to a species of vigorous, licensed and purified selfishness. The responsibilities of the government were negative; those of the individual were positive." Only Abraham Lincoln managed to fuse the deepest democratic values with what Croly called the national idea, addressing the American people not simply as atomistic individuals but as members of a collective. But after the Civil War, the Republican Party fell into the hands of the trusts. The democratic idea survived; the national idea did not. Croly concluded, like Weyl, that the new lords of the economy had hijacked the language of Jeffersonian individualism to justify the power they enjoyed in a laissez-faire system. America needed a democratic collectivism—that is, a Hamiltonian leader who, like Lincoln, could address the nation in Jeffersonian language.[12]

Croly was a more systematic thinker than Weyl. He confronted explicitly the tension between majoritarian democracy and liberal individualism that runs through the thought of Mill and other nineteenth-century British thinkers. If individual liberty is the supreme good, Croly wrote, then even a democratic state, governed by a majority, must be deprived of the power to violate those rights. Democracy must bow before liberty. Croly could not accept this outcome. "Individual freedom is important," he wrote, "but more important still is the freedom of a whole people to dispose of its own destiny." A "whole people" contains a numerical majority but implies something yet greater—Lincoln's "brotherhood of man." Democracy means government by the people, and that, in turn, means government *for* the people.[13]

For Croly, Lincoln offered the key to a synthesis of liberty and power. He cited a phrase that he attributed to Lincoln: "Equal rights for all and special privileges for none." Equal rights, by themselves, enable some men to amass great wealth and then hold on to it, as Weyl observed. In the modern economic world, Jefferson's minimal state of equal rights thus guarantees gross inequality. Individualism must be balanced by a principle of justice. That is why the state has to actively fight against "special privileges." "The democratic principle requires an equal start in the race," Croly wrote, but so long as private property is sacred, equal rights cannot guarantee equal opportunity: "It is as if the competitors in a Marathon cross-country run were denied proper nourishment or proper training." This is precisely the metaphor that President Lyndon Johnson would adopt when he unveiled his Great Society programs in 1965. In the face of gross inequality of condition, the free marketplace cannot, by itself, offer equal opportunity.[14]

The Promise of American Life quickly became required reading for the nation's elites. Croly could gain their ear in part because, unlike the democratic Weyl, he shared their prejudices. He was convinced of the biological inferiority of blacks and expressed as much sympathy for slaveholders as for abolitionists. He viewed trade unions with deep skepticism even as he wrote that economic inequality was destroying the fabric of democracy. He thought America held too many elections and wanted to replace many lower-level elected officials with appointed experts serving in government agencies. Walter Weyl had seen American life and loved it, for all that he raged against the cruelty of the mighty. Croly neither knew nor loved the world of ordinary men and women. For him, far more than for Weyl, progressivism entailed direction from above in the name of a benevolent and morally substantive vision of national welfare. Today we would call Croly a liberal technocrat.[15]

Teddy Roosevelt was progressivism's *beau idéal*. When he was suddenly elevated to the presidency by the assassination of William McKinley in 1901, Roosevelt deployed the national government to address the ills that reformers had identified. He instructed the Department of Justice to file an antitrust suit against Northern Securities, the railroad trust owned by J. P. Morgan, James J. Hill, and E. H. Harriman. He passed the Pure Food and Drug Act and set aside millions of acres for national parks. The reforms themselves were modest, but in his seven years in office Roosevelt almost single-handedly revived the Hamiltonian argument for an activist national government. In 1908 he stepped aside in favor of his friend and fellow Republican William Howard Taft. But now he was running again. For a whole generation of progressive thinkers, the election of 1912 shaped up as an epic battle between Roosevelt's Hamiltonian revival and Wilson's played-out Jeffersonian individualism.

In July 1910, Roosevelt had sent Herbert Croly the kind of letter that makes a writer swoon. "I do not know when I have read a book that I felt profitted me as much as your book on American life," Roosevelt wrote. "I shall use your ideas freely in speeches I intend to make." He then proceeded to do just that in a celebrated speech he delivered a month later in Osawatomie, Kansas. "The true friend of property," Roosevelt said, "the true conservative, is he who insists that property shall be the servant and not the master of the commonwealth." What this meant, first, was that "special interests," by which Roosevelt meant the big trusts, must be brought to heel. Corporations must be prohibited from making political contributions. The state must closely regulate not just utilities but all firms that "control necessaries of life, such as meat, oil, or coal." Roosevelt called for a graduated income tax and a sharply graduated tax on inheritance. He echoed Weyl in asserting that "no man can be a good citizen unless he has a wage more than sufficient to cover the bare cost of living, and hours of labor short enough so after his day's work is done he will have time and energy to bear his share in the management of the community." Roosevelt thus called not only for laws governing the minimum wage and maximum workweek but for laws on workers' compensation, child labor, and workplace safety. Roosevelt was careful to repudiate growing allegations among conservatives that he had become a socialist. The high point of the speech came when Roosevelt, apparently citing Croly, just as he had promised to do, endorsed the New Nationalism, which put "the national need before sectional or personal advantage." In this remarkably radical speech, Roosevelt effectively endorsed the call for a new "democratic collectivism."[16]

Teddy didn't throw his hat in the ring for the 1912 presidential election until February 1912. It was always clear that as a challenger to an incumbent president he would be a long shot, but he quickly proved that he had lost little of his appeal to the party faithful. Of the twelve states that staged GOP primaries, he won nine. But at the party convention in Chicago in June, President Taft succeeded in seating several key state delegations pledged to him, and he quickly gained the nomination. Roosevelt's forces then bolted and formed the Progressive Party, the first serious national third party since the Populists a generation earlier. Croly helped write the party platform, which sounded very much like the agenda Teddy had laid out in Osawatomie. Roosevelt secured the active help of the leading progressive intellectuals of the day—not just Croly but also Weyl, Lippmann, and others.

If the GOP was in disarray in 1912, the Democratic Party was practically ossified. The Democrats had gone into eclipse with the election of the Republican William McKinley in 1896; since then the party had fallen under the sway of William Jennings Bryan, the stem-winding Nebraska populist known as "the Great Commoner." Bryan thrilled farmers with his attacks on Wall Street but had no idea how to appeal to forward-looking middle-class Americans, who viewed him as a throwback to the age of Andrew Jackson. After losing the presidential elections of 1896, 1900, and 1908, Bryan had agreed to stand down. In his stead, party regulars settled on House Speaker Champ Clark, a poor man's Bryan known as "the Ol' Hound Dawg." But progressives had found their way into the Democratic as well as the Republican Party, and they coalesced around the governor of New Jersey, Woodrow Wilson.

As president of Princeton University from 1902 to 1910, Wilson had not been known as a reformer. He was an esteemed historian of American government, a forceful and often overbearing administrator who tended to leave his adversaries feeling bruised, a Presbyterian who gave the impression that he was in regular communion with God. Wilson was a Virginian and an heir of the Jeffersonian tradition. "Excess of government," he wrote, "is the very antithesis of liberty." Wilson regarded trade unions as a restraint on the rights of workers and believed that businesses should be regulated, if at all, by states rather than by the federal government. The language of reform most natural to him was moral. "Capital," he said, "must give over its too-great preoccupation with . . . making those who control it individually rich." Wilson was Jefferson as an evangelical rather than a deist.[17]

Wilson's traditionalism recommended him to Democratic Party bosses when the governorship of New Jersey came open in 1910. By that time Wilson had his eye on high office and allowed himself to be nominated. A novice in politics but a quick study, Wilson recognized that the spirit of reform had progressed so far that he could win only as a candidate of change. He called for modest action against the trusts and for the public regulation of utilities. As governor, he broke decisively with the bosses who controlled statewide Democratic politics, pushing through a reluctant legislature laws requiring direct primaries and curbing corrupt practices. Reformers suddenly recognized in Wilson a man who had not only the ambition and the talent to be president but a strong will that could sweep aside the forces of reaction. In early 1912, Wilson began barnstorming across the country, delivering stirring if utterly vague speeches vowing to wrest power from the interests and restore it to the people. The Ol' Hound Dawg, with the ardent support of what remained of the Jefferson-Jackson coalition—farmers and the big-city machines—remained a formidable candidate. But the wish for renewal proved stronger than nostalgia: at the party convention in Baltimore, Wilson won on the forty-sixth ballot.

The election of 1912 pitted three candidates against one another, but only two campaigned. Taft knew that he couldn't win and left the field to the other two. Roosevelt ran as the standard-bearer of the New Nationalism, an activist prepared to deploy the national government as an instrument of progress and social justice. Wilson countered Roosevelt's slogan with one of his own that pointed to his foundations in Jeffersonian thinking: the New Freedom. He tarred Roosevelt as the tribune of the corporation; in a nationalist America, Wilson declared, the individual would be "swallowed up" by the giant company and the overweening state. He, by contrast, would stand up for the contemporary version of Jefferson's yeoman farmer. The nation, he said, needed "a body of laws which will look after the men who are on the make." Wilson placed the nineteenth-century liberal tradition at the core of his economic program, as it lay at the core of his larger political vision.[18]

One issue brought out the difference between the two men in stark relief: the trusts. Like most progressives, TR argued that the trusts existed because they worked and thus needed to be regulated for the public good rather than broken up. More than that, he accepted that the future would belong to national-scale institutions rather than to local businesses, which had shaped the previous century. Local communities, and local men, lay at the core of Wilson's Jeffersonian vision of the country. He found the trusts morally intolerable and culturally repugnant but didn't have any clear idea what to do with them. Over the summer he asked Louis Brandeis, the great legal scholar and political reformer, to advise him. Brandeis believed that the progressives had simply surrendered to the self-interested assertion of the plutocrats that bigness worked better than smallness. He argued that the railroads and the other giant trusts had used their monopoly power over suppliers, and their political power over government, to tilt the playing field in their direction; the best way to make the economy competitive was to break up the big corporations and force them to compete on equal footing with smaller firms. Brandeis proposed prosecuting and dissolving the trusts, and then writing new rules to govern fair competition. It was Brandeis's genius to adapt the liberal American vision of a free market of small-scale participants to the new exigencies of the twentieth century.

This open debate between a Hamiltonian and a Jeffersonian view of the role of government was something absolutely novel in American politics, and it turned the election into a sort of referendum on the American future. Yet the two sides were closer together than their slogans implied. Both recognized that the social Darwinism that exalted the survival of the fittest could no longer govern American life; both embraced the urgent need for reform to make markets and government work for ordinary Americans. Wilson was more in tune with the nation's individualist traditions and with the feelings of ordinary citizens; Roosevelt was more prepared to make sweeping changes to rein in the forces of industrialism. They offered, in effect, two different blends of conservatism and radicalism.

Wilson's tack toward reformism won him the presidency, as it had the governorship two years earlier. He won only 42 percent of the vote (TR came in second, with 27 percent) but carried 435 of the 531 electoral votes—a resounding victory. Croly, Weyl, and Lippmann fully expected Wilson to abandon the country to the nostalgic forces of the old individualism. In fact, Wilson couldn't have done so even if he had been inclined to—which he wasn't—because the forces demanding that the state intervene in the economy were far too powerful to be resisted. The Panic of 1907, from which the country had been rescued by an infusion of private capital, had demonstrated the need for a national banking system to replace the fragmentary system that had evolved after Jackson had eliminated the Second Bank of the United States. Bankers themselves had come to accept the argument, but they wanted to control the central bank themselves. Wilson's own Bryanite wing demanded a decentralized system with no power to issue currency. The progressives favored a national system under national control. Brandeis persuaded Wilson that the national government needed to exercise overall control and have the unique power to issue currency. In the face of immense pressure, Wilson stood firm against both the bankers and the populists of his own party. On December 23, 1913, he signed the bill creating the Federal Reserve system, with regional banks under private control supervised by the Federal Reserve Board. The legislation embodied the liberal recognition that the economy had become too complex for the minimal state of Jefferson and Jackson.

The following year came the immense debate over the fate of the trusts. The progressives braced for the ultimate showdown between Hamilton and Jefferson. If the antitrust crowd got its way, Lippmann wrote, "they would be breaking up the beginning of a collective organization, thwarting the possibility of cooperation, and insisting upon submitting industry to the wasteful, the planless scramble of little profiteers." That last expression may have shed more light on the speaker than on his subject, for this brilliant young Harvard man exemplified the progressive contempt for the ordinary citizen and yen for technocratic rule. But it should have been plain by now that Wilson was not the Jeffersonian caricature of Roosevelt's campaign. The president had already abandoned the idea of dissolving the trusts. In January 1914, the Democrats introduced legislation that would ban interlocking directorates, specify unfair trade practices, and establish a trade commission that would advise the Justice Department on potential violations of law. Wilson agreed that the Federal Trade Commission (FTC), as it came to be called, should not merely advise but make law, thus planting the first shoots of the giant "administrative state" that conservatives would later denounce.

Though he had come very far from his Virginian conservatism, Wilson remained a cautious reformer. He was a racist who included only white people in his "men on the make" and oversaw the official segregation of the federal workforce. Wilson continually assured businessmen that he had no wish to antagonize them—a very different tone from

Roosevelt's—and he neutered the FTC by appointing businessmen to its board. The commission never became the watchdog that Brandeis and the progressives hoped it would be. The evangelical Wilson could not abide the idea of fixed conflicts of interest that the federal government would have to adjudicate. He saw his job as pointing to a higher good that would help people see beyond the mutual antagonism that had provoked the terrible labor violence of an earlier period. In the fall of 1914 he wrote, in a letter to his treasury secretary, William G. McAdoo, "Ten or twelve years ago the country was torn and excited by an agitation which shook the very foundations of her political life, brought her business ideals into question," and undermined "morality and good faith." That grim era, he said, had now been replaced by "a time of healing because a time of just dealing." The New Freedom had achieved its goals. Wilson had preserved much of the old liberal individualism that Weyl and Croly had tried to unmask as the self-serving ideology of the plutocracy.[19]

In the summer of 1913, Herbert Croly was approached by a young banker named Willard Straight. The latter had just returned from China, where he had served as a diplomat and then as the representative for the firms of J. P. Morgan and Kuhn, Loeb. Straight had been thrilled by *The Promise of American Life*, as so many members of the American elite had been, and was keen to meet the author. He was every bit as appalled as Croly by what he took to be Wilson's reactionary individualism, and he saw Croly as the man who could shape public opinion in a healthier—and more pro-business—direction. Straight was in a position to help Croly do so because he had married Dorothy Whitney, heir to a fabulous fortune. They hit on the idea of starting a weekly magazine of opinion. *Harper's* had fashioned itself into the organ of the New Freedom; the New Nationalism needed a voice of its own. Croly was comfortable enough with Straight's status as a forward-looking servant of the plutocracy to agree to serve as his editor. Straight was equally prepared to live with Croly's faith in state intervention in the marketplace. In the end, Straight would have to surrender more of his views than Croly.

Croly had already begun to slightly relax the rigid distinction he had drawn between the Jeffersonian and Hamiltonian views. The very title of his new book, *Progressive Democracy*, implied an effort to merge progressive principles with democratic values. He was now more prepared to rely on the wisdom of citizens, rather than on the technocratic skills of experts; he had embraced Weyl's cause of industrial democracy. It was no surprise, then, that the first person Croly asked to join the staff of the magazine-in-embryo was Weyl himself. Croly then turned to Walter Lippmann, the Harvard wunderkind who had written the remarkably self-assured *Preface to Politics* at twenty-three and had immediately followed that up with another book, *Drift and Mastery*. In the latter work, Lippmann had turned his withering glance on the New Freedom, observing that the current generation could hardly be satisfied with "making themselves masters of little businesses" when they had the opportunity to devise "administrative methods by which the great resources of the country can be operated on some thought-out plan." Lippmann still took a dim view of the "planless scramble" beneath his feet.[20]

The first issue of the *New Republic* appeared on November 7, 1914, immediately after the midterm elections. The editors acknowledged that the Democrats had fared better than expected because they had done more than expected. At the same time, Wilson had only begun to make a dent in the problem of classes and economic management. Croly reacted with astonishment to Wilson's claim in the letter to McAdoo that his modest legislative achievements had cured the nation of its ills. "Any man of President Wilson's intellectual equipment," he wrote, "who seriously asserts that the fundamental wrongs of a modern society can be easily and quickly righted as a consequence of a few laws . . . casts suspicion either upon his own sincerity or upon his grasp of the realities of modern social and industrial life." Yet even Croly had come to recognize that the president was no small-government reactionary. Early in the new year, the editors agreed with Wilson's immodest claim that the previous Congress had compiled the best legislative record since the Civil War. By some remarkable sleight of hand, the editors conceded, Wilson had persuaded his own followers that progressive policies were consistent with Jeffersonian governance. Perhaps it would be Wilson, not Roosevelt, who would achieve the long-sought synthesis between Jeffersonian means and Hamiltonian ends.[21]

By the time the first issue appeared, however, a terrible specter had all but blotted out the hopes of both the magazine's editors and the president. In August, a European war that seemed simply absurd, because it was so unnecessary, had begun. Americans were shocked at newspaper descriptions of immense armies slaughtering one another across open fields. Weyl could barely eat or sleep in the first days of the war. He was a pacifist at heart, and he was blessed with the kind of sympathetic imagination that instantly placed him among the suffering. At the same time, though Weyl was a German Jew and a lover of German culture, he never doubted for a moment that German aggression threatened European civilization and must be stopped.

The war forced Croly, Weyl, Lippmann, and other progressives to turn from domestic affairs in order to devise a foreign and military policy. They quickly concluded that the United States was endangered far less by militarism than by the unthinking pacifism of much of the left. They ridiculed the Bryanite faith that the United States could disarm and thus offer itself as a neutral arbiter of Europe's broils. In "Not Our War," the editors described Democratic isolationism as the foreign policy equivalent of reckless laissez-faire at home. Almost alone on the left, the magazine supported Wilson's campaign for "preparedness," forcing the editors to rebut allegations that they had joined the ranks of the militarists. An "intelligent pacifist," they argued, must respond to reality, not wishes. A liberal foreign policy would have to come to terms with the brutal reality of a world of predators—far less tractable even than the plutocracy at home—if it was to have any chance of shaping a more peaceful order once the war ended.[22]

The war upended the simple-minded faith in science and progress that had propelled a whole generation that had come of age in a long era of peace. The unidentified author of "Mental Unpreparedness" wrote that progressives had persuaded themselves that liberal ideals were spreading across Europe as they had across the United States. History supposedly had a pattern: states democratize and then seek social control over the economy. It was all an illusion. Nationalist fervor in Germany, one of the most forward-looking of states, had plunged Europe into war; England and France were now fighting for a bigger share of the world's colonies. The world was propelled by the selfish interests of states.[23]

By early 1916, the editors had begun to see their way clear to a synthesis of military preparedness and social and economic reform. Teddy Roosevelt had suggested in a speech in January that the nation must marshal its domestic resources, as it had begun to do with men and armaments. But Roosevelt's faith in regulation now struck the editors as inadequate to the moment; they proposed instead a nationalization of essential services, including the railroads, as well as public ownership of natural resources. The war had moved them to the right of most progressives on military policy but to the left on domestic affairs, especially on labor issues. The magazine defended the strikers who had destroyed much of downtown East Youngstown, Ohio, in the first days of 1916, and did so in deeply moving language that probably marked Weyl's authorship: "All the resentment and bitterness born of years in which excessively long and arduous labor had alternated with the shame and humiliation of begging work and bread flamed up in their hearts." They defended other striking workers who had taken up arms against company-hired goons.[24]

Croly's penchant for technocracy and Lippmann's majestic contempt for the little man had largely vanished from the pages of the *New Republic*. The magazine stood for industrial democracy for workers and civil rights for the excluded. Few subjects appeared more often in editorials than the demand for women's suffrage. Francis Hackett, a staff writer, lavished praise on the progressive warden of Sing Sing Prison, who sought to equip inmates for life on the outside—"the goal for which few prison officials have ever wisely striven in the interminable and blundering history of prisons." The magazine was moderately forward looking on race. In late 1915, the editors printed a speech on segregation by Booker T. Washington. Why, Washington asked, can white store owners move into the middle of black neighborhoods if blacks can't do the same in white neighborhoods?[25]

The magazine, like Croly himself, managed to deeply penetrate the intellectual and political elite without making much of an impression on ordinary Americans. (Circulation topped out in 1919 at 27,750.) President Wilson told a visitor that he regularly clipped and kept articles. Justice Oliver Wendell Holmes sent along comments and suggestions. The muckraking journalist Ray Stannard Baker reported from England that leading members of both the Labour and the Liberal Parties read the *New Republic* keenly. Despite some hard-hitting reportage, even by the lofty Lippmann, the magazine generally hewed to Croly's default tone of Olympian certitude. Some readers found it insufferably smug. In a letter to the editors, the radical Amos Pinchot took aim at an air of "impregnable virtue, already cast in the mould of a respectable middle age."[26]

The editors had only the most modest expectations for the Wilson administration, yet Wilson surprised them once again. Facing a difficult reelection bid in 1916, Wilson decided to move left, as he had in 1910 and 1912. In the beginning of the year he nominated to the Supreme Court his close adviser Louis Brandeis, a man feared and despised by the businessmen the president had been courting. The *New Republic* cheered this brave choice. The president pushed recalcitrant Democratic leaders to get behind a workers' compensation bill for federal employees. In July, as southern senators were blocking a bill to restrict child labor, Wilson went to the Capitol to warn them that they were damaging the party's electoral prospects. The Bourbons relented, and the bill passed. Wilson had now hijacked, and passed, a good deal of the Progressive agenda.

The editors of the *New Republic* were still in Roosevelt's corner and were counting on their man to recapture the Republican nomination. But the Republican Party wanted nothing to do with Teddy's increasingly shrill demands to enter the war in Europe and instead selected Charles Evans Hughes, the liberal-minded Supreme Court justice and former governor of New York. The Progressives renominated Teddy, but he spurned the offer—at which point the party collapsed. Facing this startling new alignment in which both progressivism and its greatest champion had faded from the scene, the editors, for the first time, began using the word "liberal" to describe themselves. They did not explain why they did so, but as they had moved closer to the Democratic Party, they may have become more comfortable with a word traditionally associated with that party. In any case, they wrote, it was not they who had changed but Wilson. The president had discarded his back-looking individualism, his opposition to women's suffrage and to military preparedness. "In Mr. Wilson's present program," the editors wrote, "there is scarcely a shred left of the fabric of his Jeffersonian revival. With every development of his policy he has been approximating to the spirit and creed of Hamiltonian nationalism." The Hamiltonian and Jeffersonian streams had now merged: to be a reformer was to be a liberal.[27]

One may question exactly how far the progressives had embraced the liberal American faith in the individual citizen. Most progressives trusted institutions more than individuals, experts more than politicians, direction from above rather than uncoordinated action from below. Most were far readier to champion the rights of women than of blacks. The conservative scholar Thomas C. Leonard describes the progressives as "illiberal reformers" in a book of the same name and notes that many of the most high-minded economists and social scientists of the day advocated the "improvement" of the racial stock through eugenics, a policy discredited only by the rise of Nazism.[28]

Politically, the *New Republic* stood on the democratic side of the progressive movement. The editors opposed Jim Crow laws and argued against eugenic programs on the grounds that no one could say whether a person was "defective" owing to birth or to poor care until the state assumed "the responsibility of giving a fair opportunity for development to every child." Nevertheless, the elitist outlook of the progressives, their faith in expertise and scientific management, stood in the way of Croly's dream of merging Jeffersonian means with Hamiltonian ends. Walter Weyl stands out among them, for he favored a program of social democracy that was both radically collectivist from the perspective of nineteenth-century liberalism and genuinely democratic.[29]

The entry of the United States into the war in April 1917 marked the end of the brief era of domestic reform. All of Wilson's energies in his second term were devoted to persuading a deeply reluctant nation to enter a war thousands of miles away, to fighting that war, and then to his great and doomed project of building a new and better world on the ashes of the old. The editors of the *New Republic* regarded Wilson's vision of a postwar world with a League of Nations at its heart as the banner under which an existential battle for a liberal world would be fought. A German victory, they wrote, would constitute a triumph not only for one nation but for the principle of autocracy, and would thus entail "a fastening upon the whole civilized world of a system of aggressive policies backed by an illiberal collective and a thorough conscription of human life." The war may have started over "a clash of empires in the Balkans," but now the question at issue was the future of humanity. For the editors, as for Wilson, American involvement in the war could be justified only as a means of spreading across the world the liberal values that shaped American life. The aspiration would be reborn a generation later, this time successfully, when a victorious United States would establish and largely administer a "liberal world order."

Walter Weyl proved to be the sublimely calm center of the *New Republic*'s frantic whirligig. As an editor, he was judicious, patient, and warmhearted—the one figure at the magazine universally admired and even loved. But Weyl had only temporarily shelved his own ambitions. He kept picking up and putting down the class conflict book. In 1915 he traveled to wartime Germany to see conditions for himself. Now the war was the great subject. Weyl was less persuaded of the merits of American involvement in the conflict than were Croly, Lippmann, and the more hawkish staff members. In the summer of 1916 he left the magazine to write *American World Policies*, which endorsed the Wilson who had promised to keep America out of war and suggested, as Wilson himself had, that the United States could best shape a postwar world by preserving its neutrality. In early 1917 he left the magazine once again to travel to Hong Kong, China, and Japan, observing the economic conditions of a part of the world he had known only secondhand. He returned and then left again in the summer to write *The End of the War*.

Weyl made clear at the outset of this work that he shared the belief of anti-militarist progressives that the war would only temporarily obscure the great question of the day, class conflict. Working men, he wrote, have seen "the war beneath the war" and will never again allow their interests to be betrayed by government in league with plutocracy. Weyl argued that the imperialism of the Allies precluded an early settlement of the war on decent terms. But he accepted, as the antiwar faction did not, that the United States really did enter the war to make the world safe for democracy, as Wilson had put it, and really might succeed in doing so. He believed, as Wilson did, that America's imperative task was to spread liberal democratic principles around the world. A new world system would have to depend on the consent of the governed. A principled internationalism would have to replace aggressive nationalism. Yet Weyl was pragmatic enough to predict the war would end with imperialist horse trading by Europe's statesmen. Liberal opinion, he observed presciently, wouldn't be able to do a thing about it.[30]

Wilson did not have the tough-mindedness to see that the world could not be refashioned according to his principles. Only when he reached Paris in January 1919 did he discover that the other major Allied leaders, Lloyd George and Georges Clemenceau, had no intention of accepting what Wilson had called "peace without victory" (an expression first coined in a *New Republic* editorial). On May 7 he signed the hated Treaty of Versailles. Germany's colonies were divided up, and she was saddled with immense indemnities. In his speeches during the war, Wilson had insisted that henceforward peoples would have the right to self-determination—to their own nations. In all too many cases he sacrificed that principle to the imperial ambitions of the victors. For the editors of the *New Republic*, who had withstood the gibes of leftist intellectuals with the claim that only by fighting the war could the United States secure a truly liberal world, Wilson's acquiescence amounted almost to treason. The editors issued their denunciation in an editorial, "Peace at Any Price," that blazed with the outrage of a betrayed faith. The treaty—an "inhuman monster"—blasted all hopes not only for a liberal postwar international order but for liberal reform in the West. The editors argued that the treaty would serve as "a complete vindication of the Marxian dogma that, as long as capitalism prevails, war necessarily operates as the instrument of class aggrandizement and popular exploitation." If liberalism—or at least "that kind of liberalism that breathes the Christian spirit," as opposed to the ruthless liberalism of laissez-faire—consents to the retrospective meaning of the war implied by the treaty, it will have committed suicide.

"Thus comes to an inglorious end," Walter Weyl wrote in "Prophet and Politician," a bitter postmortem of Paris, "the quest of Woodrow Wilson in search of a new world. There also comes to an end—for a time at least—the hopes of millions of men." Surely there was a strong element of hyperbole, of the rage of betrayal, in all this. Weyl and his colleagues had placed too much faith in Wilson—as they once had in Teddy Roosevelt—and then blamed him too personally for the disappointment of those hopes. Yet events proceeded to vindicate the editors' worst fears. Wilson returned to the United States bent on winning acceptance for the League of Nations, the glittering prize he had rescued from the wreckage of the Versailles treaty. But he was outmaneuvered at home, as he had been abroad, by men more supple than he; the Senate decisively rejected the League. Crippled by a stroke, Wilson finished his presidency as a ghost confined to the White House.[31]

The *New Republic* itself came very close to perishing in the name of its own convictions, as Croly had feared. It survived only thanks to constant infusions of cash from Dorothy Straight. The original pillars of the magazine began to fall away. Willard Straight died of influenza in late 1918. In early 1919, Teddy Roosevelt died—astonishingly, at only sixty-one. Lippmann had already left to join the war effort as an intelligence officer in France, though he would later return. Walter Weyl continued to dabble in his own projects. In September 1919 the magazine asked him to serve as its Washington correspondent. He declined. Weyl, age forty-six, already had cancer. He died on November 9. In an obituary column, the editors evoked Weyl the man rather than the polemicist. "He used to say that he could not dislike anyone he had ever met," they wrote. "The heathen might rage, but what interested him was how perfect a heathen the heathen was. His method was to comprehend, no matter where it led him."[32]

The "war beneath the war" that Walter Weyl foresaw never happened. Both the reform legislation passed during Wilson's first term and the tremendous prosperity of the twenties buffered class conflict and largely put an end to the explosive labor confrontations of the previous two decades. The "surplus" that Weyl had considered a precondition for the new democracy in fact drained the energies of reform. The United States emerged from the war not as a damaged society, as did its chief economic rivals, but as the world's foremost power, with a booming domestic market that allowed it to largely turn away from the world. Both the internationalism and the program of radical domestic change that the *New Republic* liberals had championed were lost in the giddy hullaballoo of Jazz Age America.

Yet a powerful deposit of ideas, policies, and aspirations remained. The liberals had argued that government must play an active role in the economy and must act, not as a mere interested bystander, but as a referee or even policeman in transactions between private firms and workers and consumers. They had changed the meaning of liberalism as both Madison and Mill had understood it. Preserving individual autonomy from the encroachment of the state or society could no longer be seen as the sole objective of liberal thought and policy. Neither posed the chief threat to the individual. In the democratic nations where liberal thought had arisen, autonomy was more immediately endangered by economic power than by political. Workers needed protection from employers, and that protection could come only from the state.

It was this heritage that FDR drew upon when the Depression once again exposed the gross inadequacy of laissez-faire as a governing philosophy. During the period of Republican rule in the 1920s, the term "liberal" was favored chiefly by advocates of the free market like President Herbert Hoover. FDR revived the usage as Wilson and those around him had understood it. The liberal, he said, put his faith in "the wisdom and efficacy of the will of the great majority of the people"— that is, of the common people rather than the economic elite—and was prepared to use government to secure for the ordinary citizen "the right to his own economic and political life, liberty, and the pursuit of happiness." More tellingly, and lastingly, FDR defined liberalism as less a political credo than the fundamental human impulse of concern for our fellow man. The liberal, he said at the 1936 Democratic convention, seeks to impart to government "the vibrant personal character that is the very embodiment of human charity. . . . Better the occasional faults of a Government that lives in a spirit of charity than the consistent omissions of a Government frozen in the ice of its own indifference." Listeners could hardly miss the contrast with the austere conception of liberalism they had heard from Hoover and other partisans of laissez-faire. What good was the freedom to barter your labor if there were no jobs to be had? FDR thus accomplished precisely what Herbert Croly had hoped that Teddy Roosevelt would, fusing the Jeffersonian language of individual liberty with the Hamiltonian vision of strong national government.[33]

Though no philosopher or abstract thinker, FDR offered a thoroughgoing account of the development of his outlook in a speech before the Commonwealth Club of San Francisco in the heat of the 1932 presidential election. The speech was largely written by Adolph Berle, a law professor and expert on the economy who had joined the candidate's celebrated Brain Trust. FDR began the address with a history lesson that seems to have been drawn from Weyl and Croly. At the nation's birth, men were divided between Jefferson's faith in liberty and Hamilton's vision of ordered government. Jefferson won, and for the ensuing century "individualism was made the great watchword of American life." As the machine age dawned, the new barons of industry recruited the state to their side; the purpose of government "was not to interfere but to assist in the development of industry." The pell-mell rush to exploit the continent's resources brought great prosperity along with much cruelty and suffering; the American people chose, on balance, to take "the bitter with the sweet." FDR was more comfortable with the "planless scramble" of American life than were many of the progressives. Indeed, he differed from Croly on one fundamental point: Hamilton, he said, advocated a state of "autocratic strength" and believed that "the destiny of individuals was to serve that Government . . . guided by a small group of able and public spirited citizens." Like the equally well-born Thomas

Jefferson, from whom he claimed intellectual descent, FDR was always prepared to declare a rather abstract faith in the wisdom of the common man.[34]

The rise of the trusts, Roosevelt went on, transformed the relationship between the citizen and the economy. "Like the feudal barons of old," the trusts began to "threaten the economic freedom of individuals to earn a living." (Elsewhere FDR would use the expression "economic royalists" to signify the idea that the threat of oppressive power in the modern world had passed from the state to business.) Teddy Roosevelt, said FDR, had first confronted and then conditionally accepted the trusts. Wilson, by contrast, "saw the situation more clearly. Where Jefferson had feared the encroachment of political power on the lives of individuals, Wilson knew that the new power was financial." Had the Great War not intervened, FDR claimed, Wilson might have completed the work of restoring competition to a monopolistic economy and protecting citizens from the "irresponsibility and greed" of the barons. This was a dubious history, but it served to place FDR in the line of inheritance of Jefferson and Wilson rather than Hamilton and TR.

From this political foundation, FDR was able to offer an economic analysis that sounds very much like the progressive one, and to offer solutions the progressives would have cheered. He even used Weyl's language. "A glance at the situation today only too clearly indicates that equality of opportunity as we have known it no longer exists. . . . Area after area has been preempted altogether by the great corporations. . . . We are steering a course toward economic oligarchy, if we are not there already." Thus the time has come to draft the terms of "an economic declaration of rights, an economic constitutional order."

In this new order, the right to life vouchsafed by the Declaration of Independence must include the right to "make a comfortable living," so long as one is prepared to work for it. Only the government can secure that right. Similarly, the right to property must be understood not simply as the inviolable right to keep what's yours but as the right to financial security. Indeed, "all other property rights must yield to it." If in order to protect that right "we must restrict the operations of the speculator, the manipulator, even the financier," then we would do so "not to hamper individualism but to protect it."

Roosevelt stated explicitly that he wished to devise this new economic constitutional order with the active cooperation of public-spirited men of business. At this early stage, he envisioned a less intrusive state than the one men like Croly and Weyl proposed—more Wilson than TR. "The Government should assume the function of economic regulation only as a last resort," FDR said, "to be tried only when private initiative, inspired by high responsibility, with such assistance and balance as Government can give, has finally failed." Perhaps he was trying to reassure the moguls of the Commonwealth Club; certainly by the time he took office in 1933, Roosevelt and his team had concluded that, private initiative having failed, the government needed to boldly intervene in the market through a massive program of job creation.

Roosevelt concluded the address with the question of liberty, the keystone of the democratic arch. What Jefferson called "the rights of personal competency," by which he meant the right to speak and act as you wish, "must be respected at all hazard," FDR avowed. This was no more than truism. But we also know, he said, that liberty means nothing if "one man's meat is another man's poison." The absolute right of one citizen to freedom of action ends when it threatens the freedom or well-being of another. This was precisely the dilemma that John Stuart Mill faced in *On Liberty*. Mill assigned to society the job of determining where the sphere of otherwise-inviolable freedom encroached on the liberty of others. But in the modern world, "society" means little beyond the hierarchy of power created by wealth. It is now for government, FDR said, to maintain a balance "within which every individual may have a place if he will take it."

Over the next dozen years, Roosevelt would forge the new liberal order that he foreshadowed in San Francisco. And he would do so, increasingly, in the face of a new and far more ominous ideological rival—not laissez-faire but its opposite, totalitarianism. As centrist governments in Europe gave way to fascism, or in some cases to a very shaky socialism, American liberalism came to be seen as the port in a devouring storm.

Weyl, Croly, and the progressives had barely needed to speak of the "rights of personal competency" because America was constituted in such a way as to make those rights seem impregnable. Now they were under mortal threat abroad and in jeopardy at home, as fascist sympathizers like Henry Ford, Charles Lindbergh, and Father Coughlin rose to prominence. By voting for FDR—again and again—amid the great crisis of the twentieth century, Americans affirmed their faith in personal liberty, in capitalism, and in a state that ensured that one man's meat would not be another's poison.

CHAPTER FOUR

Isaiah Berlin and the Anti-totalitarians

*From the crooked timber of humanity
no straight thing was ever made.*

—IMMANUEL KANT

A T THE VERY END OF HIS LONG LIFE, THE PHILOSOPHER ISAIAH Berlin delivered a lecture in which he explained a revelation he had had decades before. As a boy, he said, he had immersed himself in the works of Tolstoy, Dostoyevsky, and the other great Russian novelists and thinkers of the nineteenth century. All of them, he saw, devoted themselves to humanity's greatest moral questions. Why is there suffering? Why do some people oppress others? And how, conversely, could one give birth to a world of truth and of justice? Each gave a different answer, but all accepted that an answer existed. Later on, as a university student, he found that the Greeks, too, and even corrosively skeptical Enlightenment thinkers like Voltaire subscribed to a "Platonic ideal" according to which "all genuine questions must have one true answer and one only"; some path must exist toward that answer, and all true answers "must necessarily be compatible with one another and form a single whole."[1]

But what if that weren't so? What if one true answer contradicted another? Berlin described the "deep and lasting impression" made on him by Machiavelli, who accepted the moral validity of the Christian virtues but nevertheless advised rulers to behave according to the pagan code of force, guile, resourcefulness. The two could not be combined; a leader had to choose between them. Berlin then embarked on a study of eighteenth-century thinkers, including Giambattista Vico and Johann Gottfried Herder, who argued that each age, or each nation, has its own distinctive culture and thus its own values—not simply better or worse than others, but different. Berlin did not call this philosophy *relativism*, which refuses to pass judgments of value, but *pluralism*—"the conception that there are many different ends which men may seek and still be fully rational."[2]

Why was this so fundamental an insight that the seventy-nine-year-old Berlin felt moved to recount it? In what respect was it a *liberal* insight? The answer is that Berlin had passed virtually his entire life in the shadow of totalitarianism. The seductive power of totalitarian ideologies comes from the promise to magically resolve otherwise intractable problems and realize them in the form of a perfect state. "To make such an omelette," Berlin went on to say, "there is surely no limit to the number of eggs that must be broken. . . . Since I know the only true path to the ultimate solution of the problems of society, I know which way to drive the human caravan; and since you are ignorant of what I know, you cannot be allowed to have liberty of choice even within the narrowest limits, if the goal is to be reached."[3]

As a boy, Berlin had seen just enough of the Communist revolution in Russia to fill him with lasting horror, and, like Benjamin Constant, he spent his life fashioning a moderate, humane answer to the totalitarian challenge. Indeed, as an epigraph for his most famous work, *Four Essays on Liberty*, Berlin chose a biting observation from Constant: "Real beings are sacrificed to abstract being: individuals are offered up in a holocaust to the collective people." For Berlin, and for the other anti-totalitarian thinkers of the middle decades of the twentieth century, liberalism entailed the defense not just of liberty but also of the very idea of the person, of individual autonomy, from ideologies that regarded people as so many eggs to be broken in the pursuit of an inhuman ideal.[4]

Liberalism had always been shaped by the forces that most urgently threatened liberal values. Berlin understood this very well. He observed that against "an uncontrolled 'market' economy" or "ultra-individualism," liberals would make the case for state intervention. But in the face of fascist or communist totalitarianism, which threatened the disappearance of the individual, the liberal could no longer use the language of democratic collectivism that had come naturally to the American progressives. The anti-totalitarians were far more drawn to Mill's defense of the sphere of privacy, though with an urgency that would have been foreign to Mill, who had faced no monster more fearsome than Victorian conformity. "The language of Victorian England was claustrophobia," as Berlin put it in an essay on Mill. "The mass neurosis of our age is agoraphobia"—the fear of solitude and anomie that makes men flee into the arms of the utopians.[5]

Herbert Croly complained that the Jeffersonian preoccupation with individual liberty had turned government into an enemy of progress. Yet this negative understanding of liberty as freedom from encroachment was the starting point for the anti-totalitarian liberals. Berlin famously distinguished between the liberal principle of "negative" liberty and a "positive" liberty that all too often served as the primrose path to despotism. What, then, could liberalism affirm? Berlin called himself a social democrat, though his fear of the state made him a very cautious one. The Austrian economist Friedrich Hayek claimed that virtually all forms of state intervention in the economy led ineluctably to totalitarianism. Another Central European economist, Karl Polanyi, by contrast, insisted on the categorical difference between economic and political liberty and blamed both communism and fascism on the failure of the self-regulating market that Hayek had championed. And then there were men of the left, socialists like Arthur Koestler, Ignazio Silone, and, above all, George Orwell, who sought to clear a space for equality without surrendering the claims of liberty. A grave question hovered over these speculations: How could liberals counter the dark allure of communism without surrendering their own principles?

For a man who lived through the great nightmares of the twentieth century, Isaiah Berlin enjoyed a very equable life. As a seven-year-old in Petrograd (now Saint Petersburg) in 1917, he watched in fascinated horror as fifteen revolutionaries dragged away a man white with terror—a policeman under the tsar's regime. This was the first and last sign the boy saw of the violence of the Russian Revolution. The family returned to the quiet of Riga; four years later, they boarded a train for London. The elder Berlin, a timber merchant, reestablished himself quickly, and the family lacked for nothing. Isaiah excelled at Oxford, and when, at twenty-three, he was admitted as a fellow at All Souls College, the holiest of holies in the great cathedral of English academic life, he was set for life. Berlin seemed allergic to the fierce enthusiasms and antipathies of the day. He identified with the Russian novelist Ivan Turgenev, whom he described in an essay as "a cool, detached, slightly mocking observer who looks upon the tragedies of life from a comparatively remote point of view." Berlin was a creature of the common room and the salon. He had a gift for friendship, including with innumerable rich older ladies, whom he entertained with a bottomless fund of gossip. Despite the pervasive anti-Semitism in the upper spheres of British life, he never suffered a serious setback because of his religion. He had the goods that established his bona fides: wit, scholarship, polished manners, and an ardent love of his adopted country.[6]

Berlin's field was political and moral philosophy, but he did not think of himself as a philosopher standing in the line of succession from Locke and Rousseau and Mill. Rather, he studied the ideas of those thinkers like an epidemiologist tracing the path of a disease back to the source. Berlin was, in short, a historian of ideas, or, as he came to think of himself, a historian of philosophy. He did not deliver a comprehensive statement of his own views until 1952, when he delivered a series of lectures on Enlightenment and Romantic thinkers that he called "Freedom and Its Betrayal: Six Enemies of Human Liberty." These enemies included figures like Rousseau and Hegel, whom others would have classed as friends of liberty. But that was Berlin's point: the heroic idealism of the Romantic era had offered a blueprint, and a banner, for modern tyrants.

Berlin always began with a question. In the second lecture, on Rousseau, he asked where, exactly, the importance of that Enlightenment thinker lies. He then explained that, like a mathematician who has cut the knot of an ancient conundrum, Rousseau solved, or believed he had solved, the apparently intrinsic tension between liberty and authority, or legitimate power. Rousseau viewed both values as absolute: individual liberty was inalienable, but so, too, were the moral rules that govern right behavior and thus must govern society. Must one, then, continually adjust the dial between these two poles, as previous thinkers had supposed? Not at all. Both were absolute. However, Rousseau insisted, a rational man would never will for himself what was at variance with the "general will." If he did, it was not his true, natural self speaking but the self corrupted by the artifice, the pervasive falseness, of society. In a just society, liberty and authority would be fully harmonized. By this strange turn of logic, Berlin went on, Rousseau, the champion of liberty who helped inspire the French Revolution, ended by betraying the idea of liberty—just as the Revolution itself did. Berlin was hardly the first thinker to lodge this allegation; so, too, had Constant. But Berlin demonstrated the link between the apparently noble principle of the general will and the slave ideology of Lenin and Stalin in a way that no listener in 1952 could have missed:

> You want to give people unlimited liberty, because otherwise they cease to be men; and yet at the same time you want them to live according to the rules. If they can be made to love the rules, then they will want the rules, not so much because the rules are rules as because they love them. . . . So Rousseau says, "Man is born free, and yet he is everywhere in chains." What sort of chains? . . . If the chains are simply rules the very obedience to which is the most free, the strongest, the most spontaneous expression of your own inner nature, then the chains no longer bind you—since self-control is not control. Self-control is freedom.[7]

In these lectures Berlin asked how liberty, the greatest of all political values, comes to be perverted into its opposite. For the great liberal thinkers—Mill, Constant, Tom Paine, Denis Diderot—liberty meant "nonencroachment": we all should be allowed to live our lives according to our wishes so long as we do not impede the liberties of others. The liberal state plays the role of "traffic policeman," ensuring that citizens stay in their own lanes. But for Rousseau, liberty entailed willing submission to the collective good. For the German Romantics, including Johann Gottlieb Fichte and Hegel, liberty meant integrity, authenticity. To be free was to follow your inner light, at whatever cost to others not so enlightened—thus the reverence with which many of these thinkers regarded Napoleon. Fichte took this logic one step further. The true self, he argued, was no mere individual but an entity that lay beyond and, as it were, above us—a society, a nation, a people. Freedom is thus, Berlin said, "self-submission to a super-self." Fichte's mystical nationalism gives this idea a particularly nasty turn, for freedom is the collective endeavor of a people—the German people, in Fichte's mind—to realize itself. Like Hegel, Fichte recast the state as the bearer of the collective national vision. The people seek a leader with the special gifts required to lead them to their historic destiny. While freedom, for Mill, led to the liberal society, for the Romantics it led, ultimately, to Stalin and Hitler.[8]

The grain of totalitarianism is planted when we say that we can achieve all our goals through a single formula, that we can enjoy, as Rousseau insisted, absolute liberty even amidst absolute authority. Modern man, beset by agoraphobia, as Berlin put it, is drawn to the promise of an effortless resolution. The total system is beautiful and sleek, precisely because it is total. But of course it is false, for all good things do not, in fact, go together. We must choose among competing goods—so much liberty, so much equality, so much justice, and so on. There is no "right" choice; each of us will have different preferences. A liberal society does not tell us what we should wish but honors the variety of wishes. Mill remained a hero to Berlin throughout his life, in part because Mill understood the moral importance of variety—of pluralism. He defended the right of every individual to act and think according to his or her own particular and even peculiar nature. Because, Berlin wrote, Mill's view of human nature accepts individuals' "perpetual incompleteness, self-transformation and novelty, his words are today alive and relevant to our own problems," even as we have all but forgotten magisterial nineteenth-century figures like Auguste Comte and the duc de Saint-Simon who assembled dizzying, abstract systems. Berlin loved Kant's wonderful expression, "From the crooked timber of humanity no straight thing was ever made." It is the respect for human particularity that is the foundation of Berlin's anti-totalitarian liberalism.[9]

Berlin always regarded communism as a nightmare. He wrote his first book, which he began in 1933, on Marx, whom he considered a false prophet. Berlin was a liberal by personal history and by temperament. In the thirties, however, that made him a marginal voice among his contemporaries, most of whom considered liberalism a dead letter. England's Liberal Party had collapsed after World War I, its adherents joining either the Conservatives or the socialists of the Labour Party, which first came to power in 1924. The Great Depression persuaded people across the West that capitalism was not only unjust but doomed to destroy itself in wild swings of boom and bust. Whereas in the United States FDR succeeded in protecting democracy while preserving capitalism through state intervention, many British and European thinkers came to regard a collectivism of the left as the only viable alternative to a fascist collectivism of the right. In 1937, the socialist activists Sidney and Beatrice Webb published the rhapsodic *Soviet Communism: A New Civilization*, which fully accepted the Soviets' claims to have at last liberated workers from the tyranny of capital. In fact, the Soviets had begun staging their notorious show trials in 1936, but even George Bernard Shaw, a socialist who seemed proof against all forms of self-delusion, refused to accept that they were sham proceedings.

Liberalism seemed to be a fraud, as it had seemed to the American progressives in 1912. Berlin's friend and Oxford classmate Stephen Spender joined the Communist Party and in 1936 published an account of the evolution of his views titled *Forward from Liberalism*. Far from viewing liberalism as a rampart against fascism, Spender argued that the former enables the latter. Liberal democracy, he wrote, is the political instrument whereby capitalists legitimize their dominance. Voting is a fraud, for real power lies not with the politicians but with the industrialists. The failure of liberal states to deliver on the promise of equality and prosperity has led to the "apathy and despair" that serve as the emotional fuel for fascism and war—an echo of the dire prediction the *New Republic*'s editors made after Wilson signed the Treaty of Versailles. Liberal democracy cannot cure itself, Spender argued, because the gross inequality fostered by capitalism ultimately leads to fascism and war. Only by putting an end to private property can one break the cycle, for political freedom can stand only on a foundation of economic equality. Spender was prepared to accept what he blandly called "the dictatorship of an idea by the guardians of that idea during a period of reorganization when it is impossible to put the democracy into force." Stalin and his circle would serve as those guardians, withholding the liberty of the people until the end state had been achieved.[10]

Communism had a far deeper and more lasting appeal to intellectuals than did fascism, for communism promised to exalt the poor and humble the mighty. Communism offered a theory of history that both explained injustice and made justice seem inevitable. Idealists who were susceptible to the fallacy that Berlin identified—that all good things go together—could all too easily persuade themselves that the Soviets had squared the circle of equality and liberty. The allure of the Soviet Union to thinkers on the left would dim only after World War II, when the truth of the purges and the vast labor camps fully emerged, and when Russia systematically stamped out political liberty in the Eastern bloc. Only in 1949 would Spender join five other ex-Communists in contributing an essay to *The God That Failed*, a famous distillation of ideological regret.

One way of describing the liberals of 1940 is to say that they refused to accept the moral distinction between communism and fascism. The liberals made much less of the fact that communism traced its origins to the work of a great nineteenth-century thinker who wished to free the working class from the tyranny of capital, than of the fact that actual men and women in the Soviet Union had been deprived of their humanness as utterly as were Germans under Nazism. Liberal thinkers asked why that was so and by what means this new form of despotism could be checked. In *The Open Society and Its Enemies*, published in 1944, Karl Popper, an Austrian refugee and historian of science, argued, as Berlin would, that modern tyranny originated not as traditional absolutism but as a promise of emancipation.

Popper devoted much of this epic work to a doctrine he called "historicism," which regards history not as a thing made by people but as a force governed by inexorable laws that shape human destiny. Historicism satisfies the deep human wish to be absolved of responsibility for ourselves and others by ascribing agency to a force beyond ourselves. "If you know that things are bound to happen whatever you do," Popper wrote, "then you may feel free to give up the fight against them." In what Popper called the "open" as opposed to the "closed" civilization, people accept the burden of freedom and the anxiety that accompanies that recognition. "We must," Popper wrote, "bear this strain as the price to be paid for every increase in knowledge, in reasonableness, in cooperation and in mutual help, and consequently in our chances of survival, and in the size of the population. It is the price we have to pay for being human."[11]

Like Berlin, Popper looked to reason to counter the pull of the tribal, the magical, the extrahuman. Rationalism, Popper wrote, "is an attitude of readiness to listen to critical arguments and to learn from experience. It is fundamentally an attitude of admitting that '*I may be wrong and you may be right, and by an effort, we may get nearer to the truth.*'" The irrational certitudes of Hitler and Stalin, the incantatory logic that hypnotized whole populations, turned rational skepticism into the sword and shield of liberalism. In his 1947 essay "Philosophy and Politics," the philosopher Bertrand Russell asserted that "the essence of the liberal outlook lies not in *what* opinions are held, but in *how* they are held: instead of being held dogmatically, they are held tentatively, and with a consciousness that new evidence may at any moment lead to their abandonment." There is little here that Mill did not write in *On Liberty*, but in the face of murderous dogma, Mill's ethic of anti-dogmatism appears not only wise but heroic.[12]

Berlin was a philosopher while Popper was a historian of science. At the heart of his conception of an open society was not merely reason but science, a collective enterprise that depended upon the process of trial and error known as the scientific method. A liberal society, for Popper, was one where the scientific outlook had become a credo—a faith in reason that, he conceded, might be itself irrational. The open society was thus not merely a state of mind but a set of institutions. In 1979 Popper's most famous student, the investor and philanthropist George Soros, established a global network of institutions designed to propagate and promote liberal values under the banner of the Open Society Foundations. The fate of Soros's brainchild may prove that scientific rationalism offers as flimsy a democratic foundation as Berlin's pluralism. Soros has become the illiberal's piñata: Viktor Orbán, the populist leader of Hungary, Soros's birthplace, has drummed the Open Society out of the country and demonized Soros—as has Donald Trump.

The specter of state collectivism drove Popper, and to a lesser extent Berlin, to embrace the virtues of marketplace liberalism. If communism would liquidate political freedom in the name of economic justice, liberalism would restore that freedom by allowing people to exchange goods, labor, and capital according to their own preferences. The chief proponent of classical liberalism as the antithesis of totalitarian rule was the Viennese economist Friedrich Hayek. In 1932 Hayek began teaching at the London School of Economics, where he became a prominent critic of Keynesian theory and mentor to a new generation of economic liberals. In the 1940s, Hayek turned inside out the standard left-wing critique that German capitalists had made common cause with Hitler in order to smash trade unions and eliminate an interventionist state. In fact, he asserted, the German people, and German intellectuals in particular, had been conditioned to accept National Socialism by a prewar socialist consensus. Hayek regarded socialism as not merely bad economic practice but the intellectual precursor to collectivism. He captured this claim in the title of *The Road to Serfdom*, which appeared in 1944.

In his introduction, Hayek addressed himself to the English socialists who insist that fascism sprouts from the soil of capitalism. Quite the contrary, Hayek wrote: the Nazi ideology was born out of a fusion of anti-capitalist forces on the left and right, that is, Marx and Hegel on the one hand and fervent German nationalists like Oswald Spengler on the other. Hayek cited the socialist theorists of the interwar years who argued that the spontaneity and reckless individuality of free-market capitalism would have to give way to organization, planning, and collective purpose. Hayek regarded central planning with the same horror that Berlin felt for monism, the idea that there is one solution to all problems. It "united almost all the single-minded idealists," Hayek wrote, "all the men and women who have devoted their lives to a single task." And "from the saintly and single-minded idealist to the fanatic is often but a short step." The demand for total oversight of the economy inevitably leads to a popular call for an "economic dictator." Even if issued by a democratic legislature, the call for centralization of control "would probably destroy personal freedom as completely as any autocracy has ever done."[13]

Hayek argued forcefully against the idea that planning was inevitable or even effective. He observed, with Adam Smith, that planners could never know enough to efficiently determine prices and output; only the distributed mind of the marketplace could do so. *The Road to Serfdom* appeared at a time when England's Labour Party was planning a postwar regime of overwhelming state control. The case Hayek made was powerful enough that John Maynard Keynes himself wrote to say that he found *The Road to Serfdom* a "grand book." Remarkably, for the thinker most responsible for twentieth-century economic policy, Keynes added that, "morally and philosophically, I find myself in agreement with virtually the whole of it." In a 1946 essay, Orwell took quite seriously Hayek's argument that planning destroys liberty and praised a raft of recent books by classical liberals, including Peter Drucker and F. A. Voigt. (Berlin, on the other hand, noted in a letter that he was "reading the awful Dr. Hayek.")[14]

In 1947, Hayek convened a group of like-minded intellectuals at a Swiss resort. The thirty-nine founders of the Mont Pelerin Society, as it was called after the town, included Karl Popper and the foremost free-market theorists of the time—Ludwig von Mises, George Stigler, and Milton Friedman. The group's charter warned that "the position of the individual and the voluntary group are progressively undermined by extensions of arbitrary power." So much was unexceptionable. The defining feature of the group was the additional stipulation that it is "difficult to imagine a society in which freedom may be effectively preserved" without the "diffused power and initiative of the free market." Political liberty could not be sustained absent economic liberty.[15]

The Road to Serfdom was a work of prognostication as well as analysis, and history was to belie its central claims. In a preface to a new edition in 1956, Hayek was forced to acknowledge that "six years of socialist government in England have not produced anything resembling a totalitarian state." He insisted that the "psychological change" that he had foreseen had, indeed, weakened English resistance to dictatorship; yet in the years to come neither England nor any of the social democratic states of northern Europe tilted even slightly toward autocratic rule. India, the one country that truly adopted a Soviet-style planned economy, remained a raucous democracy (with, however, a stagnant economy). Hayek had insisted that economic rights could not be disentangled from political ones, since economic control meant that we would have our ends dictated to us. But that is true only of total economic control. The abolition of private property in communist states plainly deprives individuals of the means to realize their own wishes. But Hayek adopted the Leninist view summed up in the expression "if a, then b"—that is, to start down the path of socialism is, inevitably, to continue to the very end. Socialism throughout the non-communist world evolved with a mixed economy that preserved private ownership. Nor was any coercion required. Quite the contrary: the high-tax social welfare states of Scandinavia self-evidently enjoy the kind of democratic consent that Hayek imagined they were bound to sacrifice.[16]

The most forceful refutation of Hayek's thesis came from an exact contemporary, the Hungarian émigré economist Karl Polanyi. In *The Great Transformation: The Political and Economic Origins of Our Time*, also published in 1944, Polanyi took direct aim at the Austrian free-market school. He cited anthropological evidence to refute the premise that markets emerge from human nature. Adam Smith's economic man, he wrote, is a fiction. In preindustrial societies, systems of exchange serve larger social purposes. They are, in Polanyi's term, "embedded" in society; only in

Western industrial culture have society and all human goods come to be embedded in the marketplace. People seek perpetually to return markets to their natural, subordinate place in society. The laissez-faire claim that "self-regulating markets" constitute a state of nature, and government intervention an artificial impediment, has the truth exactly backward: government bureaucracies nurtured free markets from the outset, while they responded spontaneously to public demands for protection from the ravages of those markets. "*Laissez-faire* was planned," Polanyi wrote provocatively; "planning was not."[17]

Polanyi conceded that capitalism has produced prosperity. But he argued, in diametrical opposition to Hayek, that the drive for self-regulating markets wrought havoc on civilization and disrupted and immiserated entire classes. The whole system finally collapsed in the Great Depression, provoking a deadly political struggle between the two great forces of production and protection, the one embodied in financial and industrial interests and the other in the legislatures of democracies. Fascist leaders held out the promise of breaking the unbearable tension. They did so, Polanyi wrote, "at the price of the extirpation of all democratic institutions." Europe thus witnessed "the almost unbearable fact that a civilization was being disrupted by the blind action of soulless institutions the only purpose of which was the automatic increase of material welfare."[18]

Taken simply as economic theory, *The Great Transformation* seems almost as one-sided as *The Road to Serfdom*. Polanyi did not convincingly explain how labor, land, and capital, the chief factors of production, can be "re-embedded" in society without killing the goose that has laid so many golden eggs. He would, like the progressives, have regulation disperse prosperity, but societies might have to sacrifice a great deal of prosperity in order to regain something of their preindustrial equilibrium. Yet Polanyi was an economist arguing against economism; his claim is, at bottom, a civilizational one. Polanyi's assault on the "soulless institutions" of the self-regulating market bears more than a trace of Mill, who recoiled against the idea that human nature could be fulfilled by economic transactions. "Economic liberty" can never be accorded the same stature as political liberty both because market freedom, untrammeled, will always lead to grave harms and because human nature is not exhausted by economic life. In his closing chapter, "Freedom in a Complex Society," Polanyi placed market relations at the service of political liberty. In such a society, he wrote, sounding like an updated version of Mill, "spheres of arbitrary freedom" would be "protected by unbreakable rules." Economic planning—Hayek's bugbear—would strengthen individual rights. Polanyi wrote that he is not describing a utopia; he is endorsing FDR's New Deal.[19]

Anti-communists of the left, who had seen through the Soviet fraud but continued to regard capitalism as a system of exploitation, struggled to reconcile the cause of liberty with the cause of justice. By the late 1930s this group included such colossal figures as the French thinker André Gide, the Italian novelist Ignazio Silone, the ex-Communist and essayist Arthur Koestler, and George Orwell. In 1936, Orwell, then a little-known novelist, went to Spain to join the fight against the fascists who were seeking to overthrow the socialist government. Orwell fought alongside anarchists and radical trade unionists who were prepared to risk their lives not to defend democratic rights, of which they knew little, but to overthrow a despised economic order under which they had lived immemorially. Orwell shared their view of liberal democracy. In an essay published in the summer of 1937, he wrote, "You can oppose Fascism by bourgeois 'democracy,' meaning capitalism. But meanwhile you have got to get rid of the troublesome person who points out that Fascism and bourgeois 'democracy' are Tweedledum and Tweedledee."[20]

Orwell went to Spain as a radical socialist. Unlike Berlin, he cared as passionately about equality as about liberty, and he hated class privilege with a virulence that only the English could fully understand. He revered the egalitarian spirit of the revolutionaries. Yet he had witnessed the destruction of that brief experiment in democracy—not by the fascists, but by the communists. As Orwell informed the world in *Homage to Catalonia*, his harrowing account of his time in Spain, the Soviets, the Spanish government's supposed great ally, were systematically annihilating the non-Marxist opposition with a brutality equal to that of the fascists. The Communist press pumped out lies about the anti-Stalinists every bit as vile as those the right-wing press fabricated about the Loyalists. Orwell came to see the Soviets as monstrous and their supporters on the left—Spender, the Webbs, and others—as dupes.

What then? Was it necessary, Orwell asked himself, to abandon socialism, the only hope for the common man, in favor of a gradualist liberalism with capitalism at its core? Orwell was not prepared to say so. In the early spring of 1940, with Hitler's air war against England only weeks away, Orwell retreated from his earlier equation of capitalism with fascism, arguing that the old-fashioned imperialism of the Allies, ugly as it was, was not merciless, systematic, and racialized, like the new imperialism of the Nazis. Orwell backed the war effort earlier than did most radicals, and far more single-mindedly. But he did so in part because, like Walter Weyl in 1916, he could see a better future beckoning on the other side of war—a European future of democratic socialism rather than the malevolent socialism, the "rationalized caste-society," that Hitler hoped to install. Orwell neither surrendered to despair nor deluded himself about the possibilities of social justice. The world, he wrote, seemed to be hurtling toward a new version of the Spanish Inquisition. "There is very little chance we can escape it unless we can reinstate human brotherhood, without the need for a 'next world' to give it meaning. . . . We have got to be the children of God, even though the God of the Prayer Book no longer exists."[21]

It was, perhaps, no great achievement for a figure as dispassionate as Berlin to resist the beguiling illusions of the age; Orwell, who despised injustice and hungered for a better world, nevertheless fended off all temptation to self-delusion. Orwell was prepared to admit every possible evidence against his own beliefs, yet he reaffirmed them. In a 1941 essay titled "Literature and Totalitarianism," Orwell virtually anticipated Hayek's critique. Having already accepted what seemed like the inexorable progress of economic collectivism, Orwell conceded that, whether the new system is called socialism or something else, "the economic liberty of the individual, and to a great extent his liberty to do what he likes . . . comes to an end." More than that, socialism may not simply turn out to be "a sort of moralised Liberalism," where citizens will enjoy perfect political freedom even as their economic liberties are throttled. The totalitarianism of the left and right are abolishing freedom of thought itself. Will not socialism do the same? Hayek, of course, would soon predict just that. Orwell wrote that he still hoped that a democratic socialism could take shape in "those countries in which liberalism has struck its deepest roots." This may be on the order of placing himself in the hands of a Providence in which he did not believe.[22]

Orwell was wrong in supposing that modernity would demand economic collectivism, whether of the left or right, just as Hayek was wrong in prophesying that democratic socialism would lead to fascism. Socialism felt to Orwell like a political necessity as much an economic one. He believed that England's only chance to defeat Hitler was to harness the deep patriotism of the English working class, but he was not convinced that workers would keep fighting for a system in which they had to make do with crumbs.

In his majestic book-length essay, *The Lion and the Unicorn: Socialism and the English Genius*, published in early 1941, Orwell wrote, "We cannot establish anything that a Western nation would regard as Socialism without defeating Hitler; on the other hand, we cannot defeat Hitler while remaining economically and socially in the nineteenth century." Yet Orwell was far too deeply imbued with a horror of utopianism to surrender to dreams of radical transformation. The ideal state, he wrote, would "leave anachronisms and loose ends everywhere," including the monarchy and "the judge in his ridiculous horsehair wig." It would keep faith with the British belief in compromise and the rule of law. It would safeguard freedom of speech and of religion. This was democratic socialism as Orwell understood it.[23]

Unlike Orwell, Isaiah Berlin was never a man of the left. In 1949, he wrote "Winston Churchill in 1940," a frankly admiring essay on the Conservative leader. In an article largely devoted to Churchill's oratorical gifts, Berlin called him—accurately, to be sure—"the largest human being of our time." This outraged Berlin's friends on the left, who despised Churchill's booming imperialism and, like Orwell, hoped for a democratic socialism as the postwar peace dividend. But as a fervent patriot, Berlin had placed all his wartime hopes in Churchill's leadership. Nevertheless, according to his biographer, in the 1950 election Berlin did not vote for Churchill. Neither did he support Labour incumbent Clement Attlee. Berlin voted for the Liberal candidate Clement Davies, who finished a very distant third.[24]

In his work in the early 1950s, Berlin made the case for pluralism as a cardinal virtue. But pluralism was not a substantive principle so much as a doctrine of restraint, a recognition of the multiplicity, and thus mutual incompatibility, of goods. How, exactly, did this principle apply to the core problem of liberty and authority? Did the respect for pluralism dictate that everyone should be allowed to do as they wished, with the state confined to the role of traffic cop? If so, what of the demands for equality and justice that had shaken the world in the previous generation and, after all, shook it still? What was the underlying principle by which one balanced these conflicting goods?

Berlin sought to answer this question in what was to become his most famous lecture, "Two Concepts of Liberty," which he delivered upon assuming the Chichele Chair in Social and Political Theory at Oxford in late 1958. One kind of liberty had been enough for John Stuart Mill, but in the twentieth century a new and, Berlin thought, insidious understanding of freedom had gained a powerful purchase in people's minds. Today, Berlin said, an "open war" is being fought between "two systems of ideas"—liberalism and communism—founded on two very different understandings of what it means to be free.[25]

Berlin began by observing that all classical liberal thinkers have understood liberty as freedom from coercion. He called this doctrine "negative liberty" because it defines the sphere within which no external obligation may be imposed on an individual. For Berlin, as for Mill, political thinking began with the autonomy, and thus the sanctity, of the person. Indeed, in his essay "John Stuart Mill and the Ends of Life," Berlin observed that, despite Mill's dutiful effort in *On Liberty* to provide a utilitarian justification for maximum individual freedom, he plainly regarded liberty as a good in itself. People have different tastes, wishes, ideas, temperaments; the great fact of human life is not uniformity but diversity. To deprive people of their freedom to speak and behave as they wish is to deny them the fullness of their individuality. Berlin was describing Mill's thought; but he was also laying the foundation of his own. He wrote that liberal thinkers naturally disagree on the scope and nature of Mill's inviolable sphere of private thought and action, but the minimum must be understood as "that which a man cannot give up without offending against the essence of his human nature."[26]

But here Berlin made a striking observation: Mill, he said, has confused two different ideas. The idea that coercion is bad and liberty good is logically distinct from Mill's belief that individuals in conditions of liberty will be able to fully realize their own gifts and that a society marked by a commitment to freedom will reach the greatest heights of which humans are capable. The "fiery individualism" Mill held out as an affirmative good often emerged from highly disciplined societies, like the Scottish Puritans, that routinely and intentionally infringed on the sphere of private speech and behavior. Negative liberty, in turn, may flourish in the absence of the kind of self-government that Mill thought of as the end point of a truly liberal society; one need only think of the despot who leaves his subjects alone so long as they obey. The liberal wish for private space and the accompanying vision of human and social self-realization are not only not the same thing, but they may conflict with one another. One, Berlin wrote, is "freedom from"—that is, freedom from coercion—while the other is "freedom to"—that is, to lead a certain kind of life. It is this freedom that Berlin described as "positive liberty."[27]

Berlin did not simply assign the negative idea of liberty to liberalism and the positive to totalitarianism. The latter, he wrote, springs from the classically liberal "wish on the part of the individual to be his own master." What's more, negative liberty, by itself, offers no guidance on how to shape a better life, not only for oneself but for one's fellow man. Many liberals, Berlin observed, feel beleaguered and at times tormented by the

conclusion that their liberty has been purchased at the cost of the suffering of others—through, for example, an unjust economic order. They,
therefore, insist on the kinds of large-scale social changes that would lead
to "equality of liberty." Orwell, for example, thought just this way. Berlin accepted that such principles may well constitute "the foundations of
liberal morality." But, he added, crucially, they should not be described
as aspects of liberty. If you sacrifice some of your freedom, or society's
freedom, in the name of some other good, you may well have produced
more fairness or justice or common decency, but you have diminished the
stock of liberty.[28]

This sounds very much like a linguistic quibble. Why is it so important to prevent the misuse of "liberty"? Why, indeed, should one even
describe the affirmative agendas of reformers as an aspect of liberty, as
opposed to socialism or social democracy or some other set of beliefs?
Berlin's answer is that totalitarianism has learned to speak the language
of liberty, and one must distinguish between true and specious uses of
this beguiling word. Communism mocks the freedom from coercion so
dear to liberals as "bourgeois liberty"; true freedom, according to the
Leninists, requires individuals to surrender their egos to the cause of human betterment. Marxist theoreticians learned this trick from the great
Enlightenment thinkers. If one says, as Rousseau did, that, whatever you
may think you want, your true self, your rational self, *must* want to live
in accordance with this or that set of principles, then you must put aside
your puny wishes. Fichte took this dangerous claim one step further by
insisting that the individual discovers the highest form of self-realization
by submitting to the will of the group, itself the embodiment of true
freedom. "Once I take this view," Berlin concluded, "I am in a position
to ignore the actual wishes of men or societies, to bully, oppress, torture
them in the name, and on the behalf, of their 'real' selves."[29]

It sounds very much as if Berlin was saying that "positive liberty" is a
euphemism for compulsion in the name of an allegedly higher good. If
that is so, then positive liberty is not a kind of liberty at all but a cynical
appropriation of one of the most cherished principles of Western thinking. Yet Berlin wrote elsewhere in the essay that freedom means nothing

to starving peasants; they have other needs that come first. And he accepted that liberty is by no means the only good, even as he insisted that to refer to other goods as forms of liberty is specious and misleading. But if positive liberty is directed toward legitimate—indeed indispensable—goods like equality, and not simply toward sinister manipulation by fanatics and absolutists, then doesn't liberalism need an affirmative as well as a negative agenda?

Berlin accepted that this is so, but he found this path very dangerous. In a conversation with a fellow philosopher, Berlin said that "the only reason for which I have been suspected of defending negative liberty against positive is because I do think that the concept of positive liberty, which is of course essential to a decent existence, has been more often abused or perverted than that of negative liberty." Yet negative liberty is subject to its own form of abuse, not only in theory but in fact. A generation before the rise of totalitarian ideologies, Walter Weyl argued that the cult of the individual, the frontiersman, had become a source of oppression in the United States. Liberty had degenerated into heedlessness. Berlin himself said as much: "Unlimited liberty for capitalists destroys the liberty of the workers." One man's meat, as FDR said, is another man's poison.[30]

Berlin regarded totalitarianism as a far greater threat than injustice; one was a calamity, the other a serious misfortune. He was prepared to err on the side of negative liberty. Berlin thus directed people away from the inspiring and toward the circumspect, away from the organic and toward the compound, away from hope and toward fear. In "The Pursuit of the Ideal," delivered when he was seventy-seven and perhaps even more inclined to skepticism about human prospects than he had been as a younger man, Berlin concluded that the liberal society can offer the citizen no more than "trade-offs" designed to achieve an "uneasy equilibrium" among competing goods. These trade-offs themselves will be defined negatively, for the state's first obligation is to "avoid extremes of suffering." The actions to be avoided at all costs are genuinely extreme—"slavery or ritual murder or Nazi gas chambers." He had little to say about social goods, save for the suggestion that they be cautiously weighed on utilitarian scales. Here is the austere philosophy of an aging mandarin—"not the kind of thing," Berlin acknowledged, "that the idealistic young would wish, if need to be, to fight and suffer for, in the cause of a new and noble society." Berlin's recognition that all good things do not and cannot go together had rendered him virtually unable to formulate a set of principles to which the less tragically minded could subscribe.[31]

The threat of totalitarianism compelled every liberal thinker in the middle of the twentieth century to confront the tension between liberty and equality, or liberty and justice, or liberty and decency. Yet fascism and communism also posed a dire threat to something so elemental to society that political thinkers of earlier generations had barely needed to take account of it: the very idea of truth. In *Darkness at Noon*, the 1940 novel that exposed the reality of the Soviet show trials, Arthur Koestler furnished a terrifying picture of a society based on slogans universally understood to be grotesque lies. The struggle to vindicate liberal principles had to be waged not only on political or economic lines but on cognitive ones as well. This conviction lay at the core of Karl Popper's idea that the "open society" depended above all on the preservation of the spirit of scientific inquiry.

The great prophet of the totalitarian assault on truth was, of course, George Orwell, who first came to recognize the danger during the Spanish Civil War, when he saw that the newspapers of all sides described events that bore no relation to reality. In an unpublished essay apparently written in 1942, he recalled having said to Koestler, "History stopped in 1936"—the year of the Soviet show trials. Thereafter one would never know what was true and what had been fabricated. The experience, Orwell wrote, had left him with the feeling that "the very concept of objective truth is fading out of the world." This fear came more and more to preoccupy Orwell. In 1947 he wrote that because totalitarian regimes insist that the leadership is infallible, history must be perpetually rewritten in order to eliminate evidence of past mistakes. Totalitarianism thus "demands a disbelief in the very existence of objective truth." Orwell added darkly that "to be corrupted by totalitarianism one does not have to live in a totalitarian country"; one simply had to surrender to certain habits of thought.[32]

Orwell's novel *1984*, published in 1948, is many, many things, but at the core of its dystopian narrative is the struggle of one man to hold on to the freedom that lives inside his own mind even as he is surrounded, and soon swallowed up, by a totalitarian leviathan. The hero, Winston Smith, can survive anything so long as he knows that such freedom remains possible. "They could not alter your feelings," he thinks. "For that matter you could not alter them yourself, even if you wanted to. They could lay bare in the utmost detail everything that you had done or said or thought; but the inner heart, whose workings were mysterious even to yourself, remained impregnable." Winston comes to understand that he has underestimated the Party, which has dedicated itself to penetrating even the inner hearts of citizens.[33]

The Party is, of course, the Communist Party of Russia; Big Brother is Stalin; the rebel Goldstein is Trotsky. But *1984* is not a parable of Soviet society like *Animal Farm*, Orwell's 1943 novel. It is a parable of totalitarianism itself. The regime that rules Winston Smith's Oceania has reduced totalitarianism to an exact science, turning the empire into a vast jail from which no individual, and no thought, can escape—save for the boisterous, *völkisch* "proles." The Party has evolved beyond any recourse to the romantic ideologies in the name of which citizens willingly yield up their liberty; as a senior leader explains to Winston, it believes in nothing save power itself. It is totalitarianism in the name of totalitarianism.

Winston works in a branch of the Ministry of Truth that rewrites history, the totalitarian preoccupation Orwell had envisioned in his essay of a year earlier. The Party has invented a past in which England groaned under injustice. A children's textbook sports a parody-Marxist version of midcentury England: "The capitalists owned everything in the world, and everyone else was their slave. They owned all the land, all the houses, all the factories, and all the money." The Party is at pains to prove that economic freedom under capitalism was a fraud; its alleged ideology, Ingsoc, is a corruption of English socialism, from which it grew. Orwell remained a socialist to the end of his life, yet here his dystopia merges for a moment with Hayek's: the road to serfdom passes by, if it does not spring from, the elimination of economic freedom. Orwell's capacity to credit ideas that jeopardize his own never ceases to amaze. But of course the willingness to do just that was a foundation of political liberty for Orwell, as it was for Mill.[34]

Like *The Road to Serfdom, 1984* was meant as a warning to liberals: it could happen here. What Orwell feared, of course, was not socialist planning but totalitarian thinking. He feared the growing separation between language and meaning that he described in his famous essay "Politics and the English Language"—the corruption of words that in turn corrupts thought. He feared the distortion of history in the name of ideology and, above all, the abandonment of the very idea of objective truth. Orwell's worst fears were not realized, any more than Hayek's were. Totalitarianism did not expand and finally disappeared. In our own time, however, the idea of objective truth does, indeed, seem to be fading out of the world. Orwell could not imagine any force save the state that would have both the will and the capacity to eliminate truth; today's social media gives all of us access to the tools that blur and finally bury the truth, though autocratic and illiberal states have seized on those tools for their own use. In an ironic development that Orwell would have sardonically savored, the coinage "fake news," devised in order to reinforce the bright line between facts and fabrications, has been repurposed by cynics like American president Donald Trump to undermine the very idea of fact.

Liberal values never faced so dire, so existential, a threat as they did in the middle decades of the twentieth century. And because communism—unlike fascism—was not only a form of social organization but a doctrine with deep roots in European political philosophy, anti-totalitarian liberals like Berlin and Popper and (perhaps to a lesser extent) Orwell felt compelled to reconsider the foundations of liberalism in order to construct a countertheory of equal force and depth. Against Marxian collectivism they posed the sanctity of the individual and of individual freedom, and against Marx's historical materialism they insisted that people shaped their own history, including through ideas about how to act. Liberals defended a commitment to truth and reason in the face of the big lie, and to incrementalism in the face of visionary madness. It is true that the threat they faced has long since faded; ours is of a different nature. But we have learned, as they knew, that the liberal virtues of reason, pragmatism, and tolerance are always in jeopardy—not from outside forces, but from ourselves.

CHAPTER FIVE

America After the War: Liberalism as Civic Religion

*The time has arrived for the Democratic Party to
get out of the shadows of states' rights and walk
forthrightly into the bright sunshine of human rights.*

—HUBERT HUMPHREY

WHEN WORLD WAR II CAME TO AN END, AMERICANS FOUND themselves, for the first time in fifteen years, with no dragons to slay. They had weathered the Depression and defeated the Nazis. The country was no longer haunted by the specter of class warfare that had launched the first generation of liberal activism, or by the prospect of mass poverty that had given rise to the New Deal. The United States was the most prosperous society the world had ever known. The situation in which midcentury political thinkers found themselves bore a very real resemblance to the one that John Stuart Mill had confronted in the wealthy, peaceful, and thoroughly self-satisfied England of a century before. That stifling complacency had given Mill his great subject. But postwar American culture already *was* liberal in Mill's sense, for society imposed few obstacles to the individual's right to speak and behave as he or she wished.

In this new context, what could liberalism mean beyond keeping the clock of American prosperity well wound? To what threats did liberals need to respond, and to what opportunities could they point? In 1949, Arthur Schlesinger Jr., a thirty-one-year-old professor of American history at Harvard, sought to answer these questions in *The Vital Center: The Politics of Freedom*. Schlesinger aspired to refound New Deal liberalism for an age of middle-class affluence threatened less by internal forces than by the global ambitions of the Soviet Union. *The Vital Center* was the ur-text of what would come to be known as Cold War liberalism.

Schlesinger shared Isaiah Berlin's bone-deep loathing of communism but not his fear of the state. America, after all, had never known the tyranny of an autocratic government. Like his American forebears, Herbert Croly and Walter Weyl, Schlesinger regarded the state as an antidote to the national tendency toward plutocratic rule; so it had proved to be during the Depression. The rise of totalitarianism in the thirties and forties had seemed for a time to undermine the cause of freedom. Now, after the climactic defeat of fascism, liberalism had regained its "radical nerve" and rediscovered the "vital center" between "the abyss of totalitarianism" and "the jungle of private enterprise." The limited states of the liberal democracies had not proved helpless before the collectivist state, as Orwell had predicted. Quite the contrary: "Experience suggests that the limited state can resolve the basic social questions which were supposed to compel a resort to the unlimited state."[1]

The Vital Center rang in liberalism's age of triumph. Two years earlier, Schlesinger had helped found Americans for Democratic Action (ADA), an explicitly anti-communist liberal organization that attracted some of the leading thinkers of the time, including theologian Reinhold Niebuhr and economist John Kenneth Galbraith, as well as rising political stars like Minneapolis mayor Hubert Humphrey. At the 1948 Democratic convention, Humphrey had led a raucous insurgent movement to place civil rights at the very heart of the party's platform. The civil rights commitment lent a sense of deep moral purpose, beyond the rivalry with the Soviet Union, to both the party and to liberalism itself. Indeed, the two projects were intimately linked, for the essence of Cold War liberalism was the conviction that the United States could most effectively defeat communism by demonstrating to the people of the world its commitment to social justice at home. Many years would have to pass before the Democrats would redeem the pledge of 1948. But in 1964, President Lyndon B. Johnson, a champion of civil rights, would crush Barry Goldwater, a far-right conservative, and unleash a torrent of civil rights legislation.

In the thirty-six years between FDR's first term and the end of Johnson's tenure, the United States showed what a nation fully committed to liberal principles could achieve for its own people. That period ended, as we shall see in the ensuing section, with a terrible crash. Liberal hegemony may have been unhealthy for liberalism.

S chlesinger's "vital center" is not a median point along an ideological spectrum so much as a source of energy struggling against the dead weight of conventional wisdom. To the right he found little more than Babbittry. Conservatism in America, Schlesinger asserted, entails less a body of coherent ideas than the selfish interests of the businessmen who have dominated the Republican Party from the time of Taft. Schlesinger did not hesitate to call them plutocrats, but he found the postwar captains of industry less sinister than plodding. In an increasingly managerial age, these barons have lost their vital spirits—"the zest for competition, the delight in risk-taking." They are a class becalmed. "On the historical record," Schlesinger brusquely concluded, "the business community appears to lack the instinct, will, and capacity to govern."[2]

Schlesinger was much more savage about the threat from the other side—the progressive, the utopian, "the fellow traveler or the fellow traveler of the fellow traveler" who viewed the Soviet Union "as a kind of enlarged Brook Farm community, complete with folk dancing in native costumes, joyous work in the fields and progressive kindergartens." He compared these latter-day American versions of the Webbs to the dough-faces—"northern men with southern principles"—who refused to break with the South in the period before the Civil War, telling themselves that slavery was, after all, hardly worse than the factory work done in the North. The new doughfaces would happily wreck capitalism, rather than work to reform it, on the grounds that the marketplace crushed people's souls without even holding out the possibility of a glorious future, as Soviet Communism did. "This well-intentioned, woolly-minded, increasingly embittered man," Schlesinger wrote, "was made to order for Communist exploitation."[3]

Whatever appeal it had enjoyed in the depths of the Depression, American communism now looked like an absurdity. The United States in the postwar era constituted the greatest argument ever mounted for the virtues of the free market. Capitalism stood at the center of the vital center. Alarmist title notwithstanding, the economists, technocrats, and politicians who contributed essays to a 1948 volume called *Saving American Capitalism: A Liberal Economic Program* did not actually regard capitalism as seriously endangered. Rather, it needed reform. The "liberal" program they had in mind derived not from Friedrich Hayek and the free-market theoreticians but from FDR, who had proved, at least to their satisfaction, that capitalism could flourish so long as it was accompanied by an active state to temper excesses and public investment to supply public goods that the market ignored. In his "Blueprint for a Second New Deal," Chester Bowles, a prominent advertising executive who had served in senior economic positions under both Roosevelt and Truman, proposed government spending on infrastructure and "slum clearance," universal access to high-quality education, an increase in the minimum wage, and the establishment of minimum standards of public health, housing, and nutrition. Bowles treated economic development as an arrow in the Cold War quiver. "The most effective means of opposing Communism," he argued, "is a bold, dynamic program of economic, political and social reform." Schlesinger made much the same argument in *The Vital Center*.[4]

Here, in full, was American Cold War liberalism. On the one hand, mass affluence had solved the ancient problems of scarcity, as Walter Weyl had once envisioned it would. The average person could enjoy the comforts formerly available only to the few. And yet a fantasy of total fulfillment, of release from all of life's contradictions, played on the inevitable shortcomings of liberal democracy and industrial society to tempt people toward collectivism. Even at this advanced moment in human history, in this wealthiest of countries, the sphere of individual liberty had to be defended at all costs—and not from the right, but from the left. Schlesinger acknowledged that the Communist Party USA was a fringe force and warned against the growing paranoia that was soon to explode into McCarthyism. But it was the uneasy proximity of liberalism to communist-influenced progressivism that gave a hard, defining edge to the thought of the Cold War liberals.

When he ridiculed the doughface left, Schlesinger was thinking above all of Henry Wallace, an Iowa farmer and progressive, FDR's secretary of agriculture and then, from 1940 to 1944, vice president. At the Democratic convention in 1944, Hubert Humphrey led a raucous parade to champion Wallace's renomination. Humphrey was bitterly disappointed when FDR spurned Wallace for Missouri senator Harry Truman, widely derided as a machine politician and a hack. But after his repudiation, Wallace drifted further left. Like many on the left, Wallace came to view the Soviets as a conservative great power bent on defending itself rather than as a dynamic ideological force determined to advance revolutionary anti-democratic principles. Truman appointed Wallace secretary of commerce but fired him in 1946, when the latter said that the United States should accept the Soviet sphere of influence in Eastern Europe. Humphrey was shaken. "Mr. Wallace says that there are spheres of influence," he wrote to a friend. "I say this is one world." When Wallace came to Minnesota later that year, Humphrey warned him about the Communist takeover of the state's Farmer-Labor faction and asked him to speak out against it. Wallace waved him off. Humphrey was cured of any lingering illusions about both the American Communist Party and Wallace. "You can be a liberal without being a Communist," he told a gathering of supporters, "and you can be a progressive without being a Communist sympathizer."[5]

Wallace had come to view the United States as a greater obstacle to world peace than the Soviet Union. He predicted that the US would stumble into a new depression and then into outright fascism. He denounced the Marshall Plan—or "martial plan," as he called it—as a flimsy cover for the takeover of foreign policy by Wall Street and the military. Though many ADA liberals, including Humphrey, hoped Truman would somehow step aside in 1948 in favor of Justice William O. Douglas or even Dwight Eisenhower, who had never declared his party affiliation, they were united by their fear of Wallace's running as the standard-bearer of the revitalized Progressive Party. The party's platform blamed Truman for the Soviet invasion of Czechoslovakia and called for the nationalization of banks, railroads, and core industries. Wallace did just well enough in early polls to scare the ADA into an all-out campaign to discredit him as a Communist stooge—red-baiting in, they deeply felt, a good cause.[6]

Like Woodrow Wilson in 1912, Harry Truman understood that he could not get elected unless he could mobilize liberals, who constituted a crucial swing vote. And so, like Wilson, he turned himself into one. In late 1946, Truman commissioned a report on civil rights, *To Secure These Rights*, which accused the United States of moral hypocrisy in its treatment of black Americans and advocated anti-lynching legislation, the abolition of the poll tax, the establishment of a fair-employment commission, and a host of other measures. Truman put forward legislation in early 1948 incorporating many of the report's recommendations.

The chief obstacle to any such legislation lay not with the Republicans, whose progressive wing had defended civil rights since the time of Lincoln, but with an axis of senior southern Democrats in the Senate, known as the Bourbons, who could block any legislation they didn't like. Liberals knew that if the Democrats were to become the party of civil rights, the fight they needed to wage would be inside the party. The place to hold that fight would be the platform committee at the party convention that summer. With President Truman unwilling to openly champion civil rights, the chances of ramming through a statement of principle even equal to the language of the president's own report seemed vanishingly small. Nevertheless, the thirty-seven-year-old Humphrey, the vice chairman of the ADA and now running for a US Senate seat in Minnesota, decided that the time had come to make the Democratic Party the instrument of racial justice.

Humphrey was a midwestern idealist, a small-town boy born a few months later than another prairie sentimentalist, Ronald Reagan. Born above the family drugstore in Wallace, South Dakota, Humphrey inherited his disposition and his principles from his father, who twice lost his store but during the Depression tore up $13,000 in debts that his customers couldn't pay back without ruining themselves. Both father and son revered FDR. On a visit to Washington in 1935, young Hubert thrilled to the signs of the government machine whirring away on behalf of ordinary people. The Depression, he would write in his memoirs, "taught me what government can mean in terms of improving the human condition and improving the human environment."[7]

Humphrey was the kind of man who never stopped talking, never stopped shaking hands or making friends. He taught Sunday school in church while climbing up the ladder of the New Deal–era Works Progress Administration. Humphrey ran for mayor of Minneapolis in 1943 and lost. Convinced that liberals would never succeed in the state so long as they divided their vote between the Democratic and Farmer-Labor Parties, he set out to merge the two. Farmer-Labor was itself divided between rural progressives and an array of Marxist factions. Humphrey was shocked to discover that these latter were not simply far-left ideologues but disciplined flunkies for Moscow. "They twisted and turned according to the demands of the Soviet line," he would later write. But Moscow wanted fusion, so the Farmer-Laborites agreed. Now the candidate of the Democratic-Farmer-Labor Party, Humphrey ran for mayor again in 1945 as a law-and-order candidate who would bring organized crime to heel. He won, and proceeded to do just that.[8]

By 1946, the Communists had seized control of the DFL—thus Humphrey's vain warning to Wallace. Though a consensus-builder by nature, Humphrey had seen enough of domestic communism to conclude that he had to force a showdown. It proved to be a brutal struggle. When Humphrey rose to speak at the party's 1946 convention, he was shouted down as a "fascist" and "warmonger." The sergeant at arms threatened to knock his block off if he didn't sit down. Humphrey sat, but he spent the next two years systematically weeding the radicals out of the party. In 1948, the DFL, now a party of bright-eyed, youthful liberals, nominated Humphrey for the Senate. The line he had drawn was the making of him as a national figure. He was a fresh face and an irrepressible voice at a moment when the Democrats seemed to have resigned themselves to dispiriting, low-risk politics. *Time* magazine put Humphrey on the cover and called him "the number one prospect for liberalism in the country."[9]

Humphrey arrived at the national convention in Philadelphia in mid-July determined to get himself on the drafting committee for the party platform and to push for an official embrace of the ambitious civil rights agenda laid out in Truman's 1946 report. But he was a rookie in national politics; he imagined that the high-flown exhortations that made him a hero in Minneapolis would carry the day in Philadelphia. His eloquence hit a wall: even northern liberals didn't care to cross the southern Bourbons. Humphrey then drafted a watered-down version of the civil rights plank and garnered a few more votes. Some of his allies warned him that if he pushed much harder he risked splitting the party. Indeed, one of Truman's aides admonished a senior ADA figure, "You won't get fifty votes on your minority plank, and all you'll do is ruin the chances for the number one prospect for liberalism in the country." The party's entire hierarchy, not just the southern racists, opposed a strong civil rights plank. Humphrey knew that he had to be a good team player or risk his brilliant future. By the night of July 13, with an ugly floor fight looming, Humphrey was prepared to throw in the towel.

Now the ADA began pushing back. The great goal was not only to reorient the Democratic Party around the supreme moral struggle of the day but to blunt the Wallace tide. How better to do so than by showing progressives that the Democratic Party was prepared to champion the cause of civil rights? Humphrey came around before dawn the next morning. "For me personally," he later wrote, "and for the party, the time had come to suffer whatever the consequences." The vote was scheduled for that night. Relentless lobbying by the ADA had already knocked several breaches in the wall of resistance. Incredibly, Ed Flynn, the flinty Tammany boss from the Bronx, not only joined the side of the angels but promised to deliver some of the other big-city sachems as well. "We've got to stir up the interests of the minority groups in this election," he grumbled, "otherwise we're dead."[10]

That night, with 60 million Americans listening on the radio and 10 million more watching on the new medium of television, Hubert Humphrey, usually a man of far too many words, addressed the convention for eight minutes. It would be the speech of his life. "There can be no hedging," he cried, "no watering down. To those who say that we are rushing the issue of civil rights—I say to them, we are 172 years late." The cheering of thousands of delegates became a sustained roar. "To those who say this bill is an infringement of states' rights, I say this: The time has arrived in America. The time has arrived for the Democratic Party to get out of the shadows of states' rights and walk forthrightly into the bright sunshine of human rights. People—people—human beings—this is the issue of the twentieth century."[11]

The civil rights plank passed 651½ to 581½. Hubert Humphrey's bold gambit would prove to be a pivotal moment of postwar liberalism—indeed, of postwar American politics. The Democrats had now shed their nineteenth-century skin, the old Jeffersonian individualism into which the southern defense of racial domination had been stitched. The party had fashioned a new majority. Black voters who had long identified with Republicans began to vote Democratic. Ed Flynn might have been right about the 1948 election, for Truman did, of course, go on to beat Thomas Dewey by a hair. Henry Wallace, who could have drawn off crucial support, finished with only 2.3 percent of the vote. For many reasons, Democratic renewal among them, Communist Party membership, which had peaked at seventy-three thousand members in 1946, dropped to fifty-four thousand in 1949. And the solid South began to delaminate. Once the civil rights plank passed, Senator Strom Thurmond of South Carolina led a walkout of southern delegates. Thurmond ran for president at the head of the Dixiecrat Party and carried his own state as well as Mississippi, Alabama, and Louisiana—a footnote at the time, though a harbinger of far graver problems inside the Democratic Party.

Truman fully embraced the liberal vision, but southerners in the Senate blocked most of his agenda. Nevertheless, the fundamental meaning of liberalism had changed. First, the Democrats had shown that a bold, affirmative vision of government—of positive liberty, in Berlin's terms—

could serve as a weapon to defend liberal democracy against the ideological threat of communism. Second, and more consequential for the American future, liberalism had come to be associated with conscience as against class interest. During the Depression, when FDR had deployed the state on behalf of the ordinary citizen—the ordinary *white* citizen— liberalism had spoken to national majorities in the language of their own interests. By the late 1940s, the average American no longer needed to be rescued by the state; instead, the postwar vision of Schlesinger and others sought to expand the sphere of public goods in order to enrich the lives of the new middle class as well as the working class. Civil rights, however, constituted a different kind of majoritarian formula—one that spoke to Americans' sense of decency rather than their self-interest. Civil rights was, as Humphrey said, the issue of the twentieth century. The deep current of idealism and optimism in twentieth-century America found its political home in the Democratic Party. For the next two decades that spirit would sustain the party. And then it wouldn't.

In the generation after World War II, liberalism constituted not only America's civic culture but its chief export. The dream of a liberal world order had sunk deep roots among thinkers and political leaders during the First World War. Though even centrist Republicans like former president William Howard Taft hoped to replace nineteenth-century balance-of-power diplomacy with a "League to Enforce Peace," it was left to President Woodrow Wilson to draft a program of postwar governance that would, in effect, universalize America's liberal principles. Wilson believed that the world was entering a democratic age in which the security of governments, and thus the peace of the world, depended on popular legitimacy—thus his famous conviction that "the world must be made safe for democracy." The postwar order he envisioned would be founded on the liberal principles that he expounded in his "Fourteen Points" speech in 1918: transparent diplomacy, free trade, freedom of the seas, national self-determination. It was this vision that gained Wilson the decisive support of liberal internationalists who, like him, justified the decision to join the war effort on the grounds that the United States could later impose its moral vision on the European ruling classes that had thrown their citizens into a senseless meat grinder. The editors of the *New Republic* greeted Wilson's call for a declaration of war by writing exultantly, "The cause of the Allies is now unmistakably the cause of liberalism." Of Wilson they wrote, "No other statesman has ever so clearly identified the glory of his country with the peace and liberty of the world."[12]

The liberal dream evaporated in the Treaty of Versailles, for the Allies were not prepared to accept American dictation. After World War II, however, a shattered Europe was fully prepared to endorse American terms in return for American protection and support. FDR was a Wilsonian without pious illusions about human virtue. In early 1941, before the US had even entered the war, he had proclaimed that henceforth the world would have to be founded on "four freedoms": freedom of speech, freedom of conscience, freedom from want, and freedom from fear. Later that year, FDR and Churchill released the Atlantic Charter, an updated version of the Fourteen Points that committed America and Britain to the principles of nonaggression, national self-determination, secure borders, free trade, and economic cooperation.

The United States was in so dominant a position after the war that it could have ruled through a series of regional or bilateral arrangements in which Washington would be immeasurably the senior partner. Instead it chose to design institutions, including the United Nations, the World Bank, and the International Monetary Fund, in which it would be first among equals. The United States would be bound by rules and by reciprocal obligations, as all members would. Both the UN Security Council and NATO, which was founded in 1949, depended on the doctrine of collective security that Wilson had placed at the heart of the ill-fated League of Nations, though the far more hardheaded FDR insisted on providing a veto to the five permanent members of the council. Even President Truman, derided as a machine pol unworthy to succeed the sainted Roosevelt, had long carried in his wallet a copy of Tennyson's "Locksley Hall," a poem in which he imagines a "parliament of man."

In this "federation of the world," the poet wrote, "the common sense of most shall hold a fretful realm in awe / And the kindly earth shall slumber, lapt in universal law."

The new world order would be based on individual and social rights understood to be not the particular property of the West but intrinsic to human society, an idea codified in the 1948 Universal Declaration of Human Rights. The influence of the New Deal led postwar planners to focus as well on the establishment of programs of social insurance to guard against mass economic failure, unemployment, illness, old age; the UN would consist not just of a peacemaking central body but of specialized agencies devoted to public health, economic development, culture, the welfare of children, and the like. Nowhere, perhaps, did the United States make its influence felt more than in the creation of bodies designed to ensure the free circulation of capital and of goods. Economic freedom had been central to Wilson's vision; so was it for FDR and Truman. Trade barriers had proved to be a provocation to war in 1914; trade relations, by contrast, bound states to one another. In 1947, twenty-three countries signed the General Agreement on Tariffs and Trade with the goal of reducing trade barriers. A historian of the postwar order listed the essential attributes of the economic institutions designed by American and British diplomats: open, nondiscriminatory, liberal, private, cooperative, rule-bound, and governed.[13]

It is absolutely true that these institutions were ultimately weaponized as the ramparts of the West in the Cold War with Soviet Russia. The United States fostered institutions like NATO, which had not been envisioned by postwar planners, to knit together a Western alliance against Soviet encroachment. Yet as the liberal foreign policy theorist John Ikenberry noted, the original purpose of the postwar architecture "was not to deter or contain the Soviet Union but to lay the foundations for an international order that would allow the United States to thrive." Washington planners were fully prepared to let this vast machine work on its own once they had put together its parts. Indeed, the Communist menace clarified for American statesmen the civilizational ties that bound Western nations to one another. They were prepared to give every member of NATO an equal voice, not only because they knew that all the other members depended on the American military and nuclear umbrella, but also because they trusted that as liberal democracies, the states shared the most fundamental interests. "The hierarchical character of the order," Ikenberry concluded, "was more liberal than imperial."[14]

It was not only through the forging of institutions but through the deployment of its vast wealth that the United States sought to demonstrate to Europeans the superiority of liberty and free markets to state control and socialism. Between 1945 and 1947 the Truman administration poured $16.25 billion into Europe in the form of humanitarian aid, loans, grants, and concessional trade deals. In 1947, with the governments of Greece and Turkey facing indigenous communist movements, President Truman announced that henceforth the United States would "support free people who are resisting attempted subjugation by armed minorities or by outside pressures." The Marshall Plan, unveiled later that year, broadened that offer to include all of Europe. The objective, as Secretary of State George Marshall put it when he disclosed the plan, was "the revival of a working economy in the world as so to permit the emergence of political and social conditions in which free institutions can exist." Capitalism had to work if Europe was to resist the lure of communism; the Americans aimed to revitalize the European, and above all the German, industrial economy. The larger goal was to bind European states together; the funds were to be disbursed by a new body, the Organisation for European Economic Co-operation, the precursor to the European Union. Between 1948 and 1952 the Marshall Plan supplied an additional $13 billion to Europe.[15]

This vast undertaking both provided a liberal institutional framework for postwar Europe and demonstrated the virtues of the distinctively American combination of political and economic freedom.

The United States in the 1950s was notoriously complacent, conformist, and inward-looking. Twice it chose as president Dwight Eisenhower, a nice old man who promised to take care of the country and not do anything precipitate. Eisenhower was so fundamentally nonpartisan a figure that, as mentioned earlier, the Democrats seriously entertained trying to draft him in 1948. Arthur Schlesinger wrote that liberalism enjoyed no greater triumph than the endorsement of the New Deal in the Republicans' 1952 platform. And Eisenhower resisted the hard-liners in the party who wanted him to roll back Soviet gains and to join the fervid anti-Communist crusade of Wisconsin senator Joe McCarthy. In an essay titled "The Sources of American Prestige," Reinhold Niebuhr observed that America gained prestige through displays of restraint rather than raw power. Much of the world had imagined that the country was on the brink of fascism; by early 1955, when Niebuhr was writing, that was obviously not the case. Eisenhower was hardly a strong president, but he had the wisdom to use American power sparingly. "Prudence in a ruler," Niebuhr wrote, "is almost as great a source of authority as the sense of justice, because men rightly abhor the chaos of war more than the evils of injustice."[16]

Arthur Schlesinger thus seemed to have good reason to believe that Americans were either liberals or cranks. As the social and literary critic Lionel Trilling wrote in 1950, "In the United States at this time liberalism is not only the dominant but even the sole intellectual tradition. For it is the plain fact that nowadays there are no conservative or even reactionary ideas in general circulation." Conservativism constituted a body not of ideas but of "irritable mental gestures." A cottage industry of books explained why Americans were genetically liberal. Lacking a feudal class, as Harvard historian Louis Hartz wrote in 1955 in *The Liberal Tradition in America*, citizens had no use for a revolutionary ideology to justify the upending of that order. Nor, therefore, did it develop a Tory ideology seeking to restore the *ancien régime*. Americans were the secular, pragmatic, legalistic children of John Locke.[17]

Yet there was more than a trace of Harvard Square myopia, not to mention smugness, in this view. In 1947, at virtually the exact moment when Schlesinger and others were founding the ADA, leading American laissez-faire thinkers were joining Friedrich Hayek to found the Mont Pelerin Society. Economic liberalism seemed every bit as native to American soil as the political liberalism of the post-FDR Democrats. In fact, conservatism enjoyed an intellectual boomlet in the early 1950s. The New Conservatives, as they were called, were not fat cats or religious re-actionaries, though they thought of themselves as prophets in the wilder-ness. William Buckley caught the spirit of the enterprise when he wrote in the first issue of the *National Review*, in 1955, that the conservative "stands athwart history, yelling Stop." Conservatives defined themselves against the liberal consensus. In *The Conservative Mind*, Russell Kirk made the case for a Burkean traditionalism that respected "orders and classes," "tradition and sound prejudice." If the various strands of conservatism had a unifying feature, it was zealous anti-communism. Conservatives of all stripes were virtually obsessed with alleged Communist infiltra-tion at home. Almost all ranged themselves in McCarthy's camp when he began "exposing" Communist agents in academia, foundations, and the State Department. William Buckley coauthored a passionate defense, *McCarthy and His Enemies*, in 1954.[18]

"For better or for worse," wrote a historian of the period, "the domes-tic cold war branded the American Right for a generation." Conservatives backed the wrong horse. McCarthy would be defined by the famous ques-tion posed by attorney Robert Welch in the Army-McCarthy hearings of 1954: "Have you no sense of decency, sir?" Later that year the Sen-ate censured the Wisconsin senator, who would die soon thereafter. The ADA, which had swallowed loyalty tests with barely a murmur, had begun calling for McCarthy to be drummed out of the Senate in 1951. Liberals had thus found a way of balancing anti-communism with civil liberties; conservatives had not. Ideological conservatism would not become a force in the United States for several decades.[19]

America remained a liberal country, not because the country's lead-ers were prepared to enact a progressive agenda—they were not—but because both parties adhered to the core commitments of the New Deal, defended civil liberties in the crunch, and made small gestures in the direction of civil rights. Eisenhower sponsored modestly progres-sive legislation, including an increase in the federal minimum wage, expanded access to Social Security, and funding for public housing and slum clearance. He also agreed to send army troops to Little Rock in

1957 to enforce a court-ordered school desegregation plan. But the real sources of progress lay outside the executive branch. In the 1954 *Brown* decision the Supreme Court under Chief Justice Earl Warren finally put to rest the shameful principle of "separate but equal" that it had ratified in 1896 in *Plessy v. Ferguson*. The civil rights movement started in earnest the following year with the Montgomery bus boycott, which began to force northerners to acknowledge the grip that Jim Crow held over the South. Humphrey introduced civil rights bills that had no chance of passing. By the late 1950s, when the Democrats had gained strong majorities in both houses of Congress, the sense of dammed-up energies for reform made Eisenhower's grandfatherly composure feel increasingly at odds with the mood of the country. In 1960, Schlesinger wrote that "the present period of passivity and acquiescence in politics . . . is drawing to a natural end." The nation had a long list of unaddressed needs—urban redevelopment, the provision of health care, school reform, civil rights and civil liberties. The 1960s, he predicted, would offer "a sense of leadership, of motion, of hope."[20]

Schlesinger was, of course, more right than he knew. Americans had experienced astonishing material changes over the previous decade. With hourly manufacturing wages three times as high as they had been in 1940, factory workers enjoyed effective lifetime tenure at wage levels that allowed them to buy good homes and cars and take beach vacations. In the 1950s alone, disposable income nationwide grew by a third in constant dollars. The white-collar managerial class exploded in size and wealth. Americans were also growing more economically equal. The largest fraction of the economic gains made during the 1940s had gone to those in the lowest income decile, and the smallest to those at the top. And as memories of both war and Depression faded, these gains felt more and more permanent and America's ever-upward trajectory more assured.[21]

The liberalism of the New Deal had been provoked by economic failure and scarcity. In *The Affluent Society*, published in 1958, Harvard economist John Kenneth Galbraith proposed a new liberalism of abundance. Until only a generation earlier, Galbraith claimed, "economic ideas predicted pervasive unhappiness and poverty." Modern man, he argued, lived with this intellectual heritage even as the facts of life up-ended the old wisdom. Americans had experienced "a mountainous rise in well-being" as well as an increasingly fair distribution of wealth. The economy had "largely completed the work" of protecting citizens against the age-old scourge of insecurity; yet eliminating insecurity had not pro-duced a nation of idlers, as classical economics would have predicted. Americans enjoyed security *and* progress.[22]

Galbraith insisted that the economy was producing every bit as much as it needed, but it was producing the wrong things. In an age of afflu-ence, the marketplace churned out every possible gadget to satisfy the wishes of consumers but could not supply the goods on which all de-pend—cars of every type but not decent roads, or schools, or even fresh air. Was there anything, Galbraith sardonically observed, so utterly de-void of public value as the tail fin? Yet that was just what the marketplace, on its own, would produce. It would not produce "human development"; only the state could do that. As Schlesinger would later put it, Galbraith had charted the shift of liberalism from the "quantitative" problems of the New Deal to the "qualitative" problems of abundance—the question of "the quality of the life lived." It would be the job of liberals to channel the forces of abundance in order to improve the quality of life.[23]

Into this moment stepped John F. Kennedy. This figure of ro-mance, young and handsome and beguiling and driven by a ferocious ambition, embodied the spirit of the moment as sure as had FDR, his more warm-spirited predecessor in noblesse oblige. Kennedy was not a Cold War liberal. His faith in civil liberties did not equal the fervor of his anti-communism: Kennedy had not voted for the censure of Joseph McCarthy (for whom his brother Robert had briefly worked). He had never joined the ADA, and as a senator he had shown very little interest in its reform agenda.

The ADA's consensus candidate in 1960 was Hubert Humphrey, who had been waiting for his moment. "The quiescence of the Eisenhower years had cast a spell that had to be broken," he later wrote. Humphrey's vision was much more urgent than Galbraith's. The civil rights revolution that he had called for in 1948 had barely begun; he planned to use the campaign to educate Americans about the condition of those who had been left behind, above all in the nation's deteriorating cities. The great migration of blacks, Hispanics, and poor whites from the countryside to the city had produced a generation of "strangers in a strange land . . . thrust into the relatively dehumanized, indifferent sector of industrialized America." The task of liberalism was to address the suffering of those who had been left out of the great carnival of affluence. Humphrey talked about urban redevelopment, federal aid to education, and a pet project, the Peace Corps, that would send young Americans into the impoverished nations of the Third World to engage in the kind of social work that they had begun to do in America's own backward areas. On the campaign trail, however, he quickly found himself overwhelmed by the well-financed Kennedy machine. This eminently fair-minded good-government liberal was also taken aback by "an element of ruthlessness and toughness that I had trouble either accepting or forgetting."[24]

Like so many of his predecessors, Kennedy moved left in the course of his campaign in order to secure liberal votes. The platform he endorsed at the party's convention called for "equal access for all Americans to all areas of community life, including voting booths, schoolhouses, jobs, housing, and public facilities." Though in his inaugural address the new president spoke only about foreign affairs, because that was what felt most urgent to him, the speech was greeted as the declaration of a new era of activism and optimism. A new generation of Americans, Kennedy famously declared, "shall pay any price, bear any burden, meet any hardship, support any friend, oppose any foe to assure the survival and the success of liberty." America would fight not only for its own political liberty but for the economic freedom of the downtrodden. To the poor in their "huts and villages," Kennedy pledged "our best efforts to help them help themselves, for whatever period is required." He proposed talks with the Soviets on nuclear disarmament and a new spirit of cooperation between the two rivals. "Together," Kennedy said, "let us explore the stars, conquer the deserts, eradicate disease, tap the ocean depths, and encourage the arts and commerce." If that part was hooey, it was beautiful hooey.

Humphrey recorded that despite his desperate feelings of envy, "when the new President said, 'Ask not what your country can do for you, but what you can do for your country,' there suddenly seemed a kind of unity of purpose, or at least unity of determination, in the air." Under Kennedy, liberalism would be a thrilling adventure.[25]

At first, that adventure almost entirely took the form of reckless confrontations with Communism. Kennedy authorized the disastrous Bay of Pigs invasion of Cuba and then stumbled into the Cuban missile crisis before finding the wisdom and resolution to resist his own hawkish counselors and offer the Soviets a face-saving exit. Domestically, he avoided civil rights as too politically difficult and declined to endorse the kind of expensive social welfare programs that Humphrey had campaigned on. Walter Lippmann, by this stage of his life a very cautious moderate, complained that Washington looked like "the Eisenhower Administration 30 years younger."[26]

It would be fair to say that, until his last months in office, Kennedy did more to incarnate the liberal vision than to enact it. As Kennedy's growing security in the job loosened some of the restraints he had placed on himself, the president became more willing to push for federal aid to education, increases in the minimum wage, the expansion of Social Security—in short, an Eisenhower-plus agenda. It was on civil rights, however, that Kennedy began to make his mark. He endorsed school desegregation efforts, as Eisenhower had not. In 1962 he sent federal marshals to Mississippi to enforce a court order admitting a black student to Ole Miss, and then he sent troops to suppress violence by whites. And in 1963, following confrontations with Alabama governor George Wallace and Birmingham police commissioner Bull Connor, Kennedy sent to Congress a long-awaited civil rights bill. It was before Congress at the time of Kennedy's death.

Kennedy's most notable contribution to the doctrines of Cold War liberalism was a negative one: the Vietnam War. His forceful posture on Vietnam made good the promises of his inaugural address, both that America would "pay any price" to defeat Communism and that it understood the promotion of prosperity and democracy abroad as an indispensable part of that price. Kennedy waged this early stage of the conflict as a counterinsurgency war, using Green Berets not to fight but to assist local forces and help them win the sympathies of villagers. The brilliant liberal advisers he had recruited from Harvard and elsewhere assured him that South Vietnam was making steady progress toward democratic governance. Vietnam was, as two historians of the era wrote, "the liberals' war."[27]

In the wake of Kennedy's assassination, Lyndon Johnson inherited two liberal legacies in their very earliest stages—civil rights and Vietnam. It would be his fate to bring both to fruition. We will never know whether Kennedy would have pushed hard enough to pass the Civil Rights Act over southern resistance. Johnson, however, did. The former Senate majority leader and master of the dark arts of legislative negotiation hammered away at the opposition until a southern filibuster finally collapsed. The bill, which passed on July 2, 1964, outlawed discrimination in access to public places—that is, Jim Crow laws—authorized the attorney general to sue school systems to enforce desegregation orders, and barred racial discrimination by employers and unions. In a letter to Walter Lippmann, Hubert Humphrey, now LBJ's vice president, called the Civil Rights Act "without doubt the most significant piece of legislation of this century." Hyperbole was Humphrey's natural mode, but the only possible rival for that title was the 1935 act establishing the Social Security system.[28]

John Kenneth Galbraith had written that poverty had evolved from "a universal or mass affliction" to "more nearly an afterthought." If you believed, as Galbraith did at the time, that the nation's great problem was the tail fin—that is, artificially generated consumer appetite—you would not likely be alert to signs of poverty. Indeed, when they took office, Kennedy and his team were only dimly aware of the systematic deprivation that condemned one generation after another to failure and poverty. That, perhaps, explains the shock at the publication of *The Other America*, Michael Harrington's 1962 masterpiece. Harrington demonstrated that poverty was widespread and crippling, even in the affluent society. He estimated that about a quarter of the country's 190 million people lived at or below the poverty line.[29]

Johnson had known all about poverty growing up, but he thought of it as something that afflicted the "peckerwood boys" in forgotten towns and the rural beyond. Curing poverty became a crusade for him, as putting a man on the moon had been for Kennedy. In his inaugural address, LBJ declared an "unconditional war on poverty." He understood that the solution to systemic poverty lay not in economic growth, which had bypassed the poor for generations, or in New Deal–type programs of job creation. The problem, at root, was the condition in which the poor lived. Poverty was the consequence not simply of joblessness but of substandard education, housing, and health care, of degraded communities and a pervading sense of helplessness. Changing those conditions would require a vast and far-reaching effort by the federal government. In a 1965 speech at Howard University, Johnson explained that "you do not take a person who, for years, has been hobbled by chains and liberate him, bring him to the starting line of a race and then say, 'You are free to compete with all the others,' and still justly believe that you have been completely fair." Whether or not the echo of Herbert Croly was intentional, the men around LBJ shared the view of the progressive liberals that the granting of full legal rights could not, by itself, secure equality for those who had been kept at the margins of American life. Rights were necessary, but only opportunity could make them sufficient.[30]

The astonishing array of legislation passed under Johnson was designed above all to advance the principles of what he called the Great Society. The Economic Opportunity Act, which passed in August 1964, authorized almost $1 billion to fund the creation of the Job Corps to provide vocational job training and job experience to young people; established Volunteers in Service to America (VISTA), which marshaled a battery of volunteers to combat poverty at the state and local level; funded programs targeted at rural families and migrant workers; offered incentives for small businesses to hire the long-term unemployed; and created the federal Office of Economic Opportunity. Johnson had accepted the claim, advanced by the New Left, that the poor needed to have meaningful control over programs intended for their benefit; the act thus also established "community action programs" that would depend on "maximum feasible participation" by the poor themselves. In 1965, the OEO would also create both the Head Start program and the Legal Services Corporation.[31]

The second New Deal of which Schlesinger and other Cold War liberals had dreamed had been, in effect, postponed to the mid-1960s. But what they had envisioned was a program of public investment to benefit the great mass of Americans. The Great Society was something different: a boost for those who had been left behind. Politically, that was a more perilous proposition. And while the New Deal, or for that matter the Marshall Plan, had fed the fuel of government spending into a machine that had temporarily broken down and was fully expected to chug back to life, the Great Society set itself the more difficult task of helping those long marginalized to compete on an equal footing. No one really knew how to do this, which is why vogue ideas like maximum feasible participation gained such a purchase. The second New Deal was never as likely to succeed as the first.

The 1964 presidential election offered a referendum on the new activist liberalism but not on the programs themselves, which had not yet begun to operate. Barry Goldwater, an Arizona senator, wrested the Republican nomination away from Nelson Rockefeller, the leading member of the party's moderate, Eisenhower wing. Goldwater was a true ideological conservative, a Jeffersonian individualist with Friedrich Hayek's faith in the liberatory effects of free-market capitalism. The currents of Western pioneering, immigrant self-reliance, and Main Street boosterism coursed through him. Goldwater's Jewish immigrant grandfather had helped settle Arizona. His family had run Phoenix's leading department store and viewed the New Deal as an unholy, and unnecessary, violation of the spirit of American individualism. Goldwater was a Hoover man. He had grown up rich, while Humphrey's and Johnson's families had barely scraped by. "The foundations of my conservative philosophy," he would later write, "were rooted in my resentment against the New Deal."[32]

What's more, Goldwater had never shaken the anti-Communist paranoia of the fifties. He saw the threat of socialism everywhere. Goldwater called Truman a socialist and even accused Eisenhower of capitulating to socialism. When he ran for the Republican presidential nomination in 1960, he claimed that Richard Nixon, the eventual winner, had gone squishy on the New Deal and described Nixon's secret dealings with Rockefeller as the "Munich of the Republican Party." Goldwater had supported McCarthy and opposed the 1964 Civil Rights Act. In his 1960 campaign manifesto, *The Conscience of a Conservative*—ghostwritten by Brent Bozell, a *National Review* editor—Goldwater argued that the Constitution had placed powerful restrictions on the federal government, including in the operation of schools. The *Brown* decision, he insisted, was "not the law of the land." He described a progressive tax system as "repugnant to my notion of justice." Goldwater was as fervent in his opposition to communism abroad as he was to socialism at home. He called for the United States to take the offensive in the Cold War. If that meant actual war with the Soviets, Goldwater was prepared. "A craven fear of death is entering the American consciousness," he wrote darkly.[33]

Goldwater's call to arms, frightening in a way that Kennedy's heraldic trumpet never was, left him hopelessly at odds with the optimistic spirit of the age. Americans, at least outside of the South, did not feel threatened by civil rights legislation, and they trusted Johnson to defend them from communism. Goldwater's suggestion during his campaign that low-yield nuclear weapons be used to defoliate the Vietnamese jungle gave Johnson the opening he needed to depict his rival as a fanatic who could not be trusted with the presidency. Goldwater drove a nail into his own coffin when he famously declared in his speech at the 1964 GOP convention, "Extremism in defense of liberty is no vice. Moderation in the pursuit of justice is no virtue." The Founders would have nodded along. But liberty was no longer in jeopardy, and in an age of liberal consensus, "extremism" had a purely negative connotation. Goldwater was denounced as a fascist.

Johnson enjoyed an overwhelming lead in the fall of 1964. In an essay written a week before the election, Reinhold Niebuhr observed that even William Ford, grandson of the bigoted Henry Ford, had made his peace with unions and announced his support for Johnson. A rough consensus—all save the ignorant and the hopelessly self-aggrandizing, Niebuhr thought—had endorsed a vision of the "common national interest." In a comment that amounted to euphoria for so deeply skeptical a thinker, Niebuhr wrote that this embrace of the public good from all corners argued that James Madison had been "unwise in his excessive fear of 'faction.'" At that moment, even to so sober a thinker as Niebuhr, liberalism really had become America's civic religion. Only the Deep South stood apart from the national consensus: outside of Arizona, Goldwater carried almost the same states that Strom Thurmond had in 1948. The South was still fighting the Civil War while the rest of the nation looked to the future—so, in any case, it seemed at the time.[34]

In the generation after World War II, the United States had established a truly liberal order both at home and abroad. Parts of Europe had, of course, fallen prey to fascism in the 1930s, while after the war communism continued to exert a powerful hold over both intellectuals and the working class. In the mid-1960s, few Europeans would have described themselves as "liberal," for the term bore the taint of laissez-faire. Yet both European thinking and European politics would evolve toward liberalism as communism discredited itself in the last decades of the century.

CHAPTER SIX

The End of History
in Postwar Europe

There is no "socialist democracy," there is only democracy. . . .
There is no "socialist economics," there is only economics.

—Timothy Garton Ash

T HE UNITED STATES WENT TO EXTRAORDINARY LENGTHS TO
ensure that Europe would rebuild itself after World War II along
liberal capitalist lines. General Lucius Clay, the military commander of
the American zone in Germany, encouraged the growth of local newspapers and radio stations, held early elections, and fostered the rebirth of
labor unions. But vast amounts of money and political guidance had not
made liberalism take root in America's colonization of the Philippines in
the early decades of the twentieth century and would notably fail again
in Iraq a century later. Europe had deep liberal traditions—including in
states like Germany that had barely experienced democratic rule. Liberals had played a strong, at times dominant, role in German parliaments
from the middle of the nineteenth century; economic and political freedoms flourished, within limits, under the rule of the Iron Chancellor,
Otto von Bismarck.

Constitutionalism predated the rise of the modern German state. As
far back as 1848, the citizen-legislators of the Frankfurt Assembly drafted

a constitution calling for a bicameral legislature, an independent judiciary, extensive individual rights, and an emperor responsible to his ministers. (The Prussian emperor Frederick Wilhelm refused, unfortunately, to be that leader.) In designing a governing system for a liberal, democratic Germany after World War I, the drafters of the Weimar Constitution looked back to the pacts of 1848 and 1871 as well as to nineteenth-century authorities like Benjamin Constant and François Guizot. The document was meant to put a permanent end to dictatorial rule. "The German Reich is a republic," read Article 1. "Political authority emanates from the people." All Germans would be "equal before the law," and all would have the right to vote. The president would be accountable to the voters, and the chancellor to the president as well as to the parliament. "Personal liberty is inviolable," the constitution stipulated. "Censorship is forbidden." "All Germans have the right to assemble peacefully."[1]

Good constitutions do not, of course, assure good republics. In the first years of the Weimar Republic, right-wing extremists demonstrated their contempt for democratic processes by assassinating liberal and leftist leaders. Rival parties deadlocked, forcing the president to step in and suspend parliamentary process. Massive inflation drained public faith in the capacities of the state. Liberal individualism did not take root in Germany's political culture or its hierarchical society; the protections built into the Weimar Constitution thus proved hopelessly flimsy in the face of the storms of the 1920s and 1930s. By 1933, party leaders had surrendered power to Adolf Hitler. As the German historian Ralf Dahrendorf put it, "Because the new illiberalism of the National Socialists fell on the soil of an illiberal, namely an authoritarian rather than liberal tradition, it succeeded in seizing the power in Germany that it failed to achieve in more liberal countries."[2]

Germany in 1945 was not Germany in 1919. Not only its war machine but its ideology had been smashed. Germans regarded themselves with almost as much fear as their foreign proconsuls did; they were eager to confine themselves with the restraints of liberal democracy. In 1946 the states, or *Länder*, began to draw up constitutions modeled on Weimar; some added the stipulation that citizens had the right to disobey any law that violated the constitution. Most also incorporated the role of parties, and thus of an opposition, which had been absent from Weimar. In July 1948, the Allied military governors authorized the *Länder* to convene a constituent assembly to draw up a Basic Law, the equivalent of a national constitution. The Allies stipulated that the new state be federal, liberal, and democratic, but after that they stepped back. The Germans could be trusted to engage in responsible self-government. In fact, the constitution was drafted in Hanover that summer with remarkable speed and harmony.[3]

Though Weimar served as the drafters' basic framework, the most important changes they made preserved liberal governance by restraining democracy. Under the Basic Law, the president would be indirectly elected and enjoy no real power. The ability to call referenda was circumscribed. Though the parliament would hold the balance of power, it would no longer be able to bring down a government unless the opposition could muster a majority behind a new government. The Constitutional Court could ban "anti-constitutional" parties. The drafters also eliminated the one truly ruinous element of the Weimar Constitution, Article 48, which allowed the president to dissolve the parliament and rule under emergency powers in case of a threat to the state. Hitler had conducted his entire tenure under this provision. The drafters of the Basic Law had every reason to recognize the fragility of liberal democracy. They understood that, in the absence of a commitment to liberal principles, democracy could become an instrument for despotic rule. As Carlo Schmid, a leading Social Democratic legislator, put it, the framers had shown "the courage to be intolerant of those who seek to use democracy to kill it."[4]

While Germany needed to build a political as well as an economic order, much of the rest of Europe reclaimed a democratic culture with the defeat of Nazism. The Soviet threat imparted urgency to the effort and persuaded ruling elites that they needed to organize themselves both institutionally and ideologically. In May 1948, 660 delegates from across the West, including twenty current and former prime ministers, met in The Hague under the aegis of the Congress of Europe. Winston Churchill proposed that European nations draft a charter of human rights and formally dedicate themselves to its principles, just as the Atlantic Charter had served as the basis for the United Nations. Delegates added the idea of a European parliament and a court to enforce humanitarian norms. This could have been the foundation of the European Union, but Churchill's own government had no wish to surrender its sovereignty to such a supranational body. At the end of the year, however, Great Britain, France, and six other countries agreed to form the Council of Europe and to draft a human rights charter.[5]

The council never amounted to much. It did, however, codify the notion that Europe's common heritage—Greek philosophy, Roman law, Christianity, Renaissance humanism, the Enlightenment—constituted the source of the "individual freedom, political liberty and rule of law" that made Europe a sphere of liberal democracy. The council promulgated the European Convention on Human Rights, which in turn established a commission with the power to refer individual cases to a European Court of Human Rights. The rights enumerated in the convention, like those in the UN Declaration of Human Rights, drafted at much the same time, offered, in negative, a record of fascist inroads on the person: the right to be free from torture, from slavery and servitude, from arbitrary arrest; the right to a fair trial; the right to freedom of expression, conscience, assembly. To be European meant to live within the protective barrier of human rights.

Over the years the council would draw up over two hundred treaties governing the rights of European citizens. Perhaps the most prominent among them was the 1961 European Social Charter, which added social and economic rights to the classically political ones enumerated in the 1949 convention. These included the rights to "social welfare services," "appropriate facilities for vocational guidance," and "fair remuneration sufficient for a decent standard of living." These were almost certainly not the rights that Winston Churchill had in mind when he spoke at The Hague, even if some of them may be extrapolated from FDR's "freedom from want." But political liberty was no longer at risk in a peaceful and largely democratic Western Europe, any more than it had been in the America of 1910, when the progressives sought a democratic collectivism.[6]

Efforts to replace the nationalist rivalries that had twice plunged the continent into catastrophe with a federated, democratic Europe continued after the council's failure. In 1950, France's visionary prime minister Robert Schuman proposed to place France and Germany's key war industries, coal and steel, under the control of a joint authority, with membership open to other European trading partners. The goal of Schuman and his chief partner, economist Jean Monnet, was to reduce the likelihood of another war, establish trade ties among the leading European nations, and lay the foundation for a liberal, suprasovereign Europe. The following year, France, Germany, Italy, Belgium, the Netherlands, and Luxembourg formally established the European Coal and Steel Community. In 1958, the members signed the Treaty of Paris, establishing the European Economic Community, a customs union. Forty-four years later, the Common Market, as it was called, would give way to the European Union.

European governance in the aftermath of the war was thus broadly liberal; but as an idea, liberalism enjoyed nothing like the consensual support it had in the United States and (to a lesser extent) the United Kingdom. The challenge from the right had been utterly discredited, though Spain and Portugal would remain under the rule of fascist leaders until the mid-1970s. But liberalism remained a term of abuse on the left, which is to say among both intellectuals and the industrial working class. To them, as to the American progressives before World War I, liberalism served as a euphemism for social Darwinism, the ruthless philosophy of winner-take-all and devil-take-the-hindmost. Communism, by contrast, enjoyed an intellectual and moral prestige scarcely imaginable in the United States. Communist parties in Europe had gained enormous credit for the role they played in the anti-Nazi resistance. They were thought of not as a fifth column but as legitimate representatives of the interests of workers. Communist parties controlled many leading unions, and Communist mayors ran many major cities. What's more, intellectuals regarded Marxist doctrine and Marxist historical analysis as the keys to unlock the great secrets of political and economic life. Jean-Paul Sartre called Marxism "the unsurpassable philosophy of our time." European intellectuals did not use the catchall term *totalitarianism* and recoiled at Schlesinger's premise of a moral or intellectual equivalency between fascism and communism. Hannah Arendt's 1951 *Origins of Totalitarianism* was largely ignored in Europe.[7]

The first major Continental thinker to treat Arendt seriously was Raymond Aron, who in a 1954 review endorsed the book's thesis that totalitarianism, whether of the left or right, is a distinctive ideology whose essence is terror. A decade earlier Aron had written *The Future of the Secular Religions*, in which he treated Marxism not as a theoretical tool for analyzing contemporary conditions but as a "religion of salvation" whose all-too-satisfying eschatology featured the triumph of the working class—a more philosophically rigorous version of Walter Weyl's dismissal of Marx in *The New Democracy*. For Aron, as for Isaiah Berlin, liberalism meant accepting the intrinsic limitations of the world rather than seeking to make it conform to an ideal pattern. "Every advance in liberation," he wrote, "carries the seeds of a new form of enslavement." The communist fantasy of a world of equals could only lead to tyranny and failure, for hierarchy was built into life itself and was intrinsic to a modern economy. Yet Aron was a less tragic thinker than Berlin; with prudence as a guide, he argued, one could make life better through incremental reform rather than revolution. Though Aron accepted the efficiency and even justice of the marketplace, he criticized Hayek as a libertarian who could not accept the legitimate functions of the state.[8]

Yet Aron was a rather lonely figure in postwar Europe. These were largely liberal societies in which, nevertheless, liberalism as an idea was held in the uttermost contempt. Though thinkers like Aron and Jürgen Habermas broadly endorsed the European welfare state, the critics of liberalism typically reduced it to laissez-faire, which is to say, the law of the jungle. So deep was this reflex, above all in France, that as late as 1995, Jacques Chirac, the right-of-center president, could describe liberalism as "a perversion of the human spirit." Communist parties continued to play important roles in European politics. In 1972, the Socialist François Mitterrand forged the Union of the Left with the Communists, an echo of the Left Front of the 1930s. Despite the self-evident political reality, communism enjoyed far more intellectual prestige than liberalism in France.[9]

But the communist illusion could not sustain itself. First the Soviet invasion of Prague in 1968, and then the failure of the revolutionary hopes inspired by popular insurrections that year in France, Italy, and elsewhere in the West, forced all but the most determined dogmatists to abandon the fantasy of "socialism with a human face." For many intellectuals on the left, the 1974 publication of English and French translations of Aleksandr Solzhenitsyn's *Gulag Archipelago* came as a shattering revelation, for the novel demonstrated that forced labor camps belonged not to a squalid Stalinist past but to the very essence of Soviet rule. Bernard-Henri Lévy, a young leftist philosopher and journalist, would later write, with his characteristic flair for overstatement, "The Communist dream *dissolved* in the furnace of a book." An older generation of liberals found a new audience. In a 1976 essay, "Solzhenitsyn and European 'Leftism,'" Raymond Aron acidly contrasted Solzhenitsyn's exposure of the monstrous brutality committed in the name of ideology with Jean-Paul Sartre's steadfast refusal to criticize the Soviets, the Cubans, or any despots acting in the name of Marx. He called Sartre "the philosopher of ideological thinking" and observed that while Sartre and Simone de Beauvoir "have no wish to give up any of *their* freedom . . . by philosophical means they justify other men's deprivation of liberty at the hands of totalitarianism and Terror." These were the terms in which George Orwell had excoriated the British left in 1940.[10]

The old rallying cry "No enemies on the left" came to seem increasingly grotesque as Cambodian rebels schooled in Paris carried out genocide in the name of revolution and millions fled the rule of Vietnamese Communists in the late 1970s. Third World liberation movements, celebrated in the name of "Maoism," proved to be yet more brutal than the despotisms they had overthrown. In 1979, André Glucksmann, one of the young generation of anti-Communists, brought together Sartre and Aron to call for support for the "boat people" fleeing Vietnam. All this shook the old pillars, but leftist intellectuals could not fully identify either with a reactionary like Solzhenitsyn or with desperate Southeast Asians. It was only when fellow Europeans in the east began to rise up against the puppets who ruled on behalf of Moscow that a liberalism of human rights began to penetrate the Seventh Arrondissement.

On January 1, 1977, a document called Charter 77, along with a list of 242 signatories, was issued in Prague. The tract began by citing the international human rights covenants that the Soviet Union and Eastern bloc states had adopted in 1975 when they signed the Helsinki Accords, which acknowledged the postwar division of Europe. The signatories pretended to believe that their rulers had thus accepted the legitimacy of human rights and proceeded to remind them of what those principles entailed and how far they had fallen short: "The right of freedom of expression . . . is in our case purely illusory." Citizens at risk of losing their jobs if they spoke out honestly could scarcely be said to enjoy "freedom from fear." The "right to education" meant little to young people who were "prevented from studying because of their own views or even their parents'." And so on through the freedom of conscience, of assembly, of the organization of workers. The Chartists acknowledged, or rather insisted, that all citizens bore a responsibility for the maintenance of civil rights, and thus they vowed to continue pursuing a "constructive dialogue" with the authorities—a threat that could scarcely be ignored by officials accustomed to absolute control.[11]

Charter 77 was not the first rent in the fabric of the Iron Curtain. In 1970 and again in 1976, Polish workers had demonstrated against price increases and suffered at least forty deaths. But Charter 77 marked the first time that Eastern Europeans demanded the same human rights that those in the West took for granted. The following year, Polish intellectuals joined with workers to form the Workers' Defense Committee, known as KOR, to formulate demands for broad social change. These highly sophisticated thinkers used the language, and appealed to the values, familiar in the cafés of Paris and Rome. They struck a nerve even with the acolytes of Marx. In 1978, Sartre and Michel Foucault hosted a group of dissidents at the Théâtre Récamier in Paris. As Foucault would say several years later, "What's happening over there was posing (posing once again, but for the first time in quite a long time) the problem of Europe."[12]

Prague and Budapest and Warsaw weren't "over there." They were here, in Europe, and they insisted passionately on their kinship. One of the most influential essays of the time was the 1983 "Un Occident kidnappé, ou la tragédie de l'Europe centrale" by the Czech novelist and Paris expatriate Milan Kundera. Kundera sought to revive the idea of Central Europe, which had been alienated from its rightful place by Russian occupation. "The fate of Russia is not part of our consciousness," he protested. "It's foreign to us; we're not responsible for it." For that very reason, he wrote, Central Europeans experience Russian dominion not merely as "political catastrophe" but as "an attack on their civilization." Poland, Hungary, and Czechoslovakia *were* Europe. "The deep meaning of their resistance is . . . to preserve their Westernness." Indeed, he said, it was only because Europeans in the West had lost the sense that they were bound together by a common culture—by Voltaire and Beethoven rather than by politics or the marketplace—that people in Paris and Munich had lost the sense of kinship they once had with the people of Prague and Budapest. Central Europe still prized that culture: a village schoolteacher in Czechoslovakia, Kundera wrote, might keep a Picasso print on her walls. It was the role of Central Europe to remind the West of what it once had been.[13]

In 1979, Václav Havel, a playwright who had helped organize Charter 77 (and had been imprisoned in the aftermath), wrote "The Power of the Powerless," an essay in which he set forth the principles by which modern totalitarianism can be resisted. Any educated European would have immediately recognized in Havel the voice of liberalism, from Tocqueville to Mill to Berlin to Aron. Life, he wrote, "moves toward plurality, diversity, independent self-constitution and self-organization." Totalitarian ideology demands "conformity, uniformity and self-discipline." Ideology seeks to hollow out life itself, replacing lived experience with "blind automatism" carried out in the name of empty abstractions. Havel did not, however, look to Berlin's or Popper's rationalism as shelter from the storm of ideology. The answer to living a lie, he wrote, is "living with the truth." A truthful act need not be an overtly political one; indeed, it cannot be, because politics has been wholly pervaded by ideology. Almost any spontaneous, politically indifferent act, like going to a rock concert, threatens the regime. Havel endorsed the idea, first proposed by the dissident Václav Benda, of creating "parallel structures"—samizdat publications, private performances—rather than seeking, futilely, to change the existing structure. Havel wasn't proposing an escape into the personal but rather the affirmation of the personal to undermine an impersonal system. The private, irreducibly subjective self of Mill and all who came after becomes a weapon of emancipation. Here was a genuinely heroic vision of liberal individualism.[14]

The parallel society arose in Poland as it did in Czechoslovakia. In 1979, KOR, the body of workers and intellectuals, issued an edict demanding that shipyard workers in Gdańsk be permitted to form an independent trade union, which came to be called Solidarity. The signatories not only signed their names, as the Chartists had, but included their telephone numbers, if they were so lucky as to have a telephone. No one missed the message: *We will declare our views openly, without fear.* KOR was explicitly "political" in Havel's sense, but its intellectual leader, Adam Michnik, shared Havel's sense that citizens must first conquer the voice of totalitarianism inside themselves, to practice instead an ethic of honesty, respect, and moral clarity. Michnik would later be immensely proud that the Solidarity movement never practiced violence, even in response to state violence.

When the workers of the Lenin Shipyard in Gdańsk joined Solidarity and went on strike on August 17, 1980, they inscribed their demands in giant red letters on a big wooden board so that they could be read by the crowd gathered there that night. The first demand was not better pay, or bread or meat. The workers demanded recognition of their right to form independent trade unions, in accord with Convention 87 of the International Labor Organization, an agency of the United Nations. Then they sought the right to strike; then freedom of speech and publication; then the restoration of the rights of workers dismissed after earlier strikes and students expelled for political activity, and the release of political prisoners. What they wanted was full citizenship as it was understood in the West. Fifteen months later, the Polish regime would declare martial law, ban Solidarity, and arrest its leaders; but the immense hopes unleashed in that moment could not be crushed.

Banned by the regime, Solidarity went underground, survived, and emerged once again after 1986, when Soviet president Mikhail Gorbachev announced the new doctrine of *perestroika*, or openness. By the end of the decade, dissidents who had been jailed or hounded into silence in Poland, Hungary, and Czechoslovakia began to bargain for power with weakened regimes. Nineteen eighty-nine was Europe's *annus mirabilis*. Communist parties surrendered their hegemony, with more or less of a fight, to a welter of competing factions. The new governments, with more or less success, drafted new constitutions and wrote new laws that brought them into conformity with the liberal principles of Western Europe.

The peoples of Central Europe had overthrown despised regimes without violent upheaval—indeed, without bloodshed. "Refolution," the historian and essayist Timothy Garton Ash called the era—a revolution in the name of reform. Indeed, this great convulsion looked less like revolution, as Europeans understood it, than like Constant's liberal reaction to revolution, for it was waged against utopianism and collectivism, and for the right to do and say what one wished. Unlike Communism, Michnik once wrote, "Solidarity never had a vision of the ideal society. It wanted to live and let live." The non-Polish author whom Michnik most often cited was Tocqueville.[15]

The new democracies did not share the West's ambivalence about the economic dimensions of liberalism, for a despised socialism had imparted an emancipatory glow to the free market even for intellectuals who looked forward to a lifetime in smoky cafés. Timothy Garton Ash observed that while they eagerly sought to learn from the West, the new democracies also had a message for the old: "In politics they are all saying: there is no 'socialist democracy,' there is only democracy. . . . They are all saying: there is no 'socialist legality,' there is only legality. . . . They are all saying, and for the left this is perhaps the most important statement: there is no 'socialist economics,' there is only economics. . . . The general direction is absolutely plain: towards an economy whose basic engine of growth is the market, with extensive private ownership of the means of production, distribution and exchange."[16]

The new and old Europe had a reciprocal relationship that moved both in the direction of liberalism. A host of forces, the exigencies of global competition above all, had undermined the socialist dream. In 1984 François Mitterrand openly embraced—or at least accepted—a "neoliberal" policy of fiscal austerity. Mitterrand even distanced himself from the venerable French principle of *étatisme*, the state direction of the economy. At the same time, the lessons of the new democracies were hardly lost on European thinkers. In a 1990 article, "What Does Socialism Mean Today?," the German philosopher Jürgen Habermas tested various critical responses to the events of 1989 and suggested that the "liberal" one had the most explanatory power: "Liberal ideas of social organization have prevailed in the form of constitutional democracy, the market economy and social pluralism." One unambiguous lesson of these revolutionary changes, Habermas wrote, was that "complex societies" persist only if they accept "the logic of an economy that regulates itself through the market." Habermas did not regard market liberalism as incompatible with social democracy; he pointedly noted that the left must continue to counter "the indifference of a market economy to its external costs, which it offloads on to the social and natural environment."[17]

But it was the West, of course, that pulled the nations of the East into its orbit. The European Union exerted a hydraulic force on the new nations, much as the United States had on Western Europe in the years after World War II. In 1991 the EU (then technically still the European Economic Community) signed agreements with Poland, Hungary, and Czechoslovakia that envisioned free-trade relationships with the former Eastern bloc nations by the end of the decade. The EU also agreed to a program of restructuring aid for the new democracies that amounted to 5.6 billion euros, about $7 billion, between 1990 and 1998. The Union defined the expectations for new members: "Membership requires that the candidate country has achieved stability of institutions guaranteeing democracy, the rule of law, human rights and respect for and protection of minorities, the existence of a functioning market economy as well as the capacity to cope with competitive pressures and market forces within the Union." There had never been a more powerful inducement for the adoption of the principles of liberal democracy.[18]

Francis Fukuyama's famous claim that history, understood as the contest of the great ideologies, came to an end in 1989, rang true for a generation of hopeful Europeans. In the United States, where liberalism appeared to have no natural predator, that contest had barely been waged. Yet the story was not so simple, and not so reassuring. The complacent liberal consensus had begun to unravel almost as soon as its triumph had been proclaimed. The civic religion of postwar America would be challenged from both the left and the right. The United States would remain a liberal country in Fukuyama's broad sense, but Hubert Humphrey's idealistic left-of-center faith would come to feel like the relic of a more hopeful and generous time.

CHAPTER SEVEN

The Great Society Goes Up in Flames

*"Liberalism had unleashed forces that its leaders
could neither control nor keep within the
confines of traditional political negotiation."*

—THOMAS BYRNE EDSALL and MARY D. EDSALL

T HE CIVIL RIGHTS REVOLUTION CAME OF AGE IN 1965. CON-
gress passed the Voting Rights Act, which barred the use of literacy
tests in the South and, extraordinarily, required most southern states to
receive advance permission from the Justice Department before making
changes in voting laws. The law made black political representation in
the South possible for the first time since Reconstruction. The Economic
Opportunity Act, also passed in 1965, committed the government to
moving toward economic equality for blacks. The combination of the
Voting Rights Act with the Economic Opportunity Act and Civil Rights
Act, both passed the year before, collectively fulfilled the promise that
Hubert Humphrey had so brashly made at the 1948 Democratic convention. Yet the nation was terribly divided in a way that had not seemed true
only a few years before. Six days after the Voting Rights Act passed, riot-
ing broke out in Watts. Americans watched on television as this ghetto
neighborhood of Los Angeles was looted and burned over five days. The
two events had nothing to do with one another, but the proximity implied

a terrible judgment about liberal benevolence. Activism, it seemed, had not healed a terrible breach but widened it.

America's commitment to liberalism did not end in the years after the civil rights revolution. Rather, one could no longer say, as a whole generation of thinkers had, that the nation was indissolubly wedded to liberalism. This did not happen because the material conditions that had made liberalism possible had disappeared—as might be said, for example, of Weimar Germany, where economic crisis promoted an extremism of left and right. Nor did it happen because a potent ideological rival challenged political liberalism; that would come later. It would be closer to the truth to say that liberalism suffered the consequences of its own successes. A young generation raised on a stultifying diet of prosperity and self-satisfaction rebelled against liberal pieties. Black beneficiaries of civil rights legislation failed to respond with the patient gratitude white Americans expected. Liberal policies not only failed to cure black poverty but alienated the working-class whites who had once formed the base of the Democratic Party. Anti-liberalism thus became a potent political force. "Liberalism," as Thomas Byrne Edsall and Mary D. Edsall would later put it in *Chain Reaction*, their analysis of liberal decline, "had unleashed forces that its leaders could neither control nor keep within the confines of traditional political negotiation."[1]

Those forces included a left-wing radicalism that regarded Cold War liberalism as a relic of postwar America. Young people growing up in the late 1950s were neither attracted to the flame of Communism nor repelled by it. Stalin was dead, and his successor, Nikita Khrushchev, had denounced his crimes. The Soviet Union seemed more dismal than dangerous. The 1962 manifesto of the Students for a Democratic Society (SDS), known as the Port Huron Statement, portrayed liberal anti-Communism as far more dangerous than domestic Communism; the policy of containing Soviet expansion adopted by all presidents since Truman, the authors argued, had proved "more effective in deterring the growth of democracy than communism." The shadow under which the authors had grown up was not Communism but the bomb—the duck-and-cover drills, the apocalyptic books and movies such as *On the Beach*.

America's invincible complacency seemed designed to stifle the sensation of horror that lay just beneath the surface.

The real threat of a state-controlled economy had persuaded many people who did not share the laissez-faire views of a Hayek or a Friedman that free markets were essential to liberalism. But the waning of the Communist menace dimmed the moral glow of capitalism. The authors of the Port Huron Statement, who had read their Marx, or at least read about him, regarded capitalism as an instrument of exploitation and called for a vast increase in the public sector, universal access to health care, and the nationalization of banks, utilities, and key industries.

Henry Wallace would have had little to quibble with on the SDS's foreign or domestic policy. But the young radicals did not simply repudiate the liberal politics of moderation; they rejected politics as such. The authors complained of a cult of tough-mindedness that shunned idealism as naivete, and called for a revival of "utopia and hope." *Utopia* was, of course, a word that had made a generation of anti-totalitarians shudder. But these postwar Americans had been raised amid affluence and peace; they had no reason to be imbued either with a tragic sense of the inherent limits of human endeavor or with Isaiah Berlin's recognition that you cannot have all the liberty you want without sacrificing some other good, like justice. They were far more attuned to what Schlesinger and Galbraith had described as the "qualitative" problems that come with a society of abundance than to the "quantitative." A politics that proposed to change the world but did not alter personal experience constituted a kind of failure. Liberals from the time of Constant had admonished the state not to tinker with man's "refractory" nature; the New Left could not accept so limited an understanding of politics.[2]

The SDS would probably have remained a left-wing splinter group were it not for the war in Vietnam. Despite his personal doubts about whether the war could be won, Lyndon Johnson pursued the goal of victory in Vietnam with the same single-minded passion he brought to the other war, on poverty. In a speech in April 1965 announcing an escalation of the American effort, Johnson explained that young Americans were fighting halfway around the world for "the principle for which our ancestors fought in the valleys of Pennsylvania"—the cause of individual liberty and national self-determination. As he was raising troop levels, Johnson also asked Congress to authorize an investment of $1 billion to build schools and hospitals in South Vietnam and to turn the Mekong River into a source of power "to dwarf even our own TVA." Johnson was making good Kennedy's pledge to the people in the "huts and villages" as well as his rash promise to "pay any price" to defeat Communism. By the summer of 1965, the United States had 125,000 troops in Vietnam and had begun a massive bombing campaign in the north.[3]

Liberals, with few exceptions, accepted the "domino theory," which held that a Communist win in Vietnam would threaten all of Southeast Asia and beyond. The New Left did not; the war struck members of the SDS as the perfect example of America's neoimperialist policy toward Third World insurgencies. At the organization's first anti-war demonstration, held ten days after Johnson's speech, SDS president Paul Potter compared the twenty-five thousand demonstrators milling around the White House to the Vietnamese guerillas. "In both countries," he cried, "there are people struggling to build a movement that has the power to change their condition." Here was a startling new note in American life. At a time when not just liberals but the democratic socialist left was using the language of patriotism to hold America to its own best values, the young radicals described the United States as morally indistinguishable from the Soviet Union and identified with a violent Communist insurgency against an American ally. As the war effort mounted, anti-war demonstrations attracted liberals and moderates. But activists on the left also began to adopt more extreme tactics, often fighting the police at demonstrations against the draft. Campus demonstrations became more frequent, more chaotic, more violent. The war *had* to be ended; thus, wrote ex-radical Todd Gitlin, the "impulse to smash up the machine, to jam the wheels of the juggernaut, and damn the consequences." Gitlin summed up the last four years of the sixties as "a cyclone in a wind tunnel."[4]

The assault on liberalism from the left came not only from the disaffected children of affluence but also from black leaders disgusted with the peaceful incrementalism of the civil rights struggle. While the scenes of police officers beating demonstrators bloody along the march from Selma to Montgomery in early 1965 dramatized the moral power of Martin Luther King Jr.'s doctrine of peaceful disobedience, they also enraged a younger generation of black activists who wanted to fight back. Radicals replaced traditionalist moderates at the helm of the Student Nonviolent Coordinating Committee, which had played a central role in organizing civil rights protests. In June 1966, SNCC's new president, Stokely Carmichael, led a crowd in chanting, "We want black power," a new phrase that thrilled many leftists, white as well as black, and frightened many whites, liberal as well as conservative. In October of that year, Huey Newton and Bobby Seale formed the Black Panthers, a group dedicated to the armed self-defense of the black community "from racist police oppression and brutality."[5]

Cold War liberalism had positioned itself between a foggy left and a complacent right. Those lines had now dissolved; the country seemed increasingly divided between those who accepted traditional American values and those who did not. Nothing crystallized that new divide like the urban riots. Watts was no isolated event: between 1964 and 1968, riots broke out in virtually every major American city—129 in all. In 1967 alone, riots in Detroit led to the death of forty-three people; in Newark, twenty-three. Civil rights liberalism plainly had not mollified black anger; indeed, liberalism appeared to have *caused* the riots. The Supreme Court under Chief Justice Earl Warren had issued a stream of rulings that limited the right of police to interrogate suspects, guaranteed the right of the accused to counsel, and suppressed illegally obtained evidence. Liberalism seemed to have taken the side of criminals against law-abiding Americans. By 1968, 81 percent of poll respondents agreed that "law and order is breaking down in this country."[6]

Nineteen sixty-eight was the liberal Götterdämmerung. The prospect of a presidential election inflamed every tension and pushed every species of extremism yet further to the edge—and over the edge. After the Vietcong reached the gates of the American embassy during the Tet Offensive, giving the lie to the claim that victory lay "just around the corner," President Johnson announced in a March 31 speech that he would not run for president. Martin Luther King Jr.'s assassination only four days later led to a new round of riots. And two months after that, Robert F. Kennedy was murdered, extinguishing the hopes of many idealists for a Democratic rejuvenation. The language and imagery of revolutionary violence became almost commonplace. Columbia University students took over their campus and giddily trashed the office of President Grayson Kirk, who finally responded by authorizing a massive show of force by the police.

Johnson's withdrawal left Vice President Hubert Humphrey as his presumptive heir. Humphrey finally had the opportunity he had been waiting for—but at a moment when his voice could no longer be heard. Humphrey was a consummate moderate, in temperament as much as in belief, at a moment when moderation felt hopelessly banal, even spineless. He was an optimist in a dark time. And he was, of course, a liberal trying to find his way among the wreckage of liberalism. Radicals heckled him everywhere he went in the summer of 1968. Five thousand demonstrators gathered outside his hotel in Chicago, forced their way into the lobby, and poured blood in the fountain. Humphrey gamely soldiered on, collecting more delegates than his anti-war rival and fellow Minnesota senator, Eugene McCarthy.

Humphrey's career was bracketed by Democratic conventions. At the 1968 convention in Chicago, Humphrey tasted a victory more bitter than many of his defeats. By sealing off the International Amphitheatre, where the convention was held, with rings of barbed wire and thousands of police and National Guardsmen, Chicago mayor William Daley reminded both the delegates and the tens of millions of Americans watching at home of the forces ripping at the country's seams. "The whole world is watching," the militants cried, and for once they weren't exaggerating. While the cops outside battled the students and the radicals and the Yippies, Humphrey claimed his poisoned chalice in the amphitheater with a gusto that felt horribly false. On the way out, he was jostled and jeered and insulted by the crowd. "All that I had ever been as a liberal spokesman seemed lost," he later wrote despondently. "All that I had accomplished in significant progress was ignored." Humphrey would win a total of 191 electoral votes—295 fewer than LBJ had won in 1964.[7]

Richard Nixon, the Republican candidate, ran on a law-and-order platform, though on civil rights he sent only the most carefully coded signals, endorsing *Brown* while questioning whether the Supreme Court had the right to order mandatory remedies. Nixon left it to his running mate, Maryland governor Spiro Agnew, to launch fusillades at students, protesters, black radicals, and liberal pundits—"the nattering nabobs of negativism," in Agnew's choice phrase. It was Alabama governor George Wallace who explored the limits of the permissible in racial discourse. Running as an independent, Wallace offered himself as the tribune of whites who viewed themselves as the losers of a zero-sum fight over civil rights for blacks. Without explicitly questioning black aspirations for equality, Wallace ran against the liberal elites who championed those aspirations. "They have looked down their noses at the average man on the street too long," Wallace cried. Though he carried only the Dixiecrat states, Wallace won 13.5 percent of the popular vote. And he had devised the terms of a new populist rhetoric that put liberals and their minority clients on one side and ordinary, hardworking Americans on the other. Half a century later, the resentments that Wallace exploited had become so much more powerful that Donald Trump would ride to the presidency on a barely updated version of Wallace's message.[8]

White resentment fueled Wallace's candidacy and helped elect Nixon. That resentment had so many targets that the outcome seems almost overdetermined: "the kids" trashing college campuses and trampling on middle-class values; liberal judges; black welfare recipients; urban rioters. Ironically, conservative voters actually supported the single most cataclysmic liberal error, the Vietnam War; they were outraged by *opposition* to the war, which they blamed on "liberal permissiveness." The left thus managed to discredit liberalism even though young radicals regarded liberals not as allies but as impediments to real change. Many Americans blamed liberals for everything that had gone wrong.

At the core of that resentment, though, was race, whether directly, through issues like desegregation, or indirectly, through rising levels of violence and crime. Race had become the Pandora's box of liberalism; Hubert Humphrey had not understood the risks that he and the Democratic Party were courting when he decided in 1948 to press for civil rights "whatever the consequences." But would he have ducked the issue if he had known the costs? If, after all, the moral commitment of 1948 led unavoidably to the calamity of 1968—if the American people were simply unwilling to fully accept black people into the national life—then perhaps we should say that liberal idealism compelled a grave political sacrifice. The story that, while signing the Civil Rights Act, President Johnson said, "There goes the South," appears to be apocryphal; but he surely thought it, and he would be proved right.

The fact that this is a self-exculpating tale of martyrdom does not make it false. Johnson had been elected with a massive mandate in 1964 after passing historic civil rights legislation. In 1966, he still enjoyed the support of two-thirds of the country. Most Americans, at least outside the South, were prepared to accept legal equality for black people. But LBJ's "starting line" metaphor was meant to make clear that ending Jim Crow laws in the South would not be enough. Whites, in the North as well as the South, had to accept some sacrifice in order to repair the consequences of past harm. White-dominated unions had to end policies designed to keep out blacks; all-white schools had to accept blacks, and parents had to send white students to schools in black neighborhoods. The sacrifice would fall most heavily on the working-class voters who had provided the backbone of the post-1932 liberal consensus. In the words of the Edsalls, "As the civil rights movement became national, as it became closely associated with the Democratic Party, as it began to impinge on local neighborhoods and schools, it served to crack the Democratic loyalties of key white voters."[9]

Liberalism, then, may have asked more of democratic majorities than they were prepared to give. But that is only part of the truth. A deep sense of moral righteousness also prevented liberals from recognizing the shortcomings of their own great experiments. In 1965, Daniel Patrick Moynihan, an academic who had worked under both Kennedy and Johnson and had written much of LBJ's "starting line" speech, authored a Labor Department study, *The Negro Family: The Case for National Action*. Drawing on both history and recent social science findings, Moynihan argued that "the deterioration of the Negro family" had produced a "tangle of pathology" in which fatherless families, low educational levels, high unemployment, and welfare dependency reinforced one another. Racism was the ultimate, but no longer the immediate, cause of persistent black poverty. How to break that cycle was thus the question at the heart of the Great Society. Moynihan concluded that welfare was not only not the answer to that question, but part of the problem: by directing payments to single-parent families, welfare programs inadvertently encouraged fathers to leave their wives and children, and thus to accelerate the cycle of dependence.[10]

The Moynihan report, as it came to be known, was savagely condemned as a racist work that blamed black people for their own failures. Even to raise the possibility that Moynihan was on to something was to invite censure. A generation later, black leaders would acknowledge the existence of a black underclass and the role of welfare in perpetuating it. At the time, however, liberalism collectively turned its back on any honest conversation about black poverty. Moynihan himself, on the other hand, took this very intellectual failure as his new subject. In "The Crises in Welfare," published in 1968, he documented the explosion of welfare programs directed to the urban poor and the almost total lack of debate over the consequences of the aid. The chief reforms now being proposed, he observed, would expand welfare rather than correct its worst effects and encourage welfare recipients to see themselves as rights-bearing members of a new, potent interest group. In an address the year before to the ADA, of which he was a longtime member, Moynihan had targeted liberals themselves, who, he said, must "overcome the curious condescension that takes the form of defending, and explaining away, anything, however outrageous, which Negroes, collectively or individually, might do."[11]

Moynihan was a liberal who believed that liberalism had lost its moorings. No less, he was a social scientist who felt that he had witnessed a failed experiment in policy making. In a 1968 essay ironically titled "Politics as the Art of the Impossible," he wrote, "Having through all my adult life worked to make the American national government larger, stronger, more active, I nonetheless plead that there are limits to what it may be asked to do." Government "cannot provide values to people who have none, or have lost those they had." This was a truism that the social engineers of the Great Society had not contemplated. It was to become a touchstone for the community of disenchanted ex-liberals and leftists known as neoconservatives who became a force in the 1970s. Unlike them, Moynihan would never repudiate his liberal principles. The fact that this card-carrying member of the ADA had become one of the most trenchant critics of liberalism offered powerful evidence that the faithful had begun to lose their way.[12]

Liberals tended to be blind not only to the shortcomings of their own nobly intended policies but to the sacrifices they asked of nonminority, nonliberal Americans. Here the great example was school desegregation, required by the Civil Rights Act and enforced by federal courts. Mandatory plans did not begin in earnest until after a 1968 Supreme Court decision that invalidated a commonly used voluntary plan and ordered a school district to dismantle segregation "root and branch." Between 1969 and 1976, courts ordered forty-seven of the one hundred largest public school systems to submit desegregation plans. In Boston, Cleveland, Detroit, and other major cities, tens of thousands of black students were bused into previously all-white schools while smaller numbers of whites were sent in the opposite direction. Enraged white parents and students often refused to comply. In Louisville, ten thousand whites blocked schools on the first day of busing in 1975, leading to fights with police. The state governor was forced to station members of the National Guard on every bus.

Millions of white parents responded to busing by moving to suburbs, beyond the reach of busing plans, or by sending their children to all-white private schools. Though a number of midsize urban school systems did become significantly more integrated, white resistance ultimately doomed mandatory busing as a legal remedy. Again, one may say that the liberal commitment to racial justice was defeated by white hostility. But busing was a remedy ordained by liberal elites—judges, civil rights lawyers, academics, government officials—and carried out to no small degree on the backs of working- and middle-class whites who couldn't afford private schools. Some white liberals proudly sent their children to black-majority schools, but many others lived beyond the reach of desegregation plans. It was not only racism but anger at bearing the burden for abuses they did not feel they had personally committed that made people rebel against the policy. Hubert Humphrey, an ur-liberal but also a sensible midwesterner, is said to have been "dubious from the beginning" about compulsory busing.[13]

The postwar liberal consensus could not survive the struggle over civil rights. Southerners—and whites elsewhere—who could not accept the equality of black Americans would not remain in a party that championed those rights. But how great did that defection have to be? Humphrey, Johnson, and others knew they were losing the solid South; they hadn't expected to lose much of white America outside the South. Perhaps that was the unavoidable consequence of fulfilling the pledge that Democrats had made to black citizens. The spell, in any case, was broken, and a generation would pass before American liberalism could recast itself.

When Jack Kemp, the former star quarterback of the Buffalo Bills, arrived in Congress to begin his first term in 1975, the Republican Party, of which he was a lifelong member, subscribed to the economic principles of small-town shopkeepers. Since the time of Dwight Eisenhower, who boasted that he had balanced the budget three times during his tenure, the GOP had preached an orthodoxy that regarded spending more than you earned as a species of moral corruption. The watchwords of the party, now under the mild hand of President Gerald Ford, were moderation, dependability, probity. With all this, Jack Kemp was deeply impatient. Kemp had grown up in southern California watching his father, a serial entrepreneur, build a modest six-truck delivery service. The Kemps were Christian Scientists. The family's unspoken motto was "You can do anything if you think you can do it." Kemp had lived that faith: having decided at the age of five that it was his destiny to play quarterback professionally, he had, despite quite modest talent, achieved just that. Kemp brought his sunny enthusiasm and his sense of humanity's unlimited promise with him to gloomy Washington.[14]

In early 1976, Kemp was introduced to Arthur Laffer, an economist and the chief exponent of a doctrine known as supply-side economics. Laffer's theory had the charm of extreme concision. Two years earlier, while lunching with Dick Cheney, then President Ford's deputy chief of staff, he had taken out a cocktail napkin and drawn a bell curve standing on its side. Since, Laffer argued, high taxes discouraged investment and thus depressed the economy and reduced taxable revenue, the government could get as much revenue from a low tax rate, which would spur growth, as from a high rate, which would diminish it. Why not, then, lower marginal income tax rates? The idea smacked of dangerous radicalism to the economic sentinels of the Ford administration, but it hit Jack Kemp with the force of revelation. Kemp had been the rare football player who regarded economics tracts as high-grade protein. He was an amateur, but a passionate and knowledgeable one. Now he had encountered a theory that vindicated his intuitive belief that people could achieve great things if only they were freed from the shackles of the state. Soon Laffer was commuting on the red-eye from USC, where he taught, going straight to Kemp's Washington townhouse, and talking economics while Kemp, still in his bathrobe, made breakfast.[15]

What was novel about supply-side theory was not the belief that tax cuts could galvanize the economy; John F. Kennedy had cut rates almost 25 percent in 1963. But Kennedy and his team of orthodox Keynesians believed that cuts could pump gas into the economy by stimulating the demand of consumers. Supply-side theorists, by contrast, argued that it was investors and entrepreneurs—suppliers of capital and of jobs—who provided the animal spirits of the economy. A growth-oriented economic policy would remove disincentives, whether in the form of tax cuts, regulations, or minimum-wage laws. The supply-siders believed that they had, in fact, recovered old wisdom. Bruce Bartlett, Kemp's economic adviser, argued that both John Stuart Mill and Jean-Baptiste Say had been proto-supply-side theoreticians. In the twentieth century, Keynes's demand-side principles had gained virtual hegemony among both economists and politicians; but, Bartlett argued, the "stagflation" of the 1970s, when the economy went into a tailspin despite high government spending, had discredited orthodox economic theory.[16]

The supply-siders were something new in the world. They were not Cold Warriors, and they were not shills for Wall Street. They were economists like Laffer, Robert Mundell, and Paul Craig Roberts; journalistic fellow travelers like the *Wall Street Journal*'s Jude Wanniski and Robert Bartley; and legislators like Kemp and the band he quickly recruited to his side. And they were the heirs to a liberal tradition: the laissez-faire faith of the Manchester liberals, of Ludwig von Mises and Friedrich Hayek, of the Mont Pelerin Society. The essence of this new right-wing liberalism was the liberation of the individual as economic actor. Kemp and the supply-side radicals thus gave new meaning and new life to the conservative idea. They believed in change, not stasis; they were idealists, not pessimists. Kemp believed in human capacity more fervently than any liberal. "There aren't a fixed number of touchdowns to go around," as he put it in his 1979 polemic, *An American Renaissance*. The economy was operating at only one-third to one-half of its true potential. You could score far more points if only you called the right plays. You could, in fact, lift so many Americans out of poverty as to render the vast safety net built by the Democrats largely superfluous.[17]

One of the reasons why Kemp was so important to the Republican Party was that he imparted a genuinely democratic gloss to what sounded like a familiar, and cynical, giveaway to the rich. Kemp himself had succeeded in the most ferociously competitive of environments. Now he wanted to put economic power in the hands of ordinary Americans. In Kemp's hands, supply-side theory threatened the Democrats' control over the all-American narrative of egalitarianism. What's more, Kemp made the GOP sound like it was *about* something, at least something other than the maintenance of the status quo. At the Republican convention in 1976, when the party nominated the plodding Ford, Kemp delivered a speech—heard by almost no one, to be sure—in which he called on his party to sharpen rather than obscure its differences with Democrats.

"History turns on ideas," Kemp declared. "Ideas rule the world." The Republicans had an idea, if only they would seize it: unleashing private enterprise through low taxes and deregulation.[18]

In 1977, Kemp coauthored a tax-cutting bill consciously modeled on the Kennedy legislation—thus staking a claim to the legacy of the Democrats' hero. The Kemp-Roth bill proposed lowering the top personal income tax rate from 70 to 50 percent and the bottom rate from 14 to 8 percent. Kemp-Roth failed, but not before provoking an epic debate that brought many orthodox Republicans over to the supply-side camp. In 1978 the crusade enjoyed its first great victory when California voters endorsed Proposition 13, which put a tight cap on the state's property tax. The fact that in the following year state tax revenue actually increased despite the steep drop in property tax rates seemed to vindicate Arthur Laffer's most optimistic projections. Over the next few years, twenty-five states enacted some form of property tax relief.

Newt Gingrich, later the House speaker but then a GOP backbencher in the House, called Kemp "the most important Republican since Teddy Roosevelt." With the 1980 election approaching and Jimmy Carter, a very vulnerable Democrat, in the White House, Kemp's kitchen cabinet concluded that the ex-quarterback just might be able to win the nomination and carry the supply-side torch into the White House. This was always an extreme long shot; Republicans did not then have a taste for mavericks. In any case, Kemp was fired more by ideas than by ambition, and he declined to run. In late 1979, he called Congressman David Stockman, one of his key backers, to announce that he had agreed to support Ronald Reagan in exchange for a central role on policy for the supply-siders. Stockman, an ex-Marxist and Vietnam War protester, an idealist and arch-rationalist, was shocked. As Stockman would later write of Reagan, "I considered him a cranky obscurantist whose political base was barnacled with every kook and fringe group that inhabited the vasty deep of American politics." But Kemp could not be dissuaded. In January 1980, Kemp called again to say that at a meeting in LAX, he, Wanniski, and Laffer had converted the antediluvian candidate to the new gospel.[19]

Without supply-side doctrine, Reagan would have been a cheerful version of Barry Goldwater—a reactionary with a merry twinkle. But without Reagan, supply-side economics probably would have remained a hobbyhorse of economists and wonky journalists and politicians. In fact, the man and the doctrine were made for one another, for Reagan, as he said of himself, was the kind of man who would walk into a room full of horse manure and say, "Where's the pony?" Reagan was attracted to the magical aspect of supply-side doctrine, its promise to reconcile the pursuit of wealth with American egalitarianism and thus preclude the need for painful choices. He was particularly attracted to those thinkers who emphasized the traditional American values that an untrammeled free market would reward.

Reagan had first caught the eye of national Republicans in October 1964, when the Goldwater campaign paid for the national broadcast of his "Time for Choosing" speech. Describing Communism as "the most dangerous enemy that has ever faced mankind," Reagan insinuatingly asked whether "we still know the freedoms that were intended for us by the Founding Fathers." The Founders had known, he went on, that "a government can't control the economy without controlling people." They had known, too, that you cannot control people without resorting to "force and coercion." America stood at a crossroads. "How many of us realize," Reagan asked darkly, "that today federal agents can invade a man's property without a warrant?" And while collectivism beckoned at home, America practiced appeasement abroad, encouraging the Soviet government to encroach further and further on the free world until we would face the starkest of choices: surrender, or fight World War III. But Reagan had the gift, which Goldwater conspicuously lacked, of sounding terrible depths with a smile and a chuckle and a shake of his head, as if, despite it all, we could usher in a bright tomorrow with some old-fashioned American horse sense.[20]

Since that 1964 speech, Reagan had burnished his reputation by serving two terms as California's governor. By 1980, he was the candidate of the California rich, who favored government by plutocracy; of the fervent anti-Communists, who wanted to spend whatever it took to roll back an aggressive Soviet Union; of the secular, tax-cutting right-wing liberals; and of the vasty deep and all its kooks. When he had made that crack, Stockman had been thinking particularly of fringe characters like Phyllis Schlafly, a Goldwaterite whose 1964 bestseller, *A Choice, Not an Echo*, described a secret cabal of Wall Street financiers pulling the strings of American foreign and domestic policy. Stockman was also thinking of a new force: the Christian Right, led by televangelist Jerry Falwell.

Christian conservatives were America's sleeping giant. A very large fraction of Americans called themselves evangelicals, but they had not voted as a bloc. Unlike Catholics or mainline Protestants, Southern Baptists—which most evangelicals were—had generally kept clear of politics, lest a fallen world corrupt the life of the spirit. That began to change when the Supreme Court declined to prohibit abortion in the 1973 *Roe v. Wade* decision; but the real impetus was a 1978 IRS decision threatening the "Christian academies" that had sprung up in recent years with a loss of their tax-exempt status unless they could demonstrate that their purpose was not simply to allow whites to escape school desegregation. That was exactly why most of them had come into being, but the resulting wave of anger and betrayal popped the lid of evangelical restraint, even after the IRS backed off.

On his syndicated television show, *The Old-Time Gospel Hour,* Jerry Falwell had been preaching against gay rights, abortion, and other signs of what he took to be national moral decay. In 1979, after meeting with other right-wing Christian leaders, he decided to found a political organization; in an echo of Richard Nixon's "silent majority" of right-thinking Americans, Falwell called the new organization the Moral Majority. The organization's agenda would run the gamut of right-wing concerns—opposition to gay rights and abortion, to pornography and the drug culture, to the Equal Rights Amendment, communism, socialism, and humanism. In May 1980, the Moral Majority sent a letter to all members of Congress listing "95 Theses for the 1980s." Unlike Luther's theses, Falwell's had nothing to do with theology and everything to do with his conservative moral code.

By early 1980, Falwell had concluded that Ronald Reagan was the man to bear the Moral Majority's message into the White House, just as Jack Kemp was concluding that Reagan would do the same for free-market economics. At the Republican convention that summer, Reagan made a point of meeting with Falwell, Phyllis Schlafly, and several other members of the Christian Right to ask their advice on a running mate. Falwell suggested Jesse Helms, the notorious segregationist senator from North Carolina. (Reagan ultimately chose the thoroughly secular and moderate George H. W. Bush.) Alone among the three presidential candidates (including independent John Anderson) in the general election, Reagan agreed to attend a summit meeting that brought eighteen thousand conservative pastors to Dallas. There he shocked his own advisers by proposing in an interview that creationism be taught alongside evolution in the public schools. "I know you can't endorse me," he said jocularly, but "I want you to know that I endorse you and what you are doing."[21]

Reagan's alliance with Falwell and other figures on the Christian Right had two titanic effects on American politics. First, it introduced an explicitly conservative moral agenda to rival the implicit moral agenda of liberal individualism, which had served so long as a national default that it hardly seemed to be an agenda at all. The liberal agenda had been erected on Mill's proposition that people should be able to do as they wish so long as it causes no harm to others, as well as on the separation of church and state inscribed in the Constitution. Once they entered the political arena, however, evangelicals could hardly be neutral on matters that touched on individual salvation or damnation, including sex, family, abortion, and religious observance itself. And Reagan, as he had said, was prepared to endorse their agenda. As president, he would propose a constitutional amendment permitting school prayer and lend his support to an amendment overturning *Roe v. Wade*. Both went nowhere, as he knew they would, but both subjects, and much else besides, became legitimate—indeed burning—matters of national political debate. In *On Liberty*, Mill had asked why it seemed acceptable for Christians to impose their religious principles on non-Christians but not for Muslims to do so. Such hypocrisy could be justified only if one assumed Christianity was true and Islam false. Yet something like this was precisely what the Christian Right proposed to do.

The other effect, which now corrupts the very air we breathe like so much fine particulate matter, was "the introduction into political discourse of the language and logic of orthodoxy," as Falwell's biographer noted. The American republic had been founded on the idea of a secular and rational public space. Isaiah Berlin had argued that liberal society depends on an implicitly accepted value pluralism: because no single good is ultimate and unarguable, all proposed goods must be subject to debate. Theology was a trump card, for discussion ends where God's will begins. The immense power of the Christian Right as a voting bloc inside the Republican Party increasingly compelled even the party's secular elites to adopt not only the evangelical agenda but evangelical habits of reasoning. One reason Jack Kemp never became president is that he would not speak or think that way. Ronald Reagan, who effortlessly embraced both liberal individualism and illiberal moralism, spoke Falwell's language as fluently as he did Kemp's.[22]

The one thing that united the supply-side right-liberals and the evangelical anti-liberals was a deep hostility to the active state that liberalism had fostered. Reagan was their tribune. As president, he once said that "the nine most terrifying words in the English language" were, "I'm from the government, and I'm here to help." Reagan had electrified the right in 1964 by identifying the welfare state with totalitarianism. That had been Goldwater's message as well. But at the time most American voters still viewed themselves as beneficiaries of the government; the white middle class received the lion's share of federal domestic spending in the form of Social Security, Medicare, veteran's benefits, and the like. The expansion of the liberal state that had begun under Kennedy and Johnson continued under Nixon and Ford. The transition from moderate conservative Ford to moderate liberal Jimmy Carter had little effect on the underlying dynamic.

But middle-class entitlements, which arrived automatically in households, did not feel to most people like "the government." Increasingly voters identified government spending with spending on the poor. This was wildly hyperbolic, but not without a foundation in reality. In the decade after 1965, the number of households on public assistance went from 1 million to 3.5 million; the number on food stamps went from 400,000 to 17.5 million. And while the majority of recipients of both were white, the explosive growth in the programs came among blacks. White middle-class voters increasingly saw themselves as taxpayers and "others" as tax recipients.

Like the movement to refound politics on explicitly Christian values, the critique of activist liberal government had come to deeply infuse the Republican Party. That critique was most powerfully formulated by the neoconservatives, former old leftists—that is, socialist critics of liberalism—who had moved rightward throughout the 1960s. True to their roots in Marxist polemics, the neocons rooted their analysis in first principles. In a 1979 article, essayist Irving Kristol described neoconservatism as "a return to the original sources of liberal vision and liberal energy so as to correct the warped vision of liberalism that is today's orthodoxy." Kristol was the echt neocon—a graduate of City College, the Jewish hothouse of left-wing dialectics, and a brilliant sectarian in the little magazines of the day, literary-political journals like *Commentary* and *Encounter*. Kristol argued that the governing philosophy of America's Founders, shaped far more deeply by the Scottish than by the French Enlightenment, was "melioristic rather than eschatological . . . also skeptical in temper, hostile to all forms of enthusiasm . . . disbelieving in all dogmatic certainties about human nature and 'the meaning of history.'" The hallmark of liberalism, as Kristol understood the term, was a preoccupation with the good of the individual rather than of the collective.[23]

So far, one may say, Kristol made common cause with midcentury liberals like Berlin or Schlesinger. But Kristol and his fellow neocons had a different understanding of the role of the marketplace than did the mild social democrats of the postwar period. The great Scottish liberal whom Kristol had in mind was Adam Smith. Kristol observed that while Smith had no great love for businessmen or for the alleged moral virtues of the marketplace, he understood property as the great bulwark against tyranny, and thus economic liberty as the precondition for political liberty. Kristol thus aligned himself with the tradition of Hayek rather than Mill. Elsewhere, Kristol described the neocons as heirs of the progressives, who opposed big business but had faith in the productive powers of capitalism. Those, he said, were the old liberals. The new generation, by contrast, weren't liberals at all but rather radicals "acting upon a hidden agenda: to propel the nation from that modified version of capitalism we call 'the welfare state' toward an economic system so stringently regulated as to fulfill many of the traditional anticapitalist aspirations of the Left."[24]

There was a contradiction here, for one could not stand both with Hayek and with Croly, a democratic socialist. Both the progressives' democratic collectivism and the modern welfare state were wholly incompatible with the new laissez-faire ideology. Yet Kristol was one of a small group of conservative intellectuals and activists urging Jack Kemp to run for president in late 1979; David Stockman was awed to see the man he regarded as "the secular incarnation of the Lord Himself" at the planning meeting. When Ronald Reagan instead emerged as the front-runner, Kristol became, and remained, an enthusiastic supporter. The ex-leftist identified deeply with Reagan's hostility to the liberal state. From the time of Moynihan's first studies of welfare through later work on social policy by Harvard scholar (and former City College boy wonder) Nathan Glazer and others, the neocons zeroed in on the law of unintended consequences that beset great social experiments. Did the judges in their chambers ordering up drastic remedies to segregated housing patterns have any clue about the magnitude of the disruption they were mandating? No more than did the social engineers in the Johnson White House who insisted on "maximum feasible participation." Rather than call liberals to account for their blindness, as Moynihan did, the neoconservatives held up those failures as proof of the contradiction at the heart of liberalism.[25]

The neoconservatives had no truck with liberal neutrality in regard to personal behavior. Kristol argued that secular liberalism had eaten away the cultural foundations of Western society. "The current version of liberalism," he wrote, "which prescribes massive government intervention in the marketplace but an absolute laissez-faire attitude toward manners and morals, strikes neocons as representing a bizarre inversion of priorities."

His wife, Gertrude Himmelfarb, a historian of Victorian England, insisted that Victorian values, far from crushing the life force of nonconformists, as Mill had claimed, offered a solid platform of discipline, self-restraint, and family coherence upon which individuals could build a flourishing life. Secular liberals—"the new class," as Kristol called them, wryly adapting Marxist terminology—succeeded by practicing just such old-time virtues, yet preached a libertine doctrine that legitimized the ruinous trend toward unwed motherhood and loose family ties among the poor. Over time, some of the neocons, including Kristol and Norman Podhoretz, a vehement anti-liberal sectarian and the editor of *Commentary*, made their peace with the Christian Right despite the gross anti-intellectualism and provinciality of many of its leaders. Others, like Nathan Glazer and Daniel Bell, a sociologist best known for his prophetic book *The Coming of Post-industrial Society*, found that they could not stomach such an alliance and drifted back toward the center.[26]

Americans voted for Ronald Reagan despite his far-right reputation because they were sick of economic stagnation at home and mortifying failures abroad, which they associated, not without reason, with Jimmy Carter and the Democrats. They wanted the sunny uplands toward which Reagan beckoned—that "shining city on a hill." Reagan succeeded in no small part because, whatever ill befell the nation or even himself, he never failed to incarnate those hopes. But he was also an ideological leader, and he carried the hopes of his illiberal, anti-liberal, and right-liberal supporters. They wanted him to change the tenor of American life—and he did. Reagan did almost nothing to rout the forces of secular humanism or to restrict abortion. Yet his door was always open to right-wing evangelical leaders, and he regularly invoked the name of Jesus in public. Reagan legitimized the Christian conservative movement even if he did not enact its agenda.

On the tax-cutting agenda of the supply-siders, however, Reagan was as good as his word. In February 1981, he endorsed the Kemp-Roth tax cut of 10 percent a year over three years; Congress ultimately approved a three-year cut of 23 percent. Kemp and Laffer had persuaded Reagan that the cuts would pay for themselves with economic growth.

Both orthodox Republicans and more cautious supply-siders like David Stockman expected a much more modest boost to growth and demanded spending cuts to offset the lost revenue. But the vast military increase Reagan demanded, along with the unwillingness of his chief advisers to cut entitlement spending, blocked that path. Stockman, now Reagan's director of the Office of Management and Budget, predicted that the deficit would increase $600 billion over five years. In 1982, the economy not only failed to bloom as supply-siders had predicted but shrank 1.5 percent. Instead of rising, tax revenues fell 6 percent. That September Reagan was compelled to agree to a partial rollback of the cuts as well as to new taxes. Average GNP growth during Reagan's entire tenure was 3.4 percent, slightly better than under Carter, though nowhere near the average rate during the 1960s. Both the budget deficit and the national debt tripled as the United States went from the world's largest creditor to the world's largest debtor. Reagan had offered the right-liberals a laboratory for their faith; the experiment did not go well.

One thing Reagan did achieve was a drastic increase in income inequality. Reagan refused to increase the minimum wage, which remained at $3.35 per hour. At the same time, he decreased the top income tax rate from 70 percent to 50 percent and the capital gains rate from 28 percent to 20 percent. Average take-home pay continued to stagnate while changes in the economy sent ever-larger fractions of income to top managers. The result, as economist Thomas Piketty pointed out, was that the share of income taken by the richest tenth of Americans, which had remained at or below 35 percent since the high-tax era of World War II, shot up to over 40 percent by the mid-1980s. Since Reagan's time, rates of growth, unemployment, and deficits have oscillated, but inequality has steadily increased, with political consequences we are living with today.[27]

As a political matter, Reagan also provoked a crisis on the other side. Liberalism had lost its grip on the white middle class. One response was to move left and abandon the center. At the 1984 Democratic convention, the Reverend Jesse Jackson, a contender for the party's nomination, declared, "My constituency is the damned, the disinherited, the disrespected and the despised." That was not a winning formula, though neither was a played-out Democratic orthodoxy: the nominee, Walter Mondale, lost to Reagan 41 percent to 59 percent, the same margin by which FDR had defeated Hoover. The following year, a group of moderates founded the Democratic Leadership Council in the hopes of charting a path away from the precipice to which the party seemed to be heading, much as an earlier generation of liberal thinkers had founded Americans for Democratic Action to counter pro-Soviet sympathies on the left. Four years later, after another dispiriting loss, the DLC established a think tank, the Progressive Policy Institute. (By this time, *progressive* had gained acceptance as a replacement for the discredited *liberal*, just as the opposite had happened after 1916.)[28]

In September 1989 two leading figures associated with PPI, William Galston and Elaine Kamarck, published a devastating account of party failure. The "politics of inclusion" that had shaped the post-1932 liberal consensus, they wrote, "had been supplanted by 'ideological litmus tests.'" Voters have come to identify liberalism "with tax and spending policies that contradict the interests of average families; with welfare policies that foster dependence rather than self-reliance; with softness toward perpetrators of crime and indifference toward its victims; with ambivalence toward the assertion of American values and interests abroad; and with an adversarial stance toward mainstream moral and cultural values." The next presidential nominee, the authors warned, must reflect "the moral sentiments of the average American" and "offer a progressive economic message, based on the values of upward mobility and individual effort, that can unite the interests of those already in the middle class with those struggling to get there." The article signaled the exhaustion of the liberalism of civil rights and of a politics directed above all to the disinherited and the damned, or those who identified with them.[29]

In 1989, Bill Clinton, the governor of Arkansas, assumed the chairmanship of the DLC, which he had also helped found. Clinton was imbued with sixties idealism, but not with the contempt for party politics common among his peers, or with the litmus-test absolutism of movement figures. As governor of one of the nation's poorest states, he focused on economic development, job training, and education reform, often running afoul of entrenched liberal groups like the teachers' association. He had read William Julius Wilson's *The Truly Disadvantaged* and accepted Wilson's argument that structural, rather than race-specific, problems accounted for the persistence of black poverty, and he concluded that the answers lay with schools and job training, the kinds of development he was seeking to foster in Arkansas. He read up on economics and concluded that the United States had to more fully prepare itself for the international competition that was coming with globalization. He was deeply versed in the tortured debate over welfare reform. In short, Clinton was persuaded, or persuaded himself, of the substantive merits of reforms that would be politically advantageous for Democrats.

Clinton used his role as head of the DLC to both assemble and broadcast a new national agenda. In a speech at the DLC national convention in May 1991, he ticked off a list of American failures compared to other Western states—on reading scores, infant mortality, vocational opportunities, health care, rates of imprisonment. Republicans had "glorified the pursuit of greed and self-interest" while poverty rose and middle-class income stagnated. Why couldn't the Democrats take advantage of rising frustration? Why couldn't they speak to the middle class as well as the poor? Because, he said, *pace* Galston and Kamarck, those voters no longer trusted the party to protect their interests. The party needed to offer pragmatic, nonideological solutions to the real problems facing ordinary—read: white middle-class—Americans. That meant an investment in new technologies and "world-class skills" in order to compete globally; a new doctrine of "responsibility for all" that demanded a reform of welfare, because "work is the best social program this country has ever devised"; and an acceptance of the value of competition in the provision of public services. The stale left-right debate between "family values" and "public spending" must give way to a recognition that both are needed.[30]

Clinton set out to rescue liberalism from itself. He used an address to Jesse Jackson's National Rainbow Coalition convention in June 1992 to criticize Jackson for giving a forum to hip-hop artist Sister Souljah, who said in an interview after the 1992 LA riots, "If black people kill black people every day, why not have a week and kill white people?" He chose a speech before the auto workers' union to argue forcefully for the North American Free Trade Agreement, despite the antipathy of major unions to free trade. The real message in both cases was this: litmus-test liberalism is over. Orthodox liberals like New York governor Mario Cuomo castigated Clinton and the New Democrats as servants of privilege; Jesse Jackson joked that DLC stood for "Democratic Leisure Class." But when Clinton won the nomination and then the election in 1992, he plainly defeated both the unreconstructed liberals and the Republicans.[31]

There was good reason to believe, at that moment, that just as liberalism had recast itself after 1912 to accept progressive principles of economic justice, and then recast itself once again after 1948 to champion civil rights, so it was prepared for a new incarnation that would reforge its links with the middle class. In effect, having made good on the civil rights pledge, the Democrats could now return to the politics of Schlesinger's "vital center," a politics of investment that would use the state to pursue the public goods, including expanded access to health care and education, that the market would not supply. Reagan had so single-mindedly tended to the marketplace that he had allowed America to fall behind its chief competitors in supplying those crucial public goods. Clinton was calling on the country to repudiate the errors of both the left and the right.

Clinton had the enormous good fortune to preside over an economic boom that wiped out the massive deficit he inherited from twelve years of Republican rule. He had the money to make the public investments he had promised. Yet he was unable to make lasting change. At times the president proved to be his own worst enemy. His White House meetings dissolved into inconclusive all-nighters. He was of two, or three, minds about almost everything. His willingness to poll-test anything, including where he should take a vacation, gave rise to the unfair claim that he was a cynical opportunist with no core. His coterie of fellow Arkansans at times proved inept or even corrupt. He allowed the all-important debate over health care to get away from him once he made the fateful decision to let his wife Hillary run it. Above all, Clinton had an affair with an intern that ultimately led to his impeachment in 1998. A grim might-have-been continues to shroud Clinton's tenure.

Yet Clinton also encountered a form and an intensity of opposition that would have been unfamiliar to Jimmy Carter, or for that matter to Ronald Reagan. In the past, virtually all major pieces of legislation, whether those enabling FDR's New Deal agencies and programs or Ronald Reagan's 1981 tax cut, had passed with some votes from the other side. At moments of supreme national importance—for example, the investigation of Richard Nixon's actions in Watergate—party members had been prepared to abandon their president in the name of principle. Even if each party was quite certain that it and not its rival was best for the country, each acknowledged the legitimacy of the other. Only after several generations of mortal combat and then civil war did the two parties embrace this principle, which the political scientists Steven Levitsky and Daniel Ziblatt call "mutual toleration" and consider one of the pillars of liberal democracy. Bill Clinton's presidency marked the beginning of the end of mutual toleration in American politics.[32]

By this time, the Christian Right had become the most active force in the Republican Party. The Christian Coalition had 1.7 million members in over 1,700 chapters across the country. The coalition ran candidates in local elections and distributed millions of voter guides at election time. Its founder, the Reverend Pat Robertson, who had run for president in 1988, regularly railed at Bill Clinton's immorality in interviews and on his television program, *The 700 Club*. In his 1991 bestseller, *The New World Order*, Robertson explained that a conspiracy hatched by global financiers lay behind "a new order for the human race under the domination of Lucifer and his followers." Robertson helped give mainstream credibility to ideas previously associated with the lunatic fringe. And though Jerry Falwell had closed the Moral Majority, Clinton's candidacy brought Falwell back into active politics. He paid for and distributed a video, *Bill Clinton's Circle of Power*, that accused Clinton of carrying out murders and running a drug-smuggling ring.[33]

The absolutism of the religious right did not simply escape into the larger political atmosphere like a rogue virus. While Reagan had first welcomed the evangelicals, it was left to a new generation of conservative politicians to make the Republican Party the home of dogmatic absolutism. It was Newt Gingrich, above all, who gathered this toxic harvest. When Gingrich first reached Congress, in 1978, he aligned himself with the Jack Kemp wing of the GOP, the insurgents seeking to end the dismal reign of budget cutting. In his 1984 book, *Window of Opportunity*, Gingrich urged his readers to embrace the coming "information age," which would unleash individual creativity and "self-determination." Breakthroughs in biology, he predicted, would "improve and enhance nature" even as new technologies ended global food shortages. "Space travel today is where air travel was in the early 1920s," he declared. Gingrich applied Kempite visionary optimism to everything.[34]

Gingrich was not a natural zealot. He was not religiously observant, and it would later come out that he was a serial adulterer every bit the equal of his nemesis, Bill Clinton. But Gingrich recognized early on that zealotry could work for him. The incessant attacks from the religious and secular right had moved the Republican Party much further to the right than it had been when Ronald Reagan was elected. And Clinton, a child of the sixties, an ex–draft dodger, a product of Oxford and Yale, represented everything the Christian Right loathed about the liberal elite. By the end of Clinton's first year in office, 93 percent of Republicans said that the federal government no longer represented the intent of the Founders. Ordinary party members increasingly viewed Democrats, the party of government, not simply as wrong but as illegitimate.

Gingrich both fostered and exploited this milieu. He had a gift for raising the stakes: like a latter-day Oswald Spengler, he prophesied cultural doom—unless the Democrats could be ousted. "No civilization can survive long," he wrote in his 1995 book, *To Renew America*, "with twelve-year-olds having babies, fifteen-year-olds killing each other, seventeen-year-olds dying of AIDS, and eighteen-year-olds getting diplomas they can't read." Liberal situational ethics had sapped citizens' capacity to distinguish right from wrong; personal responsibility had become a thing of the past, and God himself an afterthought. Americans needed to re-read the Boy Scout handbook. Gingrich was at once a traditionalist and a futurist, a man who hoped to furnish tomorrow with the beloved relics of yesterday. Space tourism still beckoned. Wouldn't it be wonderful, Gingrich wrote, if we could build "a real Jurassic Park"? Only the dead weight of liberal delusion kept America from seizing a jet-pack future.[35]

Bill Clinton's vulnerability to charges of personal misconduct gave his rivals all the pretext they needed to adopt the new politics of absolutism. Once allegations surfaced that the Clintons had engaged in shady financial conduct in Arkansas, conservative funders paid for investigations of their activities, conservative publications featured bloodcurdling stories of alleged misdeeds, right-wing talk radio hosts filled the airwaves with conspiracy stories that had first surfaced in works like *Bill Clinton's Circle of Power*. In 1994 news outlets carried more stories on the Whitewater scandal than on all of Clinton's domestic agenda. Half of Americans believed that he and Hillary were covering up the truth. Clinton's popularity diminished even as the economy improved. Republican officials understood that they would suffer no political consequences from trying to derail his presidency. William Kristol, son of the godfather of neoconservatism and a major force in his own right, circulated a memo warning party leaders against any compromise on health-care legislation. Wrecking the centerpiece of Clinton's agenda, he added, would constitute a "monumental setback" for the Democrats. In the 1994 midterm election, the Republicans ended almost forty years of Democratic control of the House. Southern voters who had continued supporting Democratic members of Congress even as they had voted Republican for president now abandoned their ancient sympathies altogether. The Democrats lost much of the white middle-class base that Clinton and the new Democrats had struggled to regain; henceforth it would largely be the party of coastal elites, the young, and the marginalized.[36]

This was not the end of Clinton, who had branded himself "the Comeback Kid" in the 1992 election. In 1995 he countered Gingrich's demand that the budget be balanced in seven years by offering to do so in ten. Gingrich could have pocketed this remarkable concession, but his combativeness and his blind self-confidence were his undoing. Refusing to compromise, the new House speaker forced a government shutdown over the budget. Most voters blamed the Republicans for this unprecedented failure of governance; Gingrich was forced to relent. A supremely gifted politician, Clinton took everything he could get from a Congress now controlled by the other side; he preserved crucial elements of the liberal legacy, such as Medicare, and won a few modest victories. Clinton's easy victory over Bob Dole in the 1996 presidential election completed a bravura comeback from what had seemed a terminal disaster.

Clinton had made difficult and sometimes painful choices in order to reorient his party, including the passage of a tough crime bill and welfare-reform legislation that put a lifetime limit on benefits and tightened eligibility for food stamp recipients. He had done as much as he could to inoculate his party against the ideological arguments, substantive as well as specious, that Gingrich and others wielded. Then, like a heaven-sent reward, came an astonishing windfall: a supercharged economy filled the government's coffers so rapidly that in 1997 Clinton was able to present a balanced budget even as he cut taxes and increased spending. Clinton suddenly had a second chance to realize the New Democrat agenda on which he had run for office, reining in government excess while investing in public goods. He said to his aides, "FDR saved capitalism from itself. Our mission has been to save government from itself. So it can be a progressive force."[37]

That *was* the role for which Clinton was destined. No one but he could have done it in the face of such entrenched opposition. If he had succeeded, the nation's political trajectory might have looked very different. And he almost did. Clinton and Gingrich had by 1997 so thoroughly bloodied each other that each was prepared to look anew at his rival and recognize how very much they had in common—the obsession with policy as well as politics, the determination to reform their party, the faith in the future. The two men began meeting secretly in order to hammer out a plan to rescue Social Security from threatened insolvency. By the first days of 1998, they had reached the outlines of a grand bargain, which

Clinton was to unveil in his State of the Union speech. And then, on January 21, six days before the speech, the *Washington Post* broke the news that a White House intern, Monica Lewinsky, claimed that she and the president had had an affair that had begun during the government shutdown two years earlier. That put paid to any talk of bipartisan cooperation, or indeed of virtually anything at all save the spreading scandal. In December 1998, the House voted to initiate impeachment proceedings on the grounds that Clinton had lied under oath about an extramarital affair, an astonishingly frivolous deployment of the Constitution's nuclear option. Clinton would spend much of the last three years of his tenure defending himself against investigations designed to destroy his presidency.

Clinton achieved far more than is widely understood. He dramatically increased spending on Head Start and child care and expanded the Earned Income Tax Credit, a crucial source of support for the working poor, from $12.5 billion to $30.4 billion. He passed the North American Free Trade Act against great odds and organized the emergency bailout of the Mexican economy. But Clinton did not save government from itself. He drained some of the toxins from liberalism but did not institutionalize a Third Way. What's more, it soon became clear that the economic growth of the era had barely lifted middle-class incomes (or diminished poverty); income inequality, which had begun increasing under Reagan, accelerated with the Clinton boom. Clinton's willingness to place the Democrats behind what had been a Republican orthodoxy of free trade and financial deregulation created a political consensus behind policies that would later provoke a populist backlash on both the right and the left.

The Napoleonic Gingrich so exhausted his own generals that he was forced out of the speakership after the 1998 midterm election. Yet Gingrich's influence probably outlasted Clinton's, for it was he, more than any other person, who transformed politics into a war of absolutes in which compromise signifies failure. Gingrich's language was civilizational rather than theological, for he was as much a product of a culture of liberal individualism as Bill Clinton was; but for this very reason Gingrich was able to unify evangelical and secular opponents of liberalism and of

Clinton, its living incarnation. Gingrich sought to convert his congressional caucus into a warrior caste. In a memo he wrote to be distributed to all Republican candidates in the 1996 election, he listed "Optimistic Positive Governing Words" like "challenge," "learn" and "moral," as well as "Contrasting Words" to be used about Democrats—"betray," "cheat," "corrupt," "punish," and "anti-" plus words like "flag, family, child, jobs." The language of polarization would soon enough lose its power to shock. At the time, however, it was a genuine innovation. Gingrich's spokesman, Tony Blankley, compared the audiotapes his boss distributed to the cassettes circulated by Ayatollah Khomeini on his way to power in Iran.

During the sixteen years between the end of Bill Clinton's tenure and the beginning of Donald Trump's, a closely divided nation seemed to be swinging back and forth between left and right. Yet all the while, illiberal values were moving toward the center of the culture. The Republican candidate in 2000, George W. Bush, was a born-again Christian with an appealing story of religious rescue from a life of aimlessness and drinking. Religion had been equally central to Jimmy Carter's life, but Bush placed Christianity at the core of his political as well as his personal convictions. He did not hesitate to transgress implicit secular taboos. Asked in a debate about the thinker who had most heavily influenced him, Bush said, "Jesus." Bush was influenced by the Christian scholar Marvin Olasky, who argued in his 1992 book, *The Tragedy of American Compassion*, that in the fight against poverty the liberal state had usurped what had traditionally been the preserve of family, neighborhood, and church, reducing a personal and spiritual problem to a purely material one. The wish to substitute church for state was a distinctive feature of Bush's program, and indeed of his character.

The 2000 election between Bush and Vice President Al Gore ended in a dead heat, with the outcome to be determined by a recount in Florida. For the next month, the two sides waged a political and legal war over the Florida vote count, but the contest was never equal. Both Gore and his running mate, Senator Joseph Lieberman, felt an obligation to honor what they regarded as fair process; Bush and his chief lieutenants were far more ruthless, as the journalist Jeffrey Toobin wrote in his history of the recount. The "feral loathing" with which Republicans had come to regard Bill Clinton, as Toobin puts it, served not only as motivation but as a pretext to adopt any means in service of the end of winning. In one incident, later memorialized as "the Brooks Brothers riot," several hundred congressional aides and lawyers, who had flown in from around the country, created enough chaos to force an end to a recount in heavily Democratic Miami-Dade County.[38]

The immediate cause of Bush's victory was the decision by a divided US Supreme Court to block a statewide recount ordered by Florida's own high court—a decision that seemed to put an end to the Supreme Court's waning status as neutral arbiter in an increasingly partisan world. But it was the difference in the weight the two parties placed on means and ends that prolonged the process so that it could reach the court. As mentioned earlier, Steven Levitsky and Daniel Ziblatt describe mutual toleration as an essential norm; so, too, they write, is "institutional forbearance"—the principled willingness to forgo using all powers to throttle rivals. The Republicans had long since crossed that Rubicon with the endless investigations of Clinton by independent counsel Kenneth Starr and then with the impeachment process; once violated, the norm could be easily enough tossed aside. Of course, norm violation is infectious. In the aftermath of the election, 92 percent of Bush voters thought that Bush had been elected legitimately, while 11 percent of Gore voters did. Mutual intolerance was becoming, indeed, mutual.

Bush might have been remembered as a small-scale Reagan had it not been for the terrorist attacks of 9/11. The crisis triggered Bush's deep sense of religious mission as no domestic struggle ever could have. Bush became, in effect, America's first evangelical commander in chief. In his 2002 State of the Union speech, Bush famously described America's true adversary as an "axis of evil." The American people, he declared, had been "called to a unique role in human history." Many had found that "God is near." This sense that a bolt of moral light had abruptly clarified the baffling flux of life became the president's leitmotif. The parlous world of debate, the perpetual adjustment of conflicting interests and preferences, had come to seem an unaffordable luxury at a moment of supreme test. Real courage was required to insist that the rules of debate had not, in fact, been nullified. Only one senator was prepared to vote against the argumentatively titled USA Patriot Act, which vastly expanded the scope of law enforcement and intelligence agencies to pursue suspected terrorist threats.[39]

Bush's increasingly tight identification of religiosity with patriotism, and of patriotism with a bellicose foreign policy, endeared him to the Republicans' evangelical base and infuriated Democrats and moderates who had rallied to his side, albeit warily, in the immediate aftermath of 9/11. Bush became by far the most polarizing president in modern American history (though Donald Trump would later establish a new standard). By October 2005, with the Iraq war heading south, only 7 percent of Democrats supported the president, the lowest such figure recorded until that time—four points less than Richard Nixon received immediately before his resignation. At the same time, his support among Republicans remained above 90 percent, higher even than Dwight Eisenhower's at its highest point. This partisan gap, which had contracted throughout the middle decades of the twentieth century, had begun increasing with the presidency of Jimmy Carter and appeared to crest with Bill Clinton—until Bush shattered the mark.[40]

A new dimension of polarization had also begun to manifest itself: many Republicans refused to accept facts that might undermine their support of the president. In 2004, the majority of party members continued to believe that Saddam Hussein had a role in 9/11; a large majority of Republicans insisted, contrary to findings, that Saddam had had weapons of mass destruction. Among evangelicals, the figures were higher still. The national media itself had begun to polarize: conservatives increasingly watched Fox News, which reflected their worldview back to them by glossing over inconvenient facts or treating far-fetched theories as established truth. At the same time, by elevating foreign policy to the realm of the transcendent, Bush had turned politics into an existential endeavor that radically separated supporters and opponents, and he had undermined the secular pluralism that had always been understood as the precondition for liberal democracy.

Barack Obama ran for president in 2000 in order, as he often said, to cure America of its polarization. Born in 1961, Obama was far too young to have experienced the ideological convulsion of civil rights and Vietnam, whose aftershocks still seemed to be rocking the country. He quite consciously positioned himself outside that antinomy. In his 2006 book, *The Audacity of Hope*, Obama wrote that when he witnessed the titanic struggle between Bill Clinton and Newt Gingrich, "I sometimes felt as if I were watching the psychodrama of the baby boom genera-tion . . . played out on the national stage." Obama believed that ordinary Americans wanted no part of this zero-sum contest. He summoned his listeners to heed their better angels, to turn aside "the cynics, and the lobbyists, and the special interests" who had reduced government to a self-aggrandizing game, as he put it in the speech in which he announced his candidacy. The fundamental choice facing Americans was personal, not ideological. Obama spoke constantly of his personal story as a father-less black man who made it to Harvard Law School as an affirmation of the American Dream, proof that the nation could change for the better and thus a vindication of hope. In this identification of self with nation he struck a note as majestic and grandiose as Bush himself had, though without the theological cast. Obama was not above comparing himself to another "gangly, self-made Springfield lawyer" who had preserved the nation amidst civil war.[41]

Obama favored policies very little different from those of Hillary Clinton, his classically liberal rival for the party nomination: major gov-ernment investments in science, technology, and infrastructure; universal access to health care; a switch to renewable energy sources; an increase in the minimum wage; full funding for Social Security. Yet he spoke of his liberal views as Lincoln, or Teddy Roosevelt, or FDR had: not as one among several competing doctrines but as the American creed. As he said in the 2004 speech that first brought him to national attention, the belief that "I am my brother's keeper, I am my sister's keeper" knit all Americans together—except the cynics and dividers. Liberal politics was the precipitate of American decency—an ardent wish rather piously expressed as fact.[42]

Obama spent his first year in office striving desperately to ward off a full-blown recession brought on chiefly by reckless lending in the housing market and speculative investments by big banks and insurers. And he did so in the face of unyielding Republican opposition: his $787 billion stimulus package was passed by Congress with zero Republican votes. The GOP had so thoroughly discarded the principle of legitimate political contestation that Senate Minority Leader Mitch McConnell admitted, or rather boasted, that "the single most important thing we want to achieve is for President Obama to be a one-term president." Nevertheless, Obama managed to pass the stimulus package, rescue the auto industry, restore faith in the economy, and, after a prolonged struggle, pass a massive health-care reform package. It was an impressive record. Yet Obama had promised to restore Americans to themselves. He had offered his own self as a kind of medium for the realization of America's intrinsically liberal spirit. And in this regard, he failed—not because he went about it in the wrong way, but because he was wrong about America. The problem wasn't a few "cynics." It was the American people themselves.[43]

As the nomination and election of Bill Clinton had ignited a culture war that had been burning, barely noticed, beneath the surface of American life, so Obama kindled the flames of racial fear and resentment. The legacy of 1948 and 1968 now revealed itself in full. Obama understood the history very well; he had mastered the art of placating white anxiety. But he was no match for the emotions his candidacy unleashed. Conservatives propagated the rumor that Barack Hussein Obama—or Barack Hussein Muhammad Obama, as some insisted—was not Christian, despite his churchgoing habits, but Muslim. Others—most prominently, the real estate magnate and TV personality Donald Trump—declared that he was not American by birth but African, which meant that his presidency was illegitimate. The "birther" conspiracy theory dogged Obama even after he made his birth certificate public in 2011.

But Obama's otherness was hardly limited to race and religion, at least for the many Americans who loathed him. He was routinely denounced as a "socialist," a "Third World" radical who harbored deep antipathy for America despite his protestations to the contrary. According to *"You Lie!": The Evasions, Omissions, Fabrications, Frauds and Outright Falsehoods of Barack Obama*, by Jack Cashill, a journalist and producer (and PhD in American Studies), Obama, as a young Marxist, learned early on the Leninist principle of strategic lying. His heroes when young were Frantz Fanon and "Communists like Langston Hughes and Richard Wright." In June 2009, Glenn Beck told his vast following on Fox News that the president had a "deep-seated hatred of white people" and of "white culture."[44]

Conspiracy theories have always circulated at the fringes of American politics. Now they engulfed one of the two national parties. As the Republican Party base vanished into a cognitive bubble, only the rare Republican leader, such as 2008 presidential candidate John McCain, openly rejected the most outlandish stories. His running mate, Alaska governor Sarah Palin, actively encouraged them, especially in the years after the election. Several GOP members of Congress warned that Obama planned to establish a dictatorship; others repeated the birther story. The most grotesque and improbable distortions thus achieved a taken-for-granted status in the Republican rank and file. As late as 2014, 54 percent of Republicans said that "deep down," Obama was a Muslim; only 9 percent accepted that he was Christian. A poll in September 2009 found that 37 percent of party members believed that Obama was not American while another 26 percent professed to be uncertain.[45]

Because he was black, and perhaps also because he had a foreign-sounding name, Barack Obama became the focal point of Republican rage. But it wasn't all about him; perhaps most of it wasn't. Nor could it be contained inside the Republican Party, for all that the party had become the vessel for evangelical conservatives and radical libertarians. Starting in the summer of 2009, alienated and angry citizens began to gravitate toward the spontaneous protest movement known as the Tea Party. Militant protest politics in the United States had largely disappeared with the demise of the Black Panthers and Students for a Democratic Society in the early 1970s. Those groups had, of course, attacked the existing consensus from the left; the Tea Party—and the Oath Keepers and 9-12

Project and all the rest—preached revolution from the right. They were white and mostly old instead of young and racially diverse. They celebrated faith and tradition, not the body electric or the authentic self. But they shared with the sixties radicals a contempt for the incrementalism of politics, an a priori certainty of their own rightness, a preference for direct action over reflection, a willingness to believe the worst of others. The Tea Party repudiation of liberalism was as resounding as that of the radical left. But while the spirit of the 1960s had been exuberantly hopeful, the Tea Party, which germinated in the stagnant soil of economic failure, was angry and fearful.

The Tea Party began as a protest against the bailouts Barack Obama had engineered in order to rescue both individuals and major firms, even whole industries, from the wreckage of the financial crisis. Many of the original militants were veterans of the presidential campaign of Ron Paul, a libertarian gadfly. The first rallying cry, in Obama's early days in office, came in the form of a televised rant by a business reporter against Obama's plan to protect homeowners whose mortgages were underwater. This native don't-tread-on-me zeal coincided with the economic interests of powerful forces. Much of the funding and organizational muscle in the early days of the Tea Party came from groups, such as Americans for Prosperity, affiliated with the billionaire Koch brothers, who had long backed an anti-government, deregulatory agenda and who had strongly supported President George W. Bush. Plutocratic power and interest thus propelled a genuine grassroots movement into a yet more formidable force than it might have been absent that support. Over time, however, Tea Party enthusiasts migrated to issues very far from the Kochs' right-liberal orthodoxy, including a vehement hostility to immigration, free trade, and the forces of globalization.

Though hostile to elites of both parties, the Tea Party was the Republican base, with pitchforks. In the 2010 midterm elections, it propelled the GOP to a victory as shattering as the one the party had gained in 1994. Candidates identified with the Tea Party contested about 130 seats in the House and won about 40. The Republican Party that emerged from the 2010 election was not only more conservative than George W. Bush's party had been but angrier, more hostile to politics as such, less accepting of the norms of liberal democracy. The combustible rage at "Washington" eventually swallowed up conservatives as well as liberals. In the years to come, Tea Party extremists would upend orthodox Republicans, including House Majority Leader Eric Cantor. Like the Democratic Party in the 1960s, the GOP could barely contain the energies it had unleashed.

Republicans no longer accepted the structural impediments intrinsic to liberal democracy. At the federal level, where the opposition controlled the executive branch, this meant using legislative power as an instrument of blackmail. At the state level, at least where the GOP controlled both legislative and executive power, it was the judicial branch that constituted an intolerable obstacle. Newly empowered conservative majorities in state capitols passed extreme measures that courts overturned, and legislators took their revenge by attacking the autonomy of the judiciary. In North Carolina, Republicans who gained power in the 2010 election immediately sought to tilt the political playing field by passing a law that placed restrictions on voting designed to reduce minority turnout, and by drawing new district boundaries transparently designed to advantage their own party. Federal courts overturned both measures. State courts declared that laws eliminating teacher tenure and placing additional restrictions on abortion violated the state constitution. Legislators could not punish federal judges directly, but they could seek vengeance at the state level—which they promptly did by eliminating funding for judicial races, shrinking the state court of appeals to get rid of a few Democrats, and compelling all judges running for election to declare a party affiliation, making North Carolina the first state to switch from nonpartisan to partisan judicial elections since 1921. Half a dozen more measures followed. The onslaught led David Price, a veteran Democratic congressman from North Carolina, to reflect, "American democracy may be more fragile than we realized." State lawmakers in Kansas, Pennsylvania, Oklahoma, South Carolina, and elsewhere launched equally grave assaults on judicial autonomy.[46]

The judiciary is, of course, the politically neutral branch. The Framers showed the store they put by the principle of neutrality when they made the judiciary a separate and coequal branch. Important elements of the Republican Party no longer accepted that principle. Once politics is understood in theological terms, the impediment posed by neutrality becomes an intolerable violation of the will of the people—whether or not "the people" actually constitute a majority. The liberal preoccupation with impartial process can only be seen as an effort of a minority—the elites—to obstruct the will of the majority.

The rules governing the standing of the judiciary are much harder to alter at the federal level, in part because the Constitution contains explicit safeguards of judicial autonomy. For that reason, the Republican effort to reduce the courts to a partisan instrument has been confined to a series of titanic fights over personnel, above all in the Supreme Court. The Democrats have played their own brand of partisan hardball at such moments, notably during the 1987 fight over the nomination of Robert Bork to the Supreme Court. But Republicans have been prepared to ride roughshod over neutral process in a way that Democrats have not. Nothing made this more manifest than the sequence of events that followed the death of Supreme Court justice Antonin Scalia in February 2016.

Though Obama's tenure still had a year to run, Senate Majority Leader Mitch McConnell announced that Republicans would not vote on any nominee the president submitted. And when Obama carefully chose a highly respected moderate, Judge Merrick Garland, the Republicans proved as good as their word. Several leading Republicans, including presidential candidate Ted Cruz, even vowed that they would block all Supreme Court nominations should Hillary Clinton become president. The gambit succeeded, and when Donald Trump won the presidency, the Republicans were able to replace Scalia with a conservative, Neil Gorsuch. Contempt for neutral principle worked.

Implicit in McConnell's uncompromising stand was the idea that the Democratic Party had no right to rule, despite the fact that Barack Obama had twice won a clear majority of votes. One would have to go back to the era of nullification in the generation before the Civil War to find so direct a challenge by one party to the nation's constitutional order. That challenge had been decades in the making. The United States had been the bulwark of liberalism in the twentieth century. Now, in a new era, it was suffering a crisis of faith. Europe, once the beneficiary of the American export of liberalism, appeared to be more solidly grounded, thanks in part to social democratic traditions that blunted some of the worst effects of the 2008 recession. But it wasn't so. Both economic conditions and cultural patterns had become so thoroughly globalized that any virus that afflicted one part of the liberal order was bound to infect another. Illiberalism would proliferate in Europe with shocking speed.

CHAPTER EIGHT

Europe in the Grip of Nationalism

*If the price of taking the refugees is bringing fascists to power,
I hope they turn the refugees back.*

—Yoram Dinstein

EAST

In the European Solidarity Centre, the gleaming museum of the Polish uprising built with EU funds on the site of the old Lenin Shipyard in Gdańsk, a blowup of a photograph from 1980 shows the leaders of the movement in triumph after the signing of accords with Poland's Communist government. There is Lech Wałęsa, the charismatic Solidarity leader, and Jacek Kuroń, and Bronisław Geremek, and there, at the very edge, are two inconspicuous blond figures: Lech and Jarosław Kaczyński. They played a marginal role in the heroic events of the time, and they seemed to represent a marginal voice—traditionalist, insular, suspicious of the West and its secular ways. The Kaczyński twins appeared to be written out of history as Poland assumed its new place in Europe in the 1990s. And then they reappeared. Millions of Poles turned out to be far more comfortable with their nationalistic language than with the modernism—the European orientation—of the people who marched closer to Wałesa. Law and Justice, the party the Kaczyńskis founded, gained power in Poland in 2005, fell in 2007, and then regained control in 2015. The party has profoundly altered Poland's liberal trajectory. In today's Poland, the courts have lost their autonomy, the public media serves as the propaganda arm of the ruling party, and the Catholic Church has a free hand to shape social policy. The people who made Poland's peaceful revolution are demoralized and frightened. "The great objective of this government is to reorganize Poland into a Putin-like system," Adam Michnik, a philosophical as well as a political leader of Solidarity, told me. "There will be some democratic institutions to appeal to those who care about democracy, but at its core it will be Putinism."

What happened? Did Polish liberalism fail? Did it, that is, fail to deliver the freedom and prosperity it had promised? Or had the binding moment of the revolution obscured the truths that other strains remained deep in Poland and that liberalism had proved an alien growth, at least beyond an urbanized elite? Had liberalism delivered almost exactly what it had promised and failed nevertheless? "Maybe," said a melancholy Radosław Markowski, head of the Center for the Study of Democracy at the University of Social Sciences and Humanities, "this twenty-five years of democracy and liberal values in Poland is a deviant period. Perhaps we're returning to normal."

Democracy and liberal values certainly *appeared* to have become normal across Central Europe in the post-1989 period. Virtually all parties save those on the far right favored reforming institutions and practices in order to satisfy EU standards. Václav Havel, the hero of Czechoslovakia's Velvet Revolution, became the country's first president in 1989 and remained in that post until 2003. Slovakia, which peacefully separated from the Czech Republic in 1992, remained committed to democratic principles, though its leaders pursued more free-market policies than did the social democrats who surrounded Havel. In both Hungary and Poland, Communists competed on an equal footing—or more than equal, given the advantages of incumbent power—but were soundly defeated by parties affiliated with the liberation movement. The Czech Republic, Slovakia, Hungary, and Poland joined NATO in 1999 and the EU in

2004. The principles for which Havel, Wałesa, and others had fought had forged a new national identity.

But the divisions that ran through the new democracies of the East were not the same as the ones that ran through the old ones in the West. The Polish Round Table, the all-party negotiations in 1989 that led to new elections and a new government headed by Lech Wałesa, had succeeded because Communists understood that they could take their place in post-Soviet society. And they quickly did, using their webs of connections to run the new banks and privatized firms. The liberals, too, parlayed their education and cosmopolitanism into leading roles in public and political life. The division between the new elite and the mass of small-town or less-educated Poles recapitulated what Adam Michnik had described as the real cleavage inside Solidarity between the "open" and the "closed"—between those who clamored for new freedoms and those who feared them. The split manifested itself in a vicious fight over the role of ex-Communists. In 1991, one of the ministers in the government of right-wing prime minister Jan Olszewski accused Wałesa and dozens of other leading political figures of having cooperated with the Communists. Lech and Jarosław Kaczyński, who had loyally served Wałesa as both advisers and errand boys since the late 1970s, shared the hard-line view; both left Wałesa's side to join the right-wing forces. When Olszewski fell in 1992, the Kaczyńskis fell with him.

The Kaczyńskis were hard men—"closed," in Michnik's terminology. They were small-town boys whose parents had fought in the anti-Nazi and anti-Soviet resistance movements. They had become lawyers and then Solidarity activists. They worked hard, and loyally, but never cracked the inner circle of French- and English-speaking intellectuals. They were always a turbulent pair. "From the beginning," Wałesa told me, "when they were kids, they always used to pick fights. They were like Romulus and Remus. They knew how to pick fights, but sometimes they chose the wrong fights."

In 2001, the Kaczyńskis established Law and Justice, known in Polish as PiS, to appeal to those who felt left out of the liberal, cosmopolitan culture of the new Poland—Catholics who feared rising secularism; rural

and small-town folk who had seen little of the country's growing prosperity; nationalists who recoiled at taking marching orders, as they saw it,
from Brussels and Berlin; unreconciled anti-Communists. In 2005, Law
and Justice narrowly defeated the right-of-center, secular, and liberal
Civic Platform, or *Platforma*. In a separate election, Lech Kaczyński was
elected president. Jarosław, the operator, remained in the background as
party leader. The party was then sufficiently moderate and pro-European
that it held talks with Civic Platform to form a coalition government,
though the effort failed. Lech, the more worldly and gregarious of the
twins, appointed both hard-line anti-Communists and Western liberals
to his cabinet. No one doubted, though, that the reclusive Jarosław called
the shots—especially after Lech, on learning that he had been elected
president, turned to his brother on national television, snapped off a
salute, and barked, "Mr. Chairman, I report: mission accomplished." In
June 2006, Lech named Jarosław prime minister.[1]

That September, Jarosław delivered a little-noticed speech to the
conservative Heritage Foundation in Washington that offered a rare
glimpse into his resentful and even paranoid understanding of recent
Polish history. Despite political reform after 1989, Kaczyński explained
to his fervently anti-Communist audience, ex-Communists continued to
dominate Poland's "social hierarchy." The old elite had simply exchanged
its former political power for wealth. How, he asked, had these despised
anti-Polish elements gained the legitimacy to remain at the top rungs of
Polish life? Who smoothed their way? It was "the most influential por-
tion of the counterelite"—the liberals. They had agreed to be "co-opted
to the socially privileged sphere." Kaczyński had reverse-engineered a
conscious conspiracy from what were, after all, observable social facts,
and thus created a new divide in Polish society, between a small class of
elite predators and the great mass of their victims. Now, under Law and
Justice, Poland was witnessing the "tempestuous process of reconstruct-
ing social awareness, restoring history, and exposing post-Communist
legitimation myths."

But the revolution would have to wait. Law and Justice's plans ran into
resistance in Parliament and with Poland's Constitutional Tribunal, the

Kaczyńskis proved as turbulent in office as out, and in 2007 the ruling right-wing coalition collapsed amid accusations of scandal. Civic Platform won the ensuing election. A decade of stability and prosperity ensued. Poland was barely scathed by the financial crisis: the economy grew by 25 percent between 2007 and 2015, the highest rate in Europe. Poland quickly surpassed Hungary, formerly the most prosperous nation in the East, in per capita income. In 2011 voters awarded Civic Platform another term. Poland became the darling of liberal Central Europe.

The Central European counterrevolution began not in Poland but in Hungary, where Viktor Orbán, founder of the Fidesz Party, won an overwhelming victory at the polls in 2010. Like the Kaczyńskis, Orbán was a child of the revolution; he had, in fact, played a leading role in Hungary's anti-Soviet uprising. Also like them, he had grown up as a provincial, seeking a place in the elite while also resenting it. Finding no role for himself in Hungary's post-Communist government, he established his own party along traditionalist, Christian Democrat lines, with the post-1989 twist of virulent anti-Communism. He became Europe's youngest prime minister at age thirty-five in 1998—and then in 2002 suffered a mortifying defeat, as the Kaczyńskis later would, at the hands of ex-Communists. But unlike Poland, Hungary suffered a ruinous economic collapse after 2007, discrediting the ruling liberals. Hungary delivered itself into Orbán's hands in 2010.

Orbán quickly set to work undoing the reforms of the two previous decades. He pushed through Parliament a law criminalizing "imbalanced news coverage," though he backed off and produced a slightly less noxious version under EU pressure. He turned public broadcasting outlets into Fidesz mouthpieces. He passed another law requiring all religious groups to receive official approval from Parliament, thus separating favored religions—above all, Christianity—from all others. He assailed foreign nongovernmental organizations as fifth columnists and began a sustained campaign of attacks against liberal George Soros, a Jewish billionaire and philanthropist of Hungarian origin. He eliminated most of the powers of Hungary's Constitutional Court, which had blocked many of his initiatives during his first tenure. He attacked the EU even as Hungary continued to benefit from hundreds of millions of euros in subsidies annually.

Like George Wallace, Orbán formulated a new language of populism based upon a new villain. Anti-Communism was a waning force. Orbán now positioned himself against liberalism itself—the word as much as the fact. He ridiculed and threatened political liberals like Soros, founder of the Open Society Foundations and heir to the tradition of Karl Popper; socialists who had overseen the privatization of Hungary's economy in the name of liberalization; the "neoliberal" regime of free trade and the free movement of capital, which he accused of undermining Hungarian sovereignty; and the moral liberalism of secular urbanites. This, he found, struck a very deep chord. "'Liberalism' as a word to Hungarians is 100 percent negative," I was told while in Budapest by Mária Schmidt, a right-wing intellectual and anti-globalization conspiracy theorist whom Orbán favors. Orbán was able to exploit the inherent tension between liberal principle and democratic majoritarianism; he made the word "liberal" stand for an alien value system imposed on the Hungarian people by outsiders and their elite agents at home.

In 2014, Orbán gave a speech in which he described a Western world in economic and moral free fall after the 2008 economic crisis. Today's stars, by contrast, were illiberal or undemocratic states like "Singapore, China, India, Turkey, Russia." It was thus incumbent on Hungary "to abandon liberal methods and principles of organizing a society, as well as the liberal way to look at the world." The new Hungary would be democratic—that is, majoritarian—but hostile to liberal principles in politics, economics, and culture. At the level of personal morals, that entailed doing away with the principle, elemental to John Stuart Mill, that we should be free to do anything that does not violate another person's freedom. At the level of the economy, illiberalism meant using the government to protect people from the marketplace. Here Orbán's populist illiberalism came very close to returning to the Communist paternalism from which Hungary had escaped.[2]

Economic failure had prepared Hungarians for Orbán's populism. The same could not be said for Poland, though the country suffered the hollowing out of heavy industry that occurred throughout the West and especially in ex-Communist countries that had long subsidized unprofitable firms. The promise of liberal prosperity hadn't failed. Poland really had established a democracy rather than a socialist democracy and a capitalist market rather than a social market. Poles enjoyed the kind of personal autonomy that Western Europeans had been able to take for granted for several generations. Civic Platform leader Donald Tusk thought, as many intellectuals did, that after centuries of tragedy and oppression, Poland had at last sailed out into Fukuyama's calm posthistorical waters. Civic Platform promised to keep hot water in Polish taps. And it did so.

But that wasn't enough. The prosperity of the previous quarter century had been, of course, very unevenly distributed. Even if almost everyone was doing somewhat better, many felt that they were doing relatively worse, because now some were doing very well indeed. Some Poles, whether or not descendants of the Communist bureaucracy, or *nomenklatura*, lived more or less the way people did in Paris and London; Poles in small towns and rural areas lived much as they had before. But the sense of dissatisfaction was not only, and perhaps not chiefly, economic. Liberals from the time of Mill had worried that individualism, secularism, pragmatism, and economic self-interest would not be enough to bind citizens together. The Poles had fought the Nazis, the Communists, the post-Communists. Perhaps they experienced the exit from history as anticlimax. That is the view of Konstanty Gebert, a leading Polish journalist and intellectual and a former Solidarity activist. "People wanted history, they wanted glory, they wanted *meaning*," Gebert told me. Law and Justice "offered a meaning. Their meaning was, 'We'll make Poland great again.'"

In the 2015 campaign for Parliament, Law and Justice promised to protect people against the vagaries of the free market by using the state as a socialist-style piggy bank. In the name of increasing Poland's dwindling population—itself a patriotic meme—the party proposed to give parents 500 złotys (about $130) monthly for every child beyond the first. It would reverse an increase in the retirement age and raise the ceiling below which income would not be taxed. But at the heart of the campaign was the act of cultural recovery that the Kaczyńskis had always championed—the return to a true Polishness. Party leaders ran against Tusk as a tool of Brussels and Germany. Deeply tainted by Jarosław's paranoia, Law and Justice even accused the opposing party of doing the secret bidding of Russia.

The party had converted a tragedy into a conspiracy. On April 10, 2010, Lech Kaczyński, then a private citizen, had flown to Smolensk in Russia with dozens of political leaders and government officials to attend an event marking the seventieth anniversary of the murder of twenty thousand Polish military officers by the Soviet secret police—a catastrophe that devastated Poland's officer and intellectual class and has reminded Poles ever since of Soviet barbarity. On its descent into the airport, the delegation's plane crashed, and all aboard were killed. Polish and Russian investigations concluded that crew members made fatal mistakes in response to worsening weather conditions. Almost immediately, however, officials of Law and Justice cited supposed evidence that Russia had brought the plane down and that the Tusk government had conspired either in Lech's death or in covering up Russian involvement, despite the fact that several Civic Platform officials also died in the crash. Three plaques commemorating the dead were placed in front of the Presidential Palace, which became a place of vigil for the party faithful. On the tenth of every month—not just on April 10—Jarosław Kaczyński, who rarely appeared in public, stood on the sidewalk in front of the palace to deliver a speech in honor of the dead. Paranoia over Smolensk supplanted paranoia over Communists, with modern Russia taking the place of the hated Soviet Union. Law and Justice hammered away at Tusk's alleged complicity throughout the 2015 campaign.

The liberal coalition still might have won had the vast flow of refugees from Syria and elsewhere not begun streaming toward Europe in the summer of 2015. Like all of Central Europe, Poland is almost wholly white and Christian. Viktor Orbán had already plumbed popular xenophobia by violently turning back refugees seeking to cross onward and vowing never to let them seek refuge in Hungary. No refugee came anywhere near

Poland, but the government agreed to take 7,000 of the 160,000 refugees European officials were hoping to place. That was all the space Kaczyński needed. In the waning days of the election, he emerged from his backroom dealings to deliver a speech. "There are," he claimed, "already signs of emergence of diseases that are highly dangerous and have not been seen in Europe for a long time: cholera on the Greek islands, dysentery in Vienna. There is also talk about other, even more severe diseases." The speech was widely credited with helping put Law and Justice over the top. Though the party won only 38 percent of the popular vote, fragmentation among the other parties allowed it to gain an outright majority in Parliament.[3]

In early 2016, I spent several days in Siedlce, a modest city halfway between Warsaw and the border with Belarus. The economically depressed and largely rural areas in Poland's south and east had gone heavily for Law and Justice. Siedlce had the sluggish traffic and empty sidewalks of a town where not much was going on. Many of the young people had left in recent years for England and other European destinations. Over the previous six or so years, the big steel plant in town, Polimex-Mostostal, had shed half its jobs. The average monthly salary was stuck at about $700. The union leaders I talked to said that Civic Platform had ignored conservative small towns in favor of its urban base, a claim that, while apparently true, reflected the deeply ingrained, Communist-era reflex of looking to the state for all good things. This habit accentuated the understandable resentment that provincial Poles felt toward a cosmopolitan Poland whose privileges they did not share.

The border areas in the east had suffered deeply during both the Nazi and Soviet onslaughts and were thus imbued with both a passionate nationalism and a profound sense of victimization. Kaczyński's insularity, his deep suspicion of outsiders, and his resentment of elites resonated deeply there. Virtually everyone I met agreed with Kaczyński on refugees and Smolensk. Wiesław Kałuski, an official with the hospital workers' union, told me that "people should have the right to vote whether they want a Muslim as a neighbor." When I asked how he would vote, he said, "I don't know, because we've never met any Muslims." He noted, however, that if the Syrians had had any courage they would have stood and fought their oppressors, as the Poles had.

People in Siedlce identified with Jarosław Kaczyński in a way that they never could with the urban elites of Civic Platform. Zbigniew Sobolewski, a local businessman, kept pictures of the Kaczyński twins on an office wall, where they flanked a Polish eagle. When I asked him to speak of Jarosław, he warned me that he might get emotional, and he promptly started to tear up. He spoke of Kaczyński as a figure of almost Gandhian self-denial. "In personal relations," he conceded, "Jarosław Kaczyński is not such an easy person. But he is a man who is very strict in his values. At our very first meeting"—in the early 1990s—"I knew that he was the man who could save Poland."

When we spoke of Kaczyński's rivals, Sobolewski's mood blackened. He described Tusk, now the president of the European Council, the EU's executive body, as a traitor. Civic Platform, he insisted, was controlled by "the sons and daughters of those who after World War II were destroying our country."

"You mean Communists?" I asked.

"In the broad sense, yes."

Another local businessman, Leszek Kucyński, told me that while Poles in the east had traditionally fought invaders, the more worldly westerners had collaborated with them. Today, he said, "What Donald Tusk keeps saying is that there are parts of Poland that didn't fit into Europe and we have to change ourselves so that we can fit." The West, he said, is "multicultural." Nurses in England, he had heard, were forbidden to wear crosses. The French burned down their churches. The multiculturals wanted Poland to integrate into the secular West. But Poland would not capitulate to the cosmopolitans. Poland would insist on being Poland.

The present, in Siedlce, held little appeal; the past was powerful. But the usable past was not the age of "noble democracy," when the sixteenth-century parliament seized powers from the king and made Poland an island of tolerance long before the decline of absolutism elsewhere in Europe. The past was the endless struggle against invaders from east and west, culminating with the heroic resistance against the Communists. And at the very heart of that struggle, sustaining Poland through all her tribulations, was the Church. The Catholic Church served as the moral center of Poland as it had not in Western Europe since the middle of the twentieth century. The visit of the Polish pope, John Paul II, in October 1978 electrified the country and reminded Poles of bonds infinitely deeper than those claimed by their godless state. Yet the pope also spoke in the modern language of the individual self. He celebrated the "inalienable rights of man, the inalienable rights of dignity." With the pope as champion, many leading Polish prelates defied the Communist regime and stood with the people. But John Paul was no liberal; neither were the Polish priests. The battle for freedom having been won, they sought to resume their roles as guardians of the faith and defenders of orthodoxy. Law and Justice, the party of tradition, family, and morality, was their natural home, as the GOP had become the natural home for conservative evangelicals.

The leading religious authority in Siedlce was Father Kazimierc Niemerka, pastor of the Church of the Divine Mercy. Father Niemerka was a big, fleshy man with beetling black brows; his great obsessions, besides the Church, were sports and politics. He knew all about Orbán's "illiberal democracy" and said that it expressed his own views perfectly. He was, of course, a Law and Justice man. He felt that the party would return Poland to traditional family morality, including by criminalizing all forms of abortion. Father Niemerka explained Polish history to me. "Without Christianity," he said, "there would have been no Poland." Law and Justice was the party of faith, and thus of Poland. The other parties had a different definition of patriotism. They had stopped celebrating the old national holidays, like Constitution Day. They looked westward to the EU, yet few of them knew that the organization had been founded by the pious Catholic Robert Schuman, who had prayed every day before work; the new leaders of the EU presided over a godless world. And yes, Father Niemerka thought there was something very fishy about Smolensk.

Polish illiberalism, like Hungarian illiberalism, is a value system defined in opposition to a liberal status quo seen as inauthentic. What distinguishes the two is, first, Poland's intense identification with the Catholic Church, and, second, the personalities of the leaders. Polish intellectuals glumly entertain themselves by trying to limn the difference between the two. "Orbán is a cynic," said Sławomir Sierakowski, head of the Institute for Advanced Study in Warsaw, "and Kaczyński is a fanatic. Orbán can be pragmatic; Kaczyński would commit suicide on principle. Orbán respects red lines; Kaczyński crosses them." Kaczyński is, as even his acolyte Zbigniew Sobolewski conceded, not such an easy person. He has never married, and he lived with his mother until she died in 2013. He has said that his only bedtime companion is his cat, Fiona. Until recently he had neither a bank account nor a driver's license. He rarely travels and rarely addresses the public. His dark monasticism draws acolytes and fellow fanatics to his side. Lech Wałesa told me that Kaczyński attracted misfits like himself.

I had great trouble meeting any Law and Justice officials. Kaczyński almost never talks to the Western press. Most far-right European parties have a few polished members who are designated to speak to foreigners; Law and Justice does not. The party spokeswoman did not respond to emails and phone calls. Finally, however, I was able to arrange a conversation with Ryszard Terlecki, the head of the party's parliamentary caucus and one of Kaczyński's small circle of confidants. When we met, late on a Sunday evening in the dark and deserted Parliament building, I learned that Terlecki belonged to a political category that I had never before encountered: ex-hippie, anti-Communist hard-liner. Youthful dissolution had taken its toll. At sixty-seven, Terlecki was a prematurely played-out-looking man, tall and gaunt, with graven cheeks, a grizzled chin, and great bags beneath dark eyes.

Terlecki did not speak English, as virtually all senior members of the opposition did. Through a translator, he told me that he shared Kaczyński's view of recent Polish history. The post-Solidarity elite, he assured me, had made common cause with the Communists "because it was the only way they could stop the conservative Catholic movement that was rising up in Poland." Terlecki said that he was not anti-Western. The difference between Law and Justice and the opposition, he said, was that "we don't want a Poland that is a colony of the West." Terlecki meant not only that Poland should not blindly follow Germany, as he accused the previous government of doing, but also that Poland should embrace its own values, above all the conservatism of the Church and the belief in the sanctity of the family. Civic Platform, he said, had seized control of the media and the courts; Law and Justice was now taking them back. Terlecki did not accept the difference between the ruling party and the state, or for that matter between the state and society. Politics, for him, was a war of ultimate values, as it had been for the Communists. How then, I asked, could he possibly accept the idea of political compromise? Terlecki laughed dryly. "What kind of compromise do you mean?" he asked. "There's no need for one." He sounded very much like latter-day Republicans.

Terlecki reflected the party view. While Orbán often tested the water with an extreme proposal before pulling back, Law and Justice blithely steamrolled Poland's constitution. Once in office, the party moved to gain control over all those sectors that, according to Kaczyński, remained in the hands of the *nomenklatura* and their liberal allies. The new government eliminated the independence of Poland's chief prosecutor, placing him underneath the minister of justice. It passed an anti-terror law giving the police expanded access to digital data. An amended civil service law eliminated merit-based appointments for high-ranking officials, permitting them to be named by the government. And it transferred the power to pick the head of public broadcasting from a government-appointed panel to the Ministry of the Treasury. The minister promptly picked a figure who had once described himself as Jarosław Kaczyński's "bull terrier."

But the institution that bore the brunt of the Law and Justice blunderbuss was the Constitutional Tribunal, which had frustrated Kaczyński in his previous time in office. The outgoing government had made appointments to replace five of the court's fifteen judges who were scheduled to retire, a decision that was plainly unconstitutional with regard to two of the judges, whose terms expired after that of the legislature and whose replacements thus should have been picked by the new officeholders. But the new Parliament simply invalidated all five choices and picked five new judges, which was an even grosser violation of the constitutional order.

When the court refused to accept them, Andrzej Duda, the president, went ahead and swore them in anyway. And that was only the beginning. In December 2015, Parliament adopted a measure that required a vote of two-thirds of judges, rather than a majority, to render a decision binding. The law also stipulated that at least thirteen of the fifteen judges be present to hear a case. In 2017 Parliament passed legislation giving the government direct control over the judiciary and the Supreme Court.

Viktor Orbán has also brought Hungary's Constitutional Court to heel. So, as mentioned earlier, have Republican state legislators in the United States. Populists cannot brook institutions that have the power to thwart the will of political majorities. They cannot, in fact, accept their legitimacy, for if, as Ryszard Terlecki says, politics is a war of transcendent values, no institution can pretend to be a neutral arbiter. It is, in fact, the putative neutrality conferred by constitutions and laws that makes the judiciary, and especially high courts, so very dangerous a weapon. So long as they persist, so does the idea of a principle that stands above the will of the majority. The truth is that Poland's high court was not a tool of the previous government. Adam Bodnar, Poland's ombudsman, said that he lost half the human rights cases he brought before the court, including his effort to overturn a law punishing criticism of the president. The court was deeply deferential to the Church. The real reason for the crusade, Bodnar said, was, "like the Hungarian model, gaining more and more power over the government, dismantling institutions that are relevant, putting the whole state under their control."

Is it true, then, that the previous quarter century of liberal democracy was "a deviant period," as Markowski suggested? Certainly the overwhelming binding power of Solidarity and the common hatred of a totalitarian enemy exaggerated the consensus around liberal values. The Poland of 1989 was deeply conservative and deeply Catholic. Yet after throwing off the Soviet yoke, Poles experienced twenty-five years of integration with Europe, tremendous increases in prosperity, and opportunities to travel. The millions of people who now enjoy a Western European life increasingly think and act and vote like Western Europeans. But millions of others may have been prepared to accept the goods that came with membership in liberal Europe, like borderless travel and labor migration, but not the values that made it possible. And for them, the pull of the past, as well as the fear of the future, is very powerful. If the implicit appeal of Law and Justice was to "make Poland great again," the emphasis—as in the United States—fell at least as heavily on "again" as on "great"—on, that is, the gravitational pull of an imagined pre-Communist past. Liberalism in Poland had delivered what it had promised to deliver, but it wasn't enough.

Kaczyński's blunt attacks on secularism—and especially his efforts, along with the Church's, to criminalize abortion even in the case of rape or incest—have roused Poles to take to the streets. But the protests remain modest, and opposition parties remain scattered. Poland is not, after all, an authoritarian state; Warsaw and Krakow feel like European capitals, with cafés and bookstores and art galleries and unbuttoned conversation. Nevertheless, opponents of the regime believe that it is in Jarosław Kaczyński's nature to keep going until he has gone too far. At that point, Adam Michnik told me, the Polish people will awaken to the threat that the Law and Justice government poses to the liberties for which they fought for so many years. What transgression would trigger a truly national response? How much damage would be done to Polish democracy in the meantime? Michnik listened to the translation of my question and stubbed out a last cigarette. "One thing is obvious," he said. "Behind us is a wall, and we see inscribed on that wall the specter of dictatorship. We cannot go back."

WEST

The Netherlands is the most liberal country in Europe; there is no species of liberalism to which the Dutch are not committed. The panoply of modern personal liberties, including the right to choose one's sexual and gender preferences and the right to smoke marijuana, are zealously defended. Unlike most other northern Europeans, the Dutch, as a historically mercantile people, believe in free trade and free markets, and tend to elect right-of-center governments that do not harbor doubts about the merits of capitalism. Finally, Dutch law treats the rights of minorities and newcomers with the utmost seriousness. The first article of the Dutch constitution reads, "All persons in the Netherlands are treated equally in equal circumstances. Discrimination on the grounds of religion, belief, political opinion, race, or sex or on any other grounds whatsoever is not permitted."

Holland is the living proof that liberalism works. The Dutch rank very close to the top in almost everything good—prosperity, employment, literacy. A UN report recently concluded that Dutch children are, by a long shot, the happiest in the world. Dutch voters thus have every reason to continue supporting the personal and economic liberties that constitute their national birthright. They are, however, having grave doubts about the minorities in their midst; they worry that the cardinal liberal value of tolerance of the other could lead to a kind of cultural suicide pact. That is not because the Dutch are xenophobic; they do not fear outsiders as such. They do fear Islam. The rise of liberalism in Europe coincided with an era not only of prosperity but of ethnic and religious homogeneity. What happens if prosperity remains but immigration from the Islamic world continues? What about the combination of an economy that hollows out the working class *and* further immigration? At what point do cultural and economic pressures threaten liberalism?

After World War II, Dutch employers imported a steady stream of guest workers—first southern Europeans, then Turks, Moroccans, Surinamese, Antilleans, and others. The Italians and the Spaniards, as envisioned, ultimately returned home; the others stayed and brought their families. While we may imagine the Netherlands as a homogeneous country of apple-cheeked blondes, about half the population of Amsterdam, Rotterdam, and The Hague are immigrants or the descendants of recent immigrants. No other European country has so large a concentration of non-European-origin residents in its major cities.

Nevertheless, because protecting the rights of immigrants constituted one of the pillars of Dutch liberalism, the very few public figures who questioned the merits of large-scale immigration were accused of Islamophobia or fascism. The question of the other was long deemed unfit for political debate. Then in 2001 Pim Fortuyn, a scholar and public speaker, began saying the unsayable. "The Muslims should simply leave," he told an interviewer. "You should treat them like Communists during the Cold War." Muslims, Fortuyn said, did not share Dutch values; unlike newcomers from "our own cultural sphere," their insistence on clinging to and promoting their own values would threaten Dutch identity over time. Fortuyn had the courage of his convictions: he called for the repeal of the first article of the constitution. That was so gross a transgression that Fortuyn was drummed out of his own anti-immigrant party, Livable Netherlands.[4]

Fortuyn posed an entirely new sort of challenge by arguing that Dutch liberalism was at war with itself. Far from being a dour traditionalist, Fortuyn was a puckish public figure, an anti-colonialist, anti-fascist, philo-Semite; and he was gay. When, in the midst of a debate, an imam said it was clear that Fortuyn had never even talked to Muslims, Fortuyn shot back, "Sir, I sleep with them." Fortuyn used his homosexuality to reverse the usual terms of debate. Far from being an intolerant reactionary, he was a lone defender of liberal principles against both illiberal Muslims and leftists who wanted to deny him the right to speak. It was he, not the left, who was standing up for Dutch values.

In early 2002, a new party, with Fortuyn at the head, won more than a third of the vote in municipal elections in progressive, eclectic Rotterdam—a shock to the Dutch political establishment. Until that moment, Dutch politics had presented voters with a choice between a statist social democratic model and a free-market one. Now, suddenly, the question of Dutch identity had imposed itself on public debate. Fortuyn had upended the system. And then, on May 6, 2002, Fortuyn was murdered—not by an Islamic extremist but by an environmental activist. No political leader in the Netherlands had been murdered in centuries. Fortuyn became a martyr; his issue became the country's issue. In an election ten days after his death, the Pim Fortuyn List won 17 percent of the seats in Parliament, an unprecedented performance by a new party—not to mention one led by a dead man. Without Fortuyn, the party soon disintegrated, but the question of identity remained at or near the center of political debate.

In April 2017, the Dutch went to the polls. Prime Minister Mark Rutte of the center-right People's Party for Freedom and Democracy, or VVD, was seeking another term. His most dangerous opponent was Geert Wilders, Pim Fortuyn's successor as the defender of Dutch identity against immigrants and Islam. Wilders was a crude, unchecked version of his charming and erudite predecessor. He had kicked off his campaign by calling Moroccan immigrants "scum." (He softened the blow by adding, "Not all are scum.") A five-second television ad for Wilder's Party for Freedom, or PVV, showed a clip of Rutte saying, "Islam is not the problem," followed by the words, "Do you agree?" Enough Dutch voters did not agree that a month before the election the Party for Freedom was running neck and neck with the VVD. At this same moment, Marine Le Pen of France's National Front had become almost a sure bet to reach the final round of France's presidential election. Six months earlier, Americans had horrified liberal voters everywhere by electing Donald Trump as president. And only a few months before *that*, in June 2016, British voters had chosen to leave the EU. It was not a moment for complacent confidence.

In early April I spent several afternoons at the Boulevard, a popular pub in the Overschie neighborhood on the northern edge of Rotterdam. The regular crowd consisted almost entirely of older white men. I asked Willem, a craggy, blue-eyed construction manager who was nursing a beer, whether he was concerned about immigration. Willem reflected for a moment and said, "You can take over a country by war, or you can take over a country by integration." When I asked what he meant, Willem (who didn't want to tell me his last name) said that the newcomers were reproducing so rapidly that "soon there will be more immigrants than Dutch." But weren't the immigrants at least good for the economy? "You can't be good for the economy if you don't work," he said. "The Dutch work; they don't." He had often seen thuggish Moroccan kids hanging around idly downtown. The immigrants dropped out of school, he thought, and so they couldn't get jobs.

Willem's views were not universal at the Boulevard. Pieter Van Koopan, the local city councilman, said he wished most Dutch were as pious as his Muslim friends. He added, however, that he didn't understand why immigrants could jump the queue to get apartments distributed by the state. (They can't, though refugees can.) Also, he said, Africans didn't work. A different Pieter, also no last name given, said the older generation of immigrants was fine, but the young guys whined about discrimination when they didn't get what they wanted. Yet no one at the bar planned to vote for Wilders—not even Willem, who grudgingly admitted that his daughter was running as a PVV candidate. Even those who shared portions of Wilders's outlook viewed him as a crank and something of a national embarrassment. Fortunately, they could choose among several other, smaller anti-immigrant parties. Even the VVD had been taking a more and more anti-immigrant and anti-Muslim line. In January, the party had published a full-page ad in Dutch newspapers quoting Rutte telling immigrants that they should "act normal or go away." That had been pretty much Pim Fortuyn's view. First Fortuyn and then Wilders had so reshaped Dutch politics that today's center sounded like yesterday's beyond-the-pale. Many of the Dutch I talked to reminded me of American neoconservatives in the 1970s: *I* didn't change, they were saying; liberalism did.

Wilders had done a favor for mainstream parties by marginalizing himself. Formerly a free-market liberal on the right wing of the VVD, he severed his ties in 2004 over the party's willingness to consider letting Turkey join the European Union. Wilders started up the PVV in 2006, though he remains the only actual member of the party. The candidates who run on his ticket, and the staff members who cater to his whims, cannot actually join the party itself. The PVV has no platform, no spokesperson, and no formal organization. It's just Wilders. Ronald Sorenson, a former close ally, told me that Wilders had justified this bizarre structure by saying that if he opened the party to the public he would attract every crackpot in the country. It was hard to argue the point.

Wilders began receiving death threats from Islamist extremists as soon as he formed his party. He was given an elaborate security detail; he has lived ever since inside a tight cordon. Whether because of the imposed isolation, his status as a quasi cult leader, or the liberation he felt at having escaped the confines of an organized party, Wilders soon threw all rhetorical restraint to the winds. In 2007, he called the Quran "the Islamic *Mein Kampf*" and proposed that the Netherlands ban "this miserable book," as it had Adolf Hitler's text. At the same time, he began moving to the left on economic issues, calling for the socialization of the country's privatized health-care system and opposing fiscal austerity. In short, he became a modern European populist, like Viktor Orbán and France's Marine Le Pen. In recent years, Wilders has become a central figure in the informal populist internationale. In early 2017 he served as a featured speaker at a right-wing conclave in Koblenz, Germany, known as the Europe of Nations and Freedom conference. There he warned darkly of hordes of African and Muslim immigrants pouring into Europe and said, "We are fed up with the elites, who offer you a beautiful ideal world in which all cultures are morally equivalent." During various visits to the United States, Wilders met with Representatives Michele Bachmann and Steve King and other leading figures in America's nativist right. He has written regularly for Breitbart, which in turn extensively covered his 2017 campaign.[5]

Wilders's flair for the extreme virtually guarantees that the PVV cannot take power, but neither can it be extracted from the core of political debate. And the fear and resentment that gave rise to the party are more likely to grow than to shrink in the near future. This, in turn, compels a question not about politics but about migration: Was Pim Fortuyn right in saying that Muslim immigrants will not accept the fundamental tenets of liberal Dutch—and European—culture?

That suggestion is deeply insulting to the vast population of middle-class Muslims in Holland. I went to Friday prayers at the Essalam mosque—one of Europe's largest—in South Rotterdam. The mosque is considered Moroccan, though while there I met a Kurd—a Dutch citizen—and a Kosovar and a Bangladeshi, both newcomers. Essalam is dedicated to a moderate, ecumenical vision of Islam. While I was there, Albert Ringer, the rabbi of Rotterdam's Reform synagogue, came by for a chat with the imam. He told me that he had been delighted to be introduced at a recent Ramadan *iftar* as "our rabbi." Essalam's imam, Azzedine Karrat, was a soft-spoken thirty-year-old who had lived in the Netherlands since he was ten. When I told him that I was writing about integration, he said, "It doesn't make sense to speak of 'integration.' We are not immigrants. We are part of the society. When somebody asks me where I am from, I say, 'I'm a Dutch Muslim with Moroccan roots.'"

Outside, after prayers, I met Driess Terrhi, a forty-five-year-old chemical engineer who had also emigrated from Morocco with his family when he was ten. He had come to the mosque with his father, a venerable gentleman in a white skullcap, and his son, Souhail, who was getting his master's degree in psychology in the hope of doing social work. Terrhi was mystified at the resentment that immigrants had provoked. His friends were second- or third-generation Dutch-speaking professionals, like him. Like the imam, they considered themselves Dutch. "Probably," he hypothesized, the PVV types "have a low educational level, so they are competing with immigrants for jobs, and many are jobless." I told him that that was more or less what the PVV people said about immigrants. I asked Terrhi if he would vote for Denk, a new party founded by Turkish immigrants, which said it aimed to combat xenophobia. Absolutely not, he said—they were chauvinists just like the PVV, only in reverse.

But Essalam is hardly the whole story. In 2016 Maarten Zeegers, a former theology student, published a startling exposé titled, *I Was One of Them: Three Years Undercover Among Muslims.* Zeegers had penetrated the Muslim community of The Hague, which, he told me, is the most segregated in the Netherlands. A boulevard that runs down the middle of the city literally separates the immigrant half of The Hague from the native Dutch half. Zeegers found that Salafism, the fundamentalist strain of Islam that looks to the Prophet Muhammad and his followers as the sole source of guidance, was gaining ground rapidly, especially among young immigrants from Morocco, who explicitly repudiated the idea of integrating into Dutch secular society. He witnessed three pro–Islamic State demonstrations during his time in the neighborhood, though all were small. Of the three hundred Dutch citizens who went to Syria to fight for the Islamic State, Zeegers said, ninety came from his neighborhood.

He concluded that the progressive view that Muslim immigrants would integrate into Dutch society so long as discrimination ends and economic conditions improve was "sticking your head in the sand."

Dutch suburbs are not banlieues—the poor, crime-ridden, immigrant-majority housing projects that mark the outskirts of French urban centers. Dutch of Moroccan or Turkish descent don't burn cars and rampage through the streets. Nor do they carry out terrorist attacks. Though the Netherlands took in about forty-five thousand refugees in 2015, even the guys at the Boulevard said the country had an obligation to accept them (so long as they were spread evenly around and not squeezed into the immigrant neighborhood of South Rotterdam). Yet many Dutch immigrants do, in fact, live in a largely self-enclosed world. The number of neighborhoods with 50 percent or more immigrants has gone up by half since 2002. Intermarriage between Turks or Moroccans and native Dutch remains below 10 percent. Half a century after large-scale, non-European immigration began, it is hard to deny that the Netherlands has an urban underclass. Four times as many non-Western immigrants are accused of crimes as Dutch natives. Unemployment rates among them are three times as high as among natives.

Even liberal Dutch worry about the extraterritorial loyalties of their Muslim citizens. In the days following the failed coup in Turkey in the summer of 2016, thousands of Turkish immigrants and people of Turkish descent thronged the Erasmus Bridge in Rotterdam, shouting slogans on behalf of Turkish president Recep Tayyip Erdoğan and carrying placards bearing his image. Some even assaulted reporters and attacked homes said to belong to Turkish followers of Fethullah Gülen, a religious authority and former ally whom Erdoğan had accused of orchestrating the coup. It was as if they wanted to prove that Wilders was right about the refusal of Muslim immigrants to integrate into Dutch civic life. As Han ten Broeke, a senior VVD parliamentarian, said to me, "You couldn't miss the irony of Erasmus, who came to Holland because it was a haven for freedom of thought." Ten Broeke pointed out that while Dutch anxieties in the past had focused on Moroccans rather than Turks, who seemed better integrated and in any case were much appreciated as shopkeepers and taxi drivers, "even third-generation Turks turn out to be totally nationalistic." They were Turks before they were Dutch.

It is disingenuous to deny the gulf in values between secular, progressive Europeans and the pious Muslims in their midst. A 2009 Gallup poll found that 58 percent of French Muslims, versus 23 percent of French generally, identify with their religion "very strongly" or "extremely strongly." The gap was greater still in other European countries. Islamic piety, in turn, is linked to a range of other attitudes—unwillingness to tolerate blasphemy, a favorable view of sharia law, opposition to homosexuality. In a poll of British Muslims, 0 percent considered homosexuality acceptable. One expects first-generation immigrants to feel a deep attachment to the values of home but ensuing generations to adapt to the values of *their* home. The question that Europeans now ask is whether Islam is a form of identity too deeply rooted to give way to the integrative force of Western secular culture.[6]

It's noteworthy that polls typically find attitudes among sixteen- to twenty-four-year-olds more conservative than those among their elders. The Salafis whom Maarten Zeegers encountered typically came from religiously moderate backgrounds; they rebelled by staking out a more adversarial identity than their parents had. In *Islamic Exceptionalism*, journalist and scholar Shadi Hamid writes that Islam has been trying to work out an acceptable relationship between faith and governance at least since the 1920s, when the Muslim Brotherhood first rose in Egypt with the message that Muslims should seek to Islamize the secular state rather than spurn it, yet a "foundational divide" persists between the *umma*—the body of the faithful—and the state. While one can hope, he writes, that eventually Islam "will succumb, like other religions before it, to the appeals of secularization," history would argue that that is "extremely unlikely in the near to medium term."[7]

Liberal tolerance does not provide a straightforward answer to this problem. Does respect for the right to behave as you wish compel an essentially laissez-faire approach to integration? That was the Dutch instinct. Throughout the 1990s, ethnic groups were encouraged to celebrate their own backgrounds, languages, customs, and history. This came to a screeching halt when scholars—and not just Fortuyn and his followers—concluded that multiculturalism was inflaming the problem it was intended to solve. In 2000, Paul Scheffer, a Dutch Labour Party academic, wrote an immensely influential essay whose title translates more or less as "The Multicultural Disaster," which argued that progressive policy was producing a generation of immigrants who did not speak Dutch or feel like they were part of Dutch life. Since that time, government policy has emphasized integration and language training. When I visited the Globetrotter School in the vast immigrant quarter of South Rotterdam, I saw printed reminders to the elementary students posted on classroom doors: "We speak Dutch in school." The fact that such a sign was necessary in a school whose pupils are virtually all second- or third-generation children of immigrants was striking. The principal told me that, cognitively, students arrive in school one to one and a half years behind the average Dutch child.

When the Dutch went to the polls in April 2017, the center did, indeed, hold. The eccentric and isolated Wilders had stopped campaigning after uncovering a "mole" in his security staff, a Moroccan who had allegedly leaked his otherwise-secret campaign schedule to a criminal organization. The kind of florid paranoia that appeals to bitter Polish voters mortifies the stolid Dutch. In the end, Rutte's VVD placed first while the PVV finished a distant second, virtually tied with the Christian Democrats and the moderately right-of-center D66. The big story was the utter collapse of the Labour Party, which fell from 38 seats to 8 in the 150-seat Parliament. In France's presidential election the following month, the Socialists, who had won in 2012, would suffer a similarly shocking collapse, finishing in fifth place with 6 percent of the vote. Between the disintegration of the industrial economy and the resulting loss of faith in governing elites, the demographic base of Europe's working-class parties had evaporated. These voters defected either to the far-left socialists or to one of the anti-immigrant parties. For many, class identity had given way to cultural identity—just as it had in the United States.

Europe has no single answer to the problem of integration. The French insist that all newcomers assimilate to French republican ideas, above all the secular code known as *laïcité*. The British practice something more like multiculturalism. The Dutch are somewhere in between. None of these approaches can be said to have succeeded. The United States offers the model of hyphenated identity, in which newcomers' food and clothing and folklore are publicly celebrated while all are expected to adhere to core American values. But the United States has almost no lumpen Muslim population. Most members of the faith are well educated and middle class, and in any case they are spread thinly across a vast continent. The problem of Islam in Europe more closely resembles the problem of race in America, with the difference that African Americans have no collective loyalty that pulls them away from American-ness. Like race in the American context, Islam in Europe has been a rallying issue for the right while steadily eating away at the foundations of the liberal center.

REFUGEES

In the first days of September 2015, I attended a conference on global governance in Salzburg, the ancient, charming, prosperous, and deeply cultured birthplace of Mozart. This was precisely the moment when the flow of refugees from war-torn Syria to Europe began to turn into a flood. Impelled by the majestic sense of self-importance of the policy elite, we conferees put aside our work to draft an urgent statement of principles on the refugee crisis. One among our number, Yoram Dinstein, an Israeli scholar of international law, declined to go along with our demand that Europe organize itself to accommodate the refugees. He had read, as had we all, that Norbert Hofer, the young and charismatic leader of Austria's far-right Freedom Party, was rising in the polls for Austria's upcoming presidential election. Here, in the beautiful heart of Europe, European-ness itself was threatened. The refugee crisis constituted a stupendous gift to Hofer's candidacy. Dinstein said, "If the price of taking the refugees is bringing fascists to power, I hope they turn the refugees back."

Fascists are not in power in today's Europe. But the illiberal and increasingly authoritarian leaders of Hungary, Poland, and Italy have exploited fear of the refugees to strengthen their hold over the public. And far-right parties across Europe, which until 2015 had attracted modest numbers of supporters to their anti-Brussels, anti-globalization platform, have seized on the refugee issue to pose serious challenges to ruling coalitions. In Germany, where shame over the Nazi past kept racist and xenophobic parties at the very fringe of politics, the Alternative for Germany, which describes immigrants and refugees as a threat to German values, won 12.6 percent of the vote in elections in the fall of 2017 to become the country's third-largest party. In most of Western Europe, unlike the East, faith in liberal democratic values and horror at the authoritarian past have relegated the nationalists to the second tier—but just barely. In the Austrian presidential election, Hofer finished in a tie with a candidate from the Green Party; he later lost in a runoff.

The imagery of an unstemmed tide of asylum seekers and their arrival at European borders played on a vast range of feelings that until that moment had festered, but quietly, across Europe—fear of immigrants, of Islam, of a loss of sovereign control; anger at an EU considered both incompetent and overbearing. Some of these feelings were solidly grounded in reality and some were not; collectively, they constituted an unprecedented challenge to liberal democracy in Europe.

If Europe has a political center, it would be the rue de la Loi—the Street of Law—in Brussels, which is lined on both sides with the major institutions of the European Union. Though first established as a free-trading community of half a dozen nations, the EU has evolved over time into a pan-European government and the guardian of the principles of liberal democracy upon which postwar Europe was built. According to the 2007 Treaty of Lisbon, which formally established the EU, "The Union is founded on the values of respect for human dignity, freedom, democracy, equality, the rule of law and respect for human rights, including the rights of persons belonging to minorities. These values are common to the Member States in a society in which pluralism, non-discrimination, tolerance, justice, solidarity and equality between women and men prevail." That is what is meant by a Europe of law.

The European Commission, the EU's secretariat, is responsible for devising the vast range of policies by which the Europe of law conducts itself. In 2014, officials working under EU commissioner Frans Timmermans, the former foreign minister of Holland, began studying what Europe could do if the 2 million–plus refugees from Syria then sheltering in neighboring countries began coming to Europe in large numbers. In May 2015, Timmermans issued a report, *A European Agenda on Migration*, which, among other things, called on member states to triple the EU budget for naval operations to save refugees at sea, target smuggler networks, and strengthen the capacity of Greece and Italy, the chief ports of entry, to deal with mass migration. More controversially, it proposed a "mandatory and automatically triggered relocation system" to share the burden of caring for refugees across Europe in the face of an emergency. Europe was then preoccupied with the crisis precipitated when Greece threatened to leave the eurozone, and political leaders showed zero interest in addressing what seemed like a remote problem. Timmermans and his colleagues were like scientists warning about climate change before any icebergs had melted. "It ain't rocket science," as Timmermans said to me when I spoke with him in the spring of 2016. "To analyze the problem is not that difficult, and to also point to solutions isn't even that difficult. The difficulty is to get member states to come together on those solutions."

Among the universal principles to which all EU states are formally pledged is the obligation to accept refugees who reach their borders; the doctrine, rendered sacred by the terrible suffering of fleeing and expelled populations during and immediately after World War II, is enshrined in the 1951 Convention Relating to the Status of Refugees. The EU had a role in coordinating security and humanitarian response to flows of refuge seekers and administered interstate rules, such as the so-called Dublin rule, which dictates that the state refugees reach first must take responsibility for their safety. Otherwise, however, states set their own standards for accepting and caring for refugees. Timmermans was, in effect, asking states to act collectively on an issue they viewed as reserved to their own sovereign powers.

His failure, in turn, speaks to the larger paradox of the EU. Even before the refugee crisis began, anger at the usurpation of sovereignty by bureaucrats in Brussels had propelled voters to join nationalist parties and movements in much of Europe; Alternative for Germany, the party that has surged to popularity on an anti-immigrant platform, got its start by bashing Brussels. When British prime minister David Cameron made the epic mistake in 2013 of promising British voters a referendum on membership in the EU, he assumed, as did elites generally, that voters, whatever their sense of pique, would vote to maintain a relationship that had plainly brought economic benefits. But conservatives and nationalists used Brussels as the scapegoat for voter anger on immigration, on deindustrialization, on loss of national prestige, and succeeded in winning a vote on "Brexit" in 2016. The British voted with their spleens rather than their pocketbooks.

The EU is not an institution guided by democratic accountability; acutely aware of the dangers of fascist populism, Europe's leaders took care to safeguard liberal principles from anti-liberal majorities. The EU parliament is weak, while its executive and regulatory bodies are strong. That has made the EU a fat target for nationalist parties. The Dutch scholar Cas Mudde has argued that illiberal democracy is a response to the "undemocratic liberalism" of technocratic bodies like the EU. Yet the EU has little substantive authority on many issues that deeply affect the sovereignty of its members. Even during the eurozone crisis, when Brussels seemed to be dictating policy to Greece, the real decision-maker was Angela Merkel, the chancellor of Germany, whose economy is by far the largest in Europe.[8]

The problem that the refugee crisis of 2015–2016 exposed was not too much EU but too little. Every European nation reacted to the vast human flood according to its own situation and its own principles. Hungary turned water hoses and police dogs on the refugees, even though all they wanted to do was transit through on their path westward. Italy and Greece, which would have been hopelessly overwhelmed had they acted according to the dictates of the Dublin rule, waved the refugees onward without so much as registering them. Denmark made them feel as unwelcome as possible. England took shelter behind the Channel. And two countries—Germany and Sweden—accepted the obligation to welcome everyone who reached their border. *"Wir schaffen das"*—"We can do this"—Merkel famously reassured her people. She did not need to stipulate her true meaning, which was, "We *must* do this." Germany had sent 40 million Europeans fleeing for their lives. Now it could make amends and demonstrate its fidelity to the principles of Europe by welcoming the newcomers.

The EU made what turned out to be a hopeless stab at governing the response. Jean-Claude Juncker, the president of the European Commission, picked up on Timmermans's proposal for mandatory shared relocation. He proposed that the member states agree to take 160,000 of the refugees massed at Europe's borders, suggesting a quota system based on population and wealth. The four Central and Eastern European countries refused to endorse the measure. Both Viktor Orbán and Jarosław Kaczyński—then in the midst of his election campaign—brandished their opposition as proof of their refusal to kowtow to the distant emperor in Brussels. In the end, all parties ignored the pledge they had made; an apparently endless supply of refugees continued to flow through Turkey to the Balkans or Greece, and then on to northern and western Europe. For all its much-mocked status as guardian of elite values, the EU failed utterly to protect those principles against political majorities.

Germany and Sweden became the victims of their lonely commitment to international law and humanitarian principle. I happened to be in Sweden in November 2015, when the country ran out of space for refugees. I was in Malmo, the southern port city through which most refugees arrived by boat or train from Denmark. When the refugee tide had begun in early summer, Sweden had received about 1,500 people a week. By August, that number had doubled. In September, it doubled again. In October, it hit 10,000 a week, and it stayed there even as the weather grew colder. A nation of 9.5 million, Sweden expected to take as many as 190,000 refugees, or 2 percent of the population—double the per capita figure projected even by Germany. At the office of the Swedish Migration Agency at the far edge of Malmo, hundreds of refugees, who had been bused in from the train station, were queued up outside in the chill to be registered or sat inside waiting to be assigned a place for the night. Two rows of white tents had been set up in the parking lot to house those for whom no other shelter could be found. Hundreds of refugees had been put in hotels a short walk down the highway, and still more in an auditorium near the station.[9]

I asked Karima Abou-Gabal, an agency official responsible for the orderly flow of people in and out of Malmo, where the new refugees would go. "As of now," she said wearily, "we have no accommodation. We have nothing." The private placement agencies with whom the migration agency contracted all over the country could not offer so much as a bed. In Malmo itself, the tents were full. So, too, were the auditorium and hotels. Sweden had, at that very moment, reached the limits of its absorptive capacity. That evening, a senior migration official said to me, "Today we had to regretfully inform forty people that we could not find space for them in Sweden." The nation had reached its limit—physically, morally, politically.

Sweden had thrown open its doors not out of guilt, like Germany, but rather in the faith that nations, like people, must act according to their professed principles. Accepting refugees was one of the things that made Sweden Sweden. During World War II, the country had taken in the Jews of Denmark, saving much of the population. In recent decades the Swedes had embraced Iranians fleeing from the shah, Chileans fleeing from General Augusto Pinochet, and Eritreans fleeing forced conscription. Perhaps because they have been spared most of the barbarities to which Europe subjected itself over the previous century, the Swedes are a remarkably idealistic people. No one had to proclaim "*Wir schaffen das*"; the Swedes took the job for granted. Ordinary Swedes pitched in. Solicitous volunteers waited to help asylum seekers at the central train station in Stockholm, even though virtually all refugees were being processed in Malmo—where the Red Cross operated a far larger setup behind the train station. Everyone seemed calm, cheerful, organized. When I worried out loud that the country was racing off a cliff, I was reassured that Sweden had done this before and that it would do it again. It was a given that Sweden benefited from its commitment to providing shelter to those in need.

Aron Etzler, secretary general of the Left Party—formerly the Communist Party—told me that refugees "helped us build the Sweden we wanted." He meant both that refugees had become good Swedes and that the social democratic model was unthinkable without the commitment to accepting them. But wouldn't the job of integrating a vast influx of Syrians and Iraqis and Afghans be harder, more disruptive, and more expensive than it had been with a far smaller number of Iranians and Kurds? "A strong state can take care of many things," Etzler reassured me.

The Swedes did not talk about the non-Swedes the way the Dutch talked about the non-Dutch. Sweden has virtually no labor migration; almost all the outsiders have come as refugees, and thus enjoy a moral status very different from that of a Turkish shopkeeper in Rotterdam. They had earned their place in Swedish society by virtue of prior suffering. But this posed a problem for public debate. As Diana Janse, a former diplomat and now the senior foreign policy adviser to the Moderate Party (which Swedes view as "conservative"), explained to me, "We have this expression in Swedish, *åsiktskorridor*. It means 'opinion corridor'—the views you can't move outside of." Janse pointed out that some recent generations of Swedish refugees, including Somalis, had been notably unsuccessful in joining the job market. How, she wondered, would the ten thousand to twenty thousand young Afghan men who had entered Sweden as unaccompanied minors fare? How would they behave in the virtual absence of young Afghan women? But merely to raise such issues was to risk accusations of racism.

Then there was the problem of cost. Sweden then expected to spend about 7 percent of its $100 billion budget on refugees in 2016. The real number would be somewhat higher, since the costs of educating and training those who had already received asylum were not included in that figure. It was, in any case, double the 2015 budget. Where would the money come from? Many Swedes who depended on the state—in Sweden, that's everyone—feared it would come from them. A border policeman working at the Red Cross station in Malmo told me, "Last summer, my grandmother almost starved to death in the hospital, but the migrants get free food and medical care. I think a government's job is to take care of its own people first, and then, if there's anything left over, you help other people." I had heard the same view a few months earlier in Hungary.

Sweden is one of the world's wealthiest countries and is deeply imbued with Aron Etzler's faith that the welfare state can accomplish anything. But the feeling is not universal; skepticism runs deeper among the (relatively) hard-pressed. A poll released soon before I arrived found that 41 percent of Swedes thought the country was taking too many refugees, up from 29 percent just two months before. Other surveys found that older, less-educated people had more negative views of refugees than younger, better-educated ones. A few extremists had taken matters into their own hands: in October 2015, arsonists had attacked five structures set aside for refugee housing. Swedish authorities had become so jittery that I was not allowed to see any of the facilities for minors in Malmo, lest I give inadvertent clues to the addresses.

The anti-immigrant Sweden Democrats rode a wave of popularity by positioning themselves outside the opinion corridor. When I said to Paula Bieler, a member of the party's parliamentary contingent, that most Swedes seemed to welcome refugees, she shot back, "Mostly the Swedes who haven't met them. It's the top politicians and journalists who live in the center of Stockholm." That's hyperbolic, but it's true that the intelligentsia generally view the refugees as a new contribution to Sweden's tapestry of diversity, while ordinary Swedes are more inclined to worry about the effects on their own lives. The reaction against the refugees had put wind in the party's sails. Like other right-wing parties in Europe, the Sweden Democrats had tried in recent years to move away from their thuggish and quasi-fascist origins while maintaining a hard line on refugees. In the fall of 2015, a group of party members traveled to Lesbos— the Greek island that serves as the main transit point for refugees coming from Turkey—to distribute leaflets contradicting Sweden's welcoming embrace. The leaflets warned that Swedish society would never accept forced marriages and polygamy—transparent code for "Islam"—and that refugees would be housed in tents and then deported.

Costs mattered, but at bottom this was a debate not about money but about identity, as it was in Poland and in Holland. Paula Bieler described herself as a nationalist who feared that an increasingly multicultural Sweden was in danger of "losing the feeling that you live in a society that is also your home." Bieler objected not to immigrants themselves but to the official state ideology of integration, which asked Swedes as well as newcomers to integrate into a world that celebrated diversity and thus cast Sweden as a gorgeous mosaic. Were native Swedes to think of their own extraordinarily stable thousand-year-old culture as simply one among many national identities?

It was the corrosiveness of this question that led the Dutch to switch from multiculturalism to integration. The refugee crisis compelled the question of what it means to be Swedish, just as the immigration debate in Holland forced the heretofore abstruse question of what it means to be Dutch. Bieler was quite right that the Swedish elites cherish diversity as a good in itself, and regard themselves, as do all contemporary elites, as cosmopolitan. Peter Wolodarski, the boy-wonder editor of Sweden's leading newspaper, *Dagens Nyheter* (he was thirty-eight when we met), pointed out that in the 1960s, Sweden and Finland were both homogeneous, but the former had chosen the path of diversity while the latter had not. "This is a tremendous strength of Sweden," he said. "We attract people from all over the world." A leading executive of Spotify had just told him that he was able to attract top talent to Sweden precisely owing to its multicultural nature.

Cosmopolitanism is not a classical liberal virtue. It is distinct from, and more affirmative than, the obligation to tolerate differences of taste, viewpoint, or background, which the first article of the Dutch constitution is designed to protect. What Wolodarski extolled was the principle that one should actively seek out other cultures, beliefs, mores, in order to become a richer person. This is why people move to great cities, or why students at elite American universities take their junior year abroad. But for all the moral importance we attribute to it, cosmopolitanism is a lifestyle choice; people who choose to live in more homogeneous places do not regard it as a universal virtue. Finns may have stayed homogeneous because they like it that way. The idea that Sweden becomes a better place by taking refugees, or that individual Swedes profit by losing some of their Swedish-ness through contact with Bosnians and Syrians, is not going to seem very congenial to people who like Sweden just the way it is—or was. In Sweden—and in Poland and Hungary and the United States—people who view themselves as rooted tend to regard cosmopolitanism as the kind of class marker that separates them from elites. That perceived condescension and the resentment it causes stoke the engines of populism. The Brexit vote pitted cosmopolites—above all, the vast population of metropolitan London—against townsfolk who resented both the urbanites and the newcomers, from both inside and outside the EU, who had thronged to England in recent decades.

Sweden's idealists had also made a serious miscalculation. They had assumed that because 500 million Europeans *could* easily absorb a million or more Middle Eastern refugees, they *would* do so. But "Europe" had not responded; individual European countries had. And even Sweden's Scandinavian neighbors had found means to discourage the newcomers. Sweden had committed an act of unshared idealism. Margot Wallström, the foreign minister, admitted that if the rest of Europe continued to turn its back on the migrants, "in the long run our system will collapse." The long run was much shorter than she had imagined.

By the end of 2015, Sweden had taken in 160,000 refugees—30,000 less than the maximum it had projected. Then it threw in the towel. Henceforth, no one would be permitted to enter the country without proper identity documents. Since many refugees arrived without passports or other valid forms of identification, the new rules sharply curtailed the number of asylum seekers arriving overland who would be permitted to enter the country. Cross-border immigration came to an almost complete stop. Sweden accepted only refugees arriving directly from Turkey, Lebanon, and Jordan who had been cleared by the UN refugee agency. Even that wasn't the final sign of Sweden's reluctant regression to the European mean, for in January 2016 came the announcement that 80,000 refugees would face deportation. That fall, Afghanistan reached an agreement with the EU to take back refugees who had been denied asylum. The understanding was said to have been a precondition for further aid from the EU. In 2015, EU countries had received 213,000 Afghan refugees; about half of those who'd sought asylum had been turned down. Sweden's own rate dropped from 50 percent in 2015 to 28 percent the following year. In 2016 the Swedish Migration Agency also adopted a system of bone-density tests used to determine age in order to weed out false claims among Afghans who described themselves as minors. When the Danes had adopted the tests in 2015, the Swedes had declined to do so.

An experience that began as an affirmation of national character ended as a grim effort to ward off catastrophe. Sweden's deputy prime minister, Åsa Romson of the Green Party, burst into tears when she had to announce the change in policy at a televised press conference. The issue was tearing Swedish society apart in a way that an American visitor could instantly recognize from the national debate over race. "This is more of a religious issue than a political issue," said Ivar Arpi, a journalist who had become an opponent of the generous refugee policy. "People have lost friends; families are divided against one another. I have agonizing talks with my mother and little sister." I asked Arpi if he didn't fear that rejecting asylees would violate Swedishness. "Yes," he said, "it would strike to the very core of our identity. But we have forced ourselves into a corner."

Indeed, Europe had forced itself into a corner. By the fall of 2015, European publics had largely come to see the refugees not as a tug on conscience but as a threat to borders, sovereignty, public safety, budgets, and the liberal center. EU leaders began talking to Turkey about blocking the flow of refugees. In February 2016, the EU authorized Macedonia to close its borders with Greece, thus leaving refugees bottled up in the Balkans. The following month, Angela Merkel, under attack even from within her own party for the policy of "We can do it," worked with Frans Timmermans and other senior EU officials to negotiate a pact with

Turkey, which agreed to prevent refugees from crossing to Greece in exchange for up to 6 billion euros in aid to care for the refuge seekers.

The deal was fiercely denounced by human rights organizations. The NGO Médecins Sans Frontières announced that it would no longer accept funding from the EU. Timmermans said his conversations with pro-refugee activists always seemed to go the same way. "If you don't like our policies," he would say, "what do you think we should do?"

"Let the people in. Bring them to Europe."

"What country is going to support that?"

"Well, it's the right thing to do."

But what about the political consequences of doing the right thing? Were the leaders of sovereign states supposed to turn on the very concept of sovereignty? Timmermans is a bureaucrat with a former politician's habits. Poring over constituency-level voting patterns in the aftermath of the Brexit vote in June 2016, he came to understand a dark reality: the politics of migration had become so toxic that even figures like Merkel could no longer afford to do what they considered the right thing. Because European leaders had failed to act collectively when they had the chance, they left themselves with no choice but to convert Turkey into a giant sink for refugees.

The dire prediction of Yoram Dinstein, who had suggested that Europe might have to choose between closing its borders to Muslim refugees and watching the rise of nativist political leaders, may yet be proved right. In the summer of 2018, Hubert Védrine, the former French foreign minister and a Socialist, observed that if Europe cannot control the flow of immigrants, "our democracy is at risk, and we will have populism or a form of European Trumpism, country by country." Védrine issued this observation at a conference at the Château de Tocqueville, where Tocqueville wrote the second volume of *Democracy in America*. One may regard this coincidence as a grotesque irony, signifying the collapse of liberal values among Europe's own liberal leaders. Or one may conclude that the refugee crisis posed a test that liberalism was not built to withstand.[10]

Liberalism is built on social trust, which in turn requires a sense of kinship or shared values. Liberal polities can be built from diverse societies because the process of integration turns outsiders into insiders—"them" into "us." That has been, preeminently, the experience of the United States, a society with no true insiders (save Native Americans, who were systematically dispossessed by new arrivals). That has not been the experience of Europe, where many national cultures are founded on immemorial ties of language and tradition. The fact that so many refugees arrived in so short a span of time hugely exacerbated the problem of integration. That torrent posed a threat not only to the existing culture but to the security of borders, and thus to the foundations of sovereignty. As refugees rather than immigrants, the newcomers were seen as a moral obligation—a burden—rather than an economic boon. Finally, it is not at all clear that pious Syrians can become progressive Swedes or that Moroccans can become Dutch in the same way that rustic Sicilians became urbanized New Yorkers, at least not for a very long time. If that is true, Europe's progressive leaders are asking for more social trust than citizens are currently prepared to offer. The refugees and immigrants, as Geert Wilders understands very well, seem to invite liberals into a suicide pact in which they are asked to demonstrate their commitment to tolerance by tolerating illiberalism.

That is a dire forecast, but hardly an implausible one. If Europe is not to fall to "Trumpism," as Védrine put it, nations will have to act collectively to regulate and limit the flow of immigrants and refugees, and they will have to make an immense effort—as Germany is now doing—to provide education, language training, job training, and jobs to the newcomers in their midst. They will have to build bridges between the pious and the secular, the traditional and the progressive. That is the work of a generation.

CHAPTER NINE

The Populist Plutocrat

The only important thing is the unification of the people—
because the other people don't mean anything.

—DONALD TRUMP

I KNEW DONALD TRUMP—OR RATHER, I THOUGHT I DID. IN 2004 I spent weeks following Trump around in order to write a profile of him for the *New York Times Magazine*. The lies he told were so transparent that they could be almost effortlessly exposed. He said that he had owned half of the ground lease of the Empire State Building and sold it for $57.5 million. In fact, he had simply gotten paid off for withdrawing a lawsuit over the ownership. As soon as I confronted him, Trump cheerfully admitted the truth but said he had still walked away with a nice piece of change. He preened like a teen idol in front of the construction workers at his building sites—and they roared their approval. "Hey, fellas, this guy's writing for the *New York Times Magazine*. If he writes badly, will you kick the shit out of him?" It seemed funny at the time. Everything about Trump in the age of *The Apprentice* seemed ludicrous rather than menacing, including the way he imitated a Bond villain on the show. "The only thing missing is the trap door into the shark pool," I joked. In fact, Trump reminded me less of Ernst Blofeld than of a balloon in the Thanksgiving Day parade—huge and gaudy and slightly dangerous, but filled with hot air.[1]

Yet Trump really did inspire mass adoration. I described him as "a populist plutocrat" and speculated that his fans loved him, first, because he spent his money on exactly the toys they fantasized about acquiring if they had his dough—planes, helicopters, palaces, hot babes—and, second, because he held status distinctions in contempt. He assumed that the people who looked down on him really looked up to him but couldn't bear to admit the truth. He despised everyone who professed to despise him. It didn't occur to me at the time that this might qualify him for politics. Besides, Trump so hated human contact that he had to spritz himself with sanitizer after shaking hands.

I called Trump a populist, but I didn't fully appreciate his dark populist gifts—his feel for a crowd, his intuitive sense of what the crowd wanted to hear, his ability to formulate the crowd's grievance in its most elemental form. "We don't have victories anymore," he shouted when he announced his presidential bid in Trump Tower in June 2015. "We used to have victories, but we don't have them. When was the last time anybody saw us beating, say, China in a trade deal? . . . When did we beat Japan at anything? . . . The US has become a dumping ground for everybody else's problems." Even Trump's most bellicose rivals could not, or did not think to, produce anything so violent as this hailstorm of rancor. In *his* announcement speech, Republican senator Ted Cruz of Texas, Trump's obvious rival for the votes of the unappeasably resentful, told his "story," with loving tributes to parents and spouse, while invoking God, the Constitution, Thomas Jefferson, Patrick Henry, and the American Dream. Trump also mentioned the American Dream, but only to say that it was "dead." Cruz gave a Barry Goldwater speech, but Trump gave a George Wallace speech.[2]

Donald Trump changed the United States—and the world—by winning the presidency. But Trump *revealed* the United States by defeating sixteen other candidates to win the GOP nomination. The fact that Trump systematically dispatched challengers representing every possible shade of opinion and almost every possible degree of conservatism, as that word had traditionally been understood, spoke volumes about the state of mind of the one-half of the country that votes Republican. As with British voters who had endorsed Brexit, or French or German voters who the following year would abandon parties of the center-right or center-left to support nationalist extremists, something had happened to cause Republicans to embrace a candidate who poured scorn on the language and the values of liberal democracy.

We will come later to the question of just what that something was. First, however, is the matter of Trump's appeal. How did he change the understood rules of political discourse? That maiden speech offers Trump's tactics in embryo. First, he spoke to fear rather than hope. "The US has become a dumping ground." The gross domestic product is "below zero." "We're dying. We're dying." Second, the target he identified was not bad ideas but bad people—Democrats, Republican officeholders, foreigners. "The politicians" are "controlled fully by the lobbyists." "How stupid are our leaders?" "China has our jobs and Mexico has our jobs." And third, he said that only a strong man could cut down such enemies at home and abroad—and that man was himself. Trump described a kind of daydream in which "the head of Ford, who I know," moves a factory to Mexico, President Trump responds with a 35 percent tariff on the resulting imports, Mr. Ford calls "within an hour" to say "please, please, please" reverse the policy, President Trump says, "Sorry, fellas," because he doesn't need their money—and Ford, presumably, caves.

None of the other candidates in either party talked that way. Bernie Sanders, it is true, blamed the problems of the economy on Wall Street, but so, too, had FDR. Sanders did not try to terrify his listeners, did not denigrate politics as such, did not fabricate statistics, and did not offer himself as personal savior. Sanders was not, in short, a populist, as Trump was. Ted Cruz deployed the Manichaean language of conservative evangelicals and the imagery of civilizational war pioneered by Newt Gingrich, but, ever proud of his degrees from Princeton and Harvard, he was more inclined to talk down to his audience than to bellow at them. He formulated issues as issues, not as street fights. Trump made the belligerent Cruz sound almost tame.

What does it mean to say that Trump is a populist? The term does not indicate any fixed spot on the ideological spectrum. Huey Long, the former Democratic governor of Louisiana, who was assassinated in 1935, had planned to challenge FDR from the left. Argentina's Juan Perón and

Venezuela's Hugo Chávez were statists. Both Viktor Orbán and Jarosław Kaczyński promised to protect citizens against the depredations of the marketplace. What all have in common is that they pitted the people, their followers, against an "anti-people," a group conniving, usually in secret, to destroy the true interests of the people. So Joe McCarthy inveighed against the hidden Communists in the State Department and George Wallace against "pointy-headed liberals." For the populist, politics does not pit interests against one another but rather pits real interests against false ones. The "core claim of populism," as political scientist Jan-Werner Müller put it, is that "only some of the people are really the people." Müller cited a line from a Trump campaign speech that the candidate seems to have lifted, albeit in garbled form, from a populist manual: "The only important thing is the unification of the people—because the other people don't mean anything."[3]

If those who disagree with you are enemies of society, they cannot be allowed to use democratic instruments, whether the ballot or the press, on equal terms with "the people." That's why senior Republicans felt fully justified in preventing Barack Obama from nominating a Supreme Court justice in early 2016, and why state-level legislators felt justified in mounting a putsch against judges who defied their will. Democracy is thus reduced to the mechanisms of forging majorities and then imposing their will on the minority—the nightmare of liberalism from the time of Benjamin Constant. Donald Trump really was different from the sixteen men and women he defeated, even if they, too, were heirs of a generation of Republican absolutism. When President Trump talks about "the deep state" or "fake news," he means to convey the idea that opposition to his policies arises not from principled disagreement but from a conspiracy of elite forces bent on subverting the will of the people.

Trump does not avail himself of the language of illiberal democracy; abstract categories of any kind, including ideological ones, are utterly foreign to him. But from the moment he entered the race, he stood apart from his rivals in refusing to bow before the graven images of Republican right-liberalism, whether on free markets, free trade, or immigration. Trump opposed them all, and he opposed them more vociferously than did any of the other candidates. Trump seems to have understood, as figures like Jeb Bush did not, that the Reagan-era language of "opportunity," and thus of individual choice, no longer resonated with the Republican base. Trump offered not liberty but protection—walls against Mexican "rapists," tariffs against Chinese manufacturers, the cudgel of the state against industrialists planning to move factories abroad.

Liberalism depends on an expectation of progress; it is founded on shared hopefulness. The American, as Arthur Schlesinger Jr. wrote in the early 1950s, "sees few problems which cannot be solved by reason and debate; and he is confident that nearly all problems can be solved." That is why, Schlesinger went on, liberalism in America was the party of the future, and conservatism the party of the past. This continued to be the case even as America's future came to look far less rosy than it had in the years immediately after World War II. Candidates who sought to exploit the fear of racial, economic, or cultural failure—George Wallace, Ross Perot, Pat Buchanan—never won a major-party nomination. Ronald Reagan stole the liberal's thunder when he forged a market-oriented version of the national creed of optimism.[4]

Trump's rhetoric of protection, by contrast, assumes threat. In a telling exchange during the first Republican debate, in August 2015, the mild-mannered Jeb Bush took on Trump's ugly invective, saying, "We're not going on win by . . . dividing the country—saying, creating a grievance kind of environment. We're going to win when we unite people with a hopeful, optimistic message." Trump shot back, "But when you have people that are cutting Christians' heads off, when you have a world that the border and at so many places, that it is medieval times, we've never—it almost has to be as bad as it ever was in terms of the violence and the horror, we don't have time for tone." In a later speech, Trump ridiculed Bush's call for politesse, saying, "We're tired of these weak, pathetic, sad people that don't have a clue." We don't have time for tone.[5]

The invocation of the bogey of political correctness allows the populist leader to recast even the most extreme ideas as harsh truths that "everyone" knows but that genteel elites or "weak, pathetic" leaders refuse to speak out loud. When Jarosław Kaczyński tells voters that refugees carry infectious diseases or that liberals are plotting with Brussels to secularize Poland, he licenses their own dire intimations. The underlying motif is always, "They tell you that it's light, but it's dark." A typical Trump speech offers a litany of such allegedly suppressed truths. They—the government, "the politicians," the experts—tell you that the unemployment rate is 5 percent, but "the number's probably 32 percent—maybe 42 percent." Mexico is sending us their worst people. China's eating our lunch.

An effective populist intuits the forces by which his followers feel marginalized and then incarnates them as enemies. The enemy must be powerful enough to thwart the will of the people, and its confabulations should be veiled beneath a benevolent or at least neutral surface, like the Communists whom Joe McCarthy found disguised by a diplomat's pin-striped suit. Those forces "above" in turn recruit clients "below": thus George Wallace's campaign against both black welfare recipients and the liberal elites who championed their cause against the interests of "the average man on the street." Europe's nationalist leaders thundered against secular elites in Brussels and at home—and against the immigrants and refugees who poured across borders in response to an invitation from the elites.

Trump addressed the same audience Wallace had: middle-class and working-class whites who felt frustrated by economic stagnation and feared that liberal policies were putting others in front of them in line. Unlike Wallace, Trump had an international cast of threats from below on which to draw, including Mexican immigrants, Syrian refugees, and ISIS terrorists, all of whom Trump portrayed in apocalyptic terms. And what powerful actors had unleashed these demonic forces? Barack Obama and Hillary Clinton, of course. But, especially during the primary campaign, the conspiracy Trump identified was bipartisan. The nation had been led to ruin by the leadership class of both parties, "controlled fully by the lobbyists, by the donors, and by the special interests." Republicans since Reagan had turned a fire hose of contempt on Washington; Trump understood that his voters wanted to see the Republican as well as the Democratic politicians get drenched.[6]

From the outset, Trump targeted one particular elite group that provoked his followers to a white-hot fury: the media. Republicans since Richard Nixon had stigmatized the "liberal media" as an elite hostile to the interests of ordinary Americans. Newt Gingrich had honed the attack into a science. But Trump's assault was both more primal and more metaphysical. Spiro Agnew had mocked the press as "nattering nabobs of negativism"; Trump called them "dirty rotten liars." The gap between those two labels reflected not only the catastrophic decline in the assumed educational level of the American political audience but also the rise of the conceit that journalists do not simply hold liberal views but routinely fabricate the truth in order to vindicate those views. Trump attacked the media not simply as an elite profession that looked down on ordinary Americans, but as an organized vanguard propagating falsehoods on behalf of unnamed powers—"the enemy of the American people." This onslaught, utterly at variance with Trump's long career of currying favor with reporters, served a crucial defensive purpose, for the campaign depended on the propagation of lies that reporters kept menacing by their resort to facts. Trump had to maintain the narrative that he was shattering the icons of political correctness rather than inventing things out of whole cloth. The media thus needed to be unseated from its self-appointed role as guardian of the neutral empire of fact.

It wasn't until he became president that Trump recognized that he could seize hold of the vogue expression "fake news" in order to reverse its meaning—in order, in fact, to drain it of any meaning that could be harmful to him. Journalists had coined the term to describe the specious narratives that circulated on the fringes of right-wing media and social media, and to which Trump, far more than any of his Republican rivals, had given credence. Rather than trying to discredit the claim by demonstrating the truthfulness of his more outlandish assertions, Trump began to use "fake news" to describe any claim critical of his own veracity, including, above all, the claim that he was peddling fake news. Whether one should ascribe this tactic to a perverse genius for controlling the political narrative or to something more like animal instinct, the effect was to undermine all truth claims and reduce legitimate disputes over accuracy to an unresolvable duel of self-interested assertions.

It is quite possible that the most lasting damage Donald Trump will do—unless he manages to provoke a major war—will be to poison the cognitive or epistemological foundations of liberalism. The liberal faith in free speech presupposes a baseline rationality, so that more speech, and more untrammeled speech, enables the collective search for truth. Mill proposed a sort of ethics of truth seeking, obliging each of us not only to protect the speech rights of those with whom we disagree but to test our own point of view against the strongest version of rival claims. The free-speech argument rests on a doctrine of intellectual humility: we need to remain open to the possibility that we are wrong and our rival is right. Mill, of course, was addressing "society." He could not have anticipated the totalitarian era in which states would seek to gain control over the truth. It was left to the generation of Berlin, Popper, and Orwell to assert that only an unswerving commitment to reason could defend society from unscrupulous leaders prepared to exploit the beast in man.

It is not authoritarianism but populism that constitutes America's native threat to the freedom of speech and thought. Populism virtually requires a conspiratorial cast of mind, since the populist asserts that dark forces are foiling the will of the people. Perhaps Americans are culturally predisposed to fits of irrationality. In his 2017 book *Fantasyland: How America Went Haywire*, the essayist and novelist Kurt Andersen traced the national history of conspiratorial thinking back to witch burning and thence to New Age cults. But our darkest moments have come when political leaders have seized on those suspicions. The historian Richard Hofstadter, a scholar of the populist movement, described how deeply conspiratorial thinking had shaped political culture in his famous 1964 essay, "The Paranoid Style in American Politics." The immediate inspiration for the book was the extremist sentiment whipped up by Barry Goldwater, which Hofstadter saw as a reenactment of the populist moment. The cognitive bubble built by Newt Gingrich and his allies among evangelical conservatives has made paranoia a largely right-wing phenomenon in the United States. The left may have loathed George W. Bush, but few thought that he had rigged the 2000 election or that he would refuse to step down after two terms—much less that he had masterminded a murder ring or was the spawn of Satan, as right-wing leaders claimed about Bill and Hillary Clinton, respectively.

American politics have been immune to totalitarianism, but hardly to totalitarian habits of thought. Donald Trump didn't invent the politics of irrationality; rather, he imported it from the margins of American political life to the mainstream. Trump occupied, in effect, the opposite end of the epistemological spectrum from the evangelicals. Rather than insisting upon the absolute and invariable nature of truth, he undermined the very idea of truth by eliminating from it the criterion of factuality. If stupid or corrupt leaders were lying about the depth of America's economic problems, then it was truer to say that the unemployment rate was 32 percent than that it was 5.3 percent. If Americans were angry about immigration, then the truth was that Mexico was sending rapists—even if it wasn't. Truth had to do with how you felt, not with correspondence to a realm of facts outside yourself. For Trump himself, truth was whatever advanced his interests, while "fake news" was information adverse to his interests. He seemed to believe that the strong man creates his own reality rather than submit to a publicly accepted one. Perhaps that partly explains his deep admiration for Vladimir Putin, a leader who has mastered the dark art of reshaping reality.

It was above all in this sense that Trump differed from predecessors like Newt Gingrich, whose cynical linguistic code—Republicans "challenge" the status quo while Democrats "betray" the voters—was designed to tip the scales, or to reframe the truth, in a contest of persuasion. Trump did not recognize the scales. He emptied language of agreed meanings; persuasion, for him, meant operating beneath the level of reason, where fear and anger fester. Trump's language was stunningly impoverished; he typically used the vocabulary of a nine-year-old. But even this does not fully express the difference between Trump and those who came before. Words were not his sole, or maybe even chief, medium. Trump tended with exquisite care to what Max Weber would have called his charismatic aura—a matter of imagery rather than language. His campaign appearances had an elaborate aesthetic, one that seemed to draw equally on the orchestrations of Nazi propagandist Leni Riefenstahl and the Super Bowl halftime show. Trump dropped down out of the sky in his personal helicopter, or his personal plane, while the thousands gathered below gaped in wonder.

The bombastic atmosphere of the Trump rally was designed to raise the candidate far above the level of the democratic citizen. So, perhaps, do most mass political spectacles. But democratic candidates, and above all populist ones, typically balance awe with intimacy, superiority with equality. The populist stands with the crowd against the elite. ("I'm a fish in the ocean," India's Narendra Modi used to declare when he was running against Rahul Gandhi, scion of India's foremost political family. "He's a fish in the aquarium.") Yet Trump remained far above his audience. He barely bothered to talk about them. He talked about himself—about the deals he had made, the celebrities he knew, the corporate titans who kowtowed to him. "I know so much from *The Apprentice*. Boy, was I the greatest of all ratings? Was I the greatest? You know I have a big chunk of *The Apprentice*. I get a lot of the profits from *The Apprentice*." Trump offered awe unalloyed by the pretense of equality. This was the bizarre twist on populism I had glimpsed in 2004: Trump offered his followers a kind of privileged access to the plutocratic sphere, a ticket to the skybox. He mixed up a cocktail of resentment and envy that proved intoxicating.

Is Donald Trump a democratic figure? If democracy refers to a political system that ascribes sovereignty to individual citizens and allocates power through elections, then we should grant that Trump, and Jarosław Kaczyński and Viktor Orbán, are indeed democrats. After all, they gained power fair and square. Some of them fiddled with electoral mechanisms, but the breadth of their appeal cannot be wished away. They won because they expressed the majority will, or something very close to it. For this reason, political scientist Yascha Mounk argues that "populism is both democratic and illiberal"; that is, "it both seeks to express the frustration of the people and to undermine liberal institutions." What is happening, Mounk says, is that liberalism and democracy are coming apart. Put otherwise, liberal principles are increasingly losing their mass support. The fact that Viktor Orbán thinks so, too, does not make the diagnosis wrong.[7]

CHAPTER TEN

Why Did One-Half of America Choose Illiberal Democracy?

W HAT IS THE MAJORITY WILL THAT DONALD TRUMP'S VIC-
tory disclosed? Or, to put it more exactly, since Trump did not
win a majority of the national vote, or anything approaching the vote of
a majority of the American people, why did Republican voters choose the
candidate who held liberal democratic values most deeply in contempt?
Trump is, of course, a very gifted salesman who knows how to exploit the
immense capital of his celebrity. Yet even as singular a figure as Trump
could not have trampled liberal and democratic norms with impunity unless those norms had been profoundly compromised by his predecessors
over the last generation; he stood, as it were, on the shoulders of giants.
Rush Limbaugh and Sarah Palin and a steady diet of Fox News had long
since taught Republican voters to demonize Democrats. Leaders from
the time of Newt Gingrich had inculcated the principle that the goal of
Republican rule justified any and all means. The Tea Party had removed
whatever stigma attached to trafficking in conspiracy theories. Theocrats
had normalized apocalyptic language. Racists—cheered on by Trump
himself—had openly disputed the legitimacy of the first black president.
The norm that Steven Levitsky and Daniel Ziblatt call "mutual toleration" had long since eroded.

The relationship between leaders and voters in a democracy is reciprocal: George Washington, Abraham Lincoln, and FDR addressed Americans in such a way as to raise them to a higher level, thus enabling their own leadership. Over the last generation, by contrast, the Republican leadership class had licensed the worst instincts of its followers, creating a downward spiral in which those leaders had to keep up with the forces they had unleashed by behaving ever more recklessly. Newt Gingrich begat Tom DeLay, a far-right congressman from Texas who served as majority leader until he was indicted for money laundering and conspiracy; DeLay in turn begat hollering xenophobes like Steve King. "The enemy of normal Americans" in the era of Bill Clinton devolved to "You lie!" in the era of Barack Obama. Obama tried to speak to Americans' better angels but found that "better angels" had become an archaism; he wound up fuming about guns and religion. Donald Trump may have ventured where no one before him had dared to go; still, by the time he stood for office, what had once been shocking had become routine.

Liberal norms erode when leaders treat them as obstacles to their ambitions. Yet that is too comforting a story, at least for beleaguered liberals. Illiberal leaders in a democracy need an audience that has come to regard liberal principles as foreign to their own lives. Donald Trump could not have succeeded if he had not spoken to deep feelings. The language of fear defeated the language of hope because so many voters were fearful—and angry and frustrated. Why? The most obvious answer is economic stagnation. The devastating recession of 2008 knocked millions out of work and threatened the livelihoods of still more. Yet the fear and resentment that Donald Trump exploited in 2016 predated that moment. Middle-class incomes had begun to stagnate in the 1970s. Rising inequality meant that the economy could grow without improving the prospects of ordinary Americans. Median income just before the recession was lower than it had been five years earlier. The benefits of growth were going to shareholders and top executives at home and to developing countries abroad.

In *The Retreat of Western Liberalism*, Edward Luce, a veteran correspondent for the *Financial Times*, published a chart, devised by economist

Branko Milanović, that shows the global distribution of growth since 1989. The poorest half of the world's people, which includes the middle class as well as the poor in places like China and India, has enjoyed an average of about 70 percent income growth over the last three decades. The richest tenth, which is to say Western elites, has also enjoyed vertiginous growth. Only those around the eightieth percentile, which is to say Western middle classes, have seen little or no benefit from the forces of globalization. In the three prior decades, as Luce observes, middle-class citizens in the West enjoyed "almost metronomic gains" that doubled their standard of living every generation. Then that growth went elsewhere. "The West's souring mood," Luce notes, "is about the psychology of dashed expectations rather than the decline in material comforts."[1]

The United States, in this respect, is no different from Western Europe. Left-of-center parties in France, Holland, and elsewhere have collapsed because much of their blue-collar base either moved up to the front office or down to the welfare rolls as factories closed up or left for Asia. Many of those dispossessed workers migrated to nationalist parties of the right, as in the United States they migrated to Donald Trump. All of these parties oppose free trade. Their new constituents don't need any persuasion on the subject; as Luce demonstrates, they have good reason to feel victimized by globalization. The same is true with immigration, for newcomers compete in what feels like a zero-sum scramble for the dwindling supply of decent manufacturing jobs. Immigrants and refugees pose, or at least are seen to pose, both an economic and a cultural threat.

But the United States is different from Western European nations in one very important respect: thanks in no small part to the influence of free-market conservatives over the last forty years, the United States offers far less protection for those who fall through the cracks of the economy, or fear they will. Jobless benefits in the United States are both scantier and briefer in duration than they are almost anywhere in northern Europe. Americans who lose their job typically lose their health benefits as well, and health care purchased on the open market is more expensive in the United States than almost anywhere else in the world.

The high cost of a college education means that the son or daughter of an unemployed or underemployed worker cannot go to college without taking out a very large loan. The vocational training and retraining system is a patchwork. For any adult, especially one with children, the loss of a job is a catastrophe, but in the United States the catastrophe is even more dire, and the sense of vulnerability that comes with job insecurity is so much the greater.

This helps explain a paradox. By the time Donald Trump was elected, the American unemployment rate had dropped to 4.5 percent, one of the lowest levels in the West. (The rate in France was approximately double.) The widespread impression that Donald Trump was lifted to the White House by unemployed coal miners and steelworkers is a myth. Both in the primaries and in the general election, only about a third of his supporters had a household income at or below the national median of $50,000. White voters without a college degree earning under the national median—a basic definition of the "white working class"—constituted only a quarter of his voters. Yet economic security, save for the most credentialed, is a thing of the past in the postindustrial economy. Today's insurance claims adjuster knows that he or she could be tomorrow's shelf stocker, at half the income and few of the benefits. The same is true across the West, but the American economy offers fewer job protections and a weaker safety net. The sense of economic insecurity grows even when the economy does.

It was optimism that made the vital center hold together: you might have only graduated from high school, but your kids would go to college; you might live in a cramped ranch house in a subdivision, but your kids would be able to build their own place in a better neighborhood with good schools. Over the last generation, however, the escalator of social mobility has almost stopped working. More than nine in ten Americans born in 1940 could count on a life better than the one their parents knew; for those born in 1980, the figure was one in two. If, in other words, you were thirty-six years old at the time of the 2016 election, you had only an even chance of doing better than your parents had. Average annual economic growth had fallen from 3–4 percent to 2 percent. And those gains were increasingly going to executives, owners, and shareholders—to capital rather than labor.

Middle-income Americans need not look backward in time to their parents' era to see the frustrating glitter of an unattainable prosperity; they can look all around them. Radical inequality may be tolerable when your own prospects are rising, but not when you feel stuck. Populism first took root in America at the end of the nineteenth century, when rapid industrialization allowed capitalists to accumulate massive fortunes while upending the settled patterns of farm life and immiserating millions of factory workers. The top 1 percent earned more than the bottom 50 percent. The progressive income tax flattened out wealth at the top while steady economic growth and a redistribution of wealth from capital to labor increased prosperity at the bottom, underwriting the consensual liberalism of the postwar era. But over the last four decades, capital has won an increasingly large share of income. Today the top 1 percent own half the nation's wealth; as recently as 1989, the figure was 30 percent. In 1980, the top 1 percent earned twenty-seven times the average income of the bottom half; by 2017, they earned eighty-one times as much.

Not only does the path above seem blocked, but a frightening path below now looms. As the economists Anne Case and Angus Deaton have shown, mortality rates among middle-aged non-Hispanic whites have been rising since the beginning of the twenty-first century. Case and Deaton show that mortality rates have continued to drop for American blacks and Hispanics, and for the middle-aged everywhere in the industrialized world; college-educated white Americans have also shown improving figures. But the health of less-educated whites has suffered a drastic reversal. That group is not suffering more from cancer or heart disease but from "deaths of despair"—drug overdoses, alcoholism, suicide. Conservatives like Charles Murray have ascribed this tightening knot of failure to a crisis of values similar to the one Daniel Patrick Moynihan described among impoverished blacks in 1965. Case and Deaton carefully avoid that language but speak instead of the "cumulative disadvantage" that comes of low levels of education, the loss of dependable factory work, the decline of traditional religion, low rates of marriage, and high rates of divorce. The skyrocketing incidence of opioid abuse is a symptom of despair, just as heroin addiction was among the black poor two generations ago.[2]

The fear of economic eclipse exacerbates the fear of racial or demographic eclipse. In the United States, as across the West, the relative ethnic homogeneity of the postwar years has given way to a diversity that threatens white majorities. After a half century of liberal immigration policy, 14 percent of Americans in 2016 had been born abroad, a level last reached in the first decades of the twentieth century—at which point popular pressure led Congress to shut off the spigot of immigration. Owing to a combination of rising immigration and high birth rates among immigrants, on the one hand, and declining birth rates and increasing mortality rates among whites on the other, whites are expected to become a minority in the United States by 2045. Liberals welcome this diversity. They, too, have an identity politics, which they call cosmopolitanism. More rooted, traditionally minded Americans don't share this view, any more than Swedes or Dutch do. Trump polled especially well in suburban and small-town areas that had long been monoethnic and had recently experienced significant, though not massive, immigration. Brexit supporters, similarly, were concentrated not in England's polyglot cities but in the once-all-white towns where Poles or Kurds or Spaniards now staffed the pubs. These are places where ethnic diversity is a fact, but not a value.

In short, the fuse had been lit for a politics of white resentment. But resentment of whom? In the late nineteenth and early twentieth centuries, farmers and factory workers directed their fury at Wall Street—the capitalists who pulled the strings of the new global marketplace. The millions of voters, young people above all, who flocked to the campaign of Bernie Sanders, shocking most political analysts—not to mention the campaign of Hillary Clinton—shared that fury at the fat cat. A 2016 poll found that only 42 percent of Americans eighteen to twenty-nine years of age support capitalism, while 33 percent prefer socialism. The vital center is plainly giving way not only to the right but to the left, as it has not since the 1960s. Yet Sanders could not mobilize a majority of Democrats, as Donald Trump, the plutocratic populist, did almost effortlessly with Republicans. Trump harnessed popular anger and turned it against not Wall Street (save fitfully) but liberal elites and their alleged clients—black people, immigrants, refugees, and the bureaucratic conspirators of the "deep state."[3]

Why was Trump more successful than Sanders? In *Strangers in Their Own Land*, anthropologist Arlie Hochschild observes that Louisiana Cajuns, among whom she spent several years starting in 2013, once looked to Huey Long for salvation from their economic woes but then looked to the Tea Party and to Governor Bobby Jindal, a small-government, tax-cutting conservative. Louisiana ranks close to dead last on measures of educational attainment, child well-being, and public health. Why not, then, flock to a new big-government populist promising a chicken in every pot? When Hochschild put this question to Bob Hardey, a small-town mayor, he told her, "I've had enough of *poor me*. I don't like government paying unwed mothers to have a lot of kids, and I don't go for affirmative action." Hardey regarded government as a mechanism of unjust redistribution to undeserving beneficiaries. Like his neighbors, he looked to the private sector as the source of opportunity and advancement. The Louisiana of 1935 didn't offer a lot of good private-sector jobs, but today petrochemical firms line the Gulf Coast.[4]

Hochschild has a deeper point to make. She notes that in his 2004 book, *What's the Matter with Kansas?*, Thomas Frank claimed that Republicans had hoodwinked working-class voters into buying free-market economic policies that harmed their interests by seducing them with cultural issues such as abortion, school prayer, and gun control. As an economist, Frank treated economic interests as objective and values as merely personal; by ignoring the former in favor of the latter, his subjects showed signs of what Marxists used to call "false consciousness." But Hochschild considers her subjects' sense of who they are—their values—to be every bit as real as their economic status. If they say they are voting according to who they are, perhaps we should listen more closely to their narrative. Hochschild describes this narrative as the "deep story" that situates them within their own community and the larger world.[5]

Hochschild summarizes the movie that runs in her subjects' heads as follows: "You are patiently standing in a long line leading up a hill, as in a pilgrimage. You are situated in the middle of this line, along with others who are also white, older, Christian, and predominantly male, some with college degrees, and some not. Just over the brow of the hill is the American Dream, the goal of everyone." But the line has stopped moving; you are stuck. A life of stoicism has taught you not to complain. But then "you see *people cutting in line ahead of you*." Like Mayor Hardey, you see black beneficiaries of welfare and affirmative action moving up without having to play by the rules. And not just them—"women, immigrants, refugees, public sector workers." They even have their own president, the biracial Barack Obama. How did *he* rise so high so fast? They've all cut in line ahead of you. "But it's people like *you* who have made this country great. . . . You resent them, and you feel that it's right that you do."[6]

The deep story of small-town Louisiana is not the same as the deep story of, say, suburban Cleveland. But some elements are universal enough to contain lessons worth heeding. One is that values cannot be reduced to bias or prejudice, to be cured by a bracing dose of fact. Values like the stoicism and self-reliance by which Hochschild's subjects set great store are not more ephemeral than material interests. Because their own faith is founded on reason, science, secularism, liberals have trouble understanding values as fundamentally constitutive of the self; their own values, such as cosmopolitanism, strike them as self-evidently good for all and thus as universal goods rather than particularistic values. In fact, cosmopolitanism orients liberals just as rootedness orients Cajuns. They will be attracted to the party that markets itself as the defender of endangered values—even if the marketing campaign is disingenuous.

The relationship between the economy and identity as causal factors of the rise of illiberalism is complicated and reciprocal. If you feel that the horizon of prosperity is receding, you will look for someone to blame. For a brief moment in the 1960s, the Democrats were able to practice a politics of self-sacrifice because America's material bounty rendered the costs bearable: giving more to historically disadvantaged citizens did not mean having less for yourself. That did not last, and perhaps could not have lasted. As white voters came to feel that they were on the wrong end of a zero-sum transaction, they turned against both the Democratic Party and black Americans. Today, the future looks much more grim for the white middle class than it did forty years ago. Most of the reasons why that is so have to do with large historical phenomena rather than with other people. But those forces are hard to grasp and hard to counter. If Fox News and Donald Trump tell you that you're falling behind because liberal beneficiaries are cutting ahead of you in line, you may well seize on that answer.

The fact that this narrative is deeply felt and rests upon a bedrock of traditional values does not, of course, make it true. Louisiana has long since gutted its social services, including welfare. No one is dining out on their meager allotment of food stamps. Louisiana's terrible public health problems, as Hochschild points out, have much to do with the toxic environment produced by the oil and gas firms that benefit from the state's low-tax, low-regulatory climate. Like Thomas Frank's Kansans, Hochschild's Cajuns would be materially better off with different policies and a different kind of state government. But that may not be decisive for them, any more than it was for the supporters of Law and Justice.

And this raises a fundamental question about liberalism and the extent to which liberals may be complicit in their own predicament. Liberals from the time of Mill have sought to shield society from the conforming pressure of social values and thus to protect the sanctity of personal choice. Yet like Tocqueville, Mill feared that a secular and individualistic society would lose the orienting force of a "fixed point" that "men agreed in holding sacred." Liberals have never been able to fully solve this dilemma. Modern liberals have dealt with it by insisting on the universality of their own values, thus reducing the realm of values to a set of unarguable propositions. But that's a delusion. Cosmopolitanism is a value. Sexual freedom is a value. In *Why Liberalism Failed*, Patrick Deneen points out that liberalism has an "anthropology," which is to say, a theory of human nature. Liberals regard humans as autonomous beings, standing apart from their fellow humans and from nature. Liberals believe that the supreme test of the value of a thing is our desire for it.

Many traditions, including the Catholic tradition that shapes Deneen's own view, regard a person's "relational" nature—toward family, community, tradition, faith—as no less precious than his or her autonomy. Deneen argues that the real freedom offered by liberal culture since the nineteenth century is the freedom to gratify appetite and satisfy ambition free from the old constraints, and protections, of custom.[7]

That feels like an overbroad account. After all, the Trump supporters whom Arlie Hochschild spent time with regarded themselves as old-fashioned American individuals, pursuing their individual wishes free from the clutches of the state, and liberals as collectivists, enemies of liberty. If both they and their cultural adversary count as liberals, then we should recognize, as Tocqueville did, or for that matter Arthur Schlesinger or Louis Hartz, that liberal individualism has not been foisted on America by elite philosophers but flourishes naturally in its soil. Both the Cajuns and the liberals they despise would strain at the confines of the organic society, rooted in deference to authority, that Deneen offers as an alternative.

Yet it's also true, as Deneen observes, that the putatively value-free meritocratic culture that liberals have established looks to many nonliberals, including Hochschild's subjects, like a racket. Deneen has coined the word *liberalocracy* to describe the elite beneficiaries of a high-status program of child-rearing and education. It is, Deneen damningly notes, almost as closed a system as aristocracy once was—and much harder to gainsay. Modern liberals, after all, succeed not by virtue of birth but by accruing the kind of merit that comes of attending elite schools and moving on to mandarin professions such as law or banking. And then they pass these advantages on to their children. Deneen sardonically describes this hereditary meritocracy as liberalism's greatest achievement, since a system built on impersonal considerations of "merit" is impervious to attack in the language of liberal individualism. Is it any wonder that the losers stew in their resentment, waiting for the Viktor Orbán or Donald Trump to set their frustrations aflame? Liberalism thus begets illiberalism.

One reason why most liberals failed to see the depth of the populist backlash is that they did not see secular, meritocratic individualism as one of various possible arrangements of society—that is, as a system of values—but rather as the natural order of modern life. In the traditional and often nativist values held by many working-class nonliberals, they saw only a sop for losers in the meritocratic struggle. As Barack Obama put it during the 2008 campaign, "They get bitter, they cling to guns or religion or antipathy to people who aren't like them or anti-immigrant sentiment or anti-trade sentiment as a way to explain their frustrations." That is both true and insufficient. The discomfort with a culture in which goods, people, and ideas freely circulate across the globe, upending old patterns, cannot simply be dismissed as reactionary nostalgia. Liberalism has to find a way of addressing it.[8]

We tend to ascribe the rise of illiberalism in the United States and Europe to either economic or cultural causes, or to the interplay between them. We may argue about who or what is responsible for those factors and thus about how best to address them. But liberalism has depended not only on economic progress and a rough consensus on values but also on what I earlier referred to as cognitive or epistemological conditions—the broad acceptance of a neutral space of fact that makes meaningful political debate possible. In this regard, and above all in the United States, the liberal order has radically eroded. We now have two parallel realities, one for Republicans and one for Democrats. While trust in the media has declined sharply over the last twenty years, the distrust itself has become polarized. A 2018 Ipsos poll found that 68 percent of Democrats, but only 29 percent of Republicans, believe that the press is well intentioned. Almost half of Republicans agree with President Trump that "the news media is the enemy of the American people."[9]

Political polarization now drives cognitive polarization because the extremism of the right depends on an a priori, ideological view of subjects like global warming and immigration, about which a great deal of data and a large body of facts have accumulated. Adherents must repudiate not only specific data but the very idea of data. This is not true, at least not yet, on the other side. Democratic voters not only did not choose a fabricator as their candidate for president; they did not have a fabricator to choose. MSNBC does not present conspiracy theories as fact, as Fox News does. Political professionals have not defected from MSNBC, as they have, in growing numbers, from Fox. Stuart Stevens, who served as chief strategist for Mitt Romney in 2012, told *Politico* that in the 1960s leftist radicals had "railed about government conspiracies and called for violent opposition. They called themselves Weathermen. Now the same is happening, and they call themselves conservative commentators."[10]

The cognitive threat to liberalism may prove to be even more pernicious, and more drug-resistant, so to speak, than the economic or cultural one. Sustained and widespread economic growth could lower the temperature of working-class anger and diminish the appeal of a racialized nationalism, but Americans might still remain locked in their cognitive bubbles. Elements of the left may become as isolated and self-referential as much of the right already is. It is possible to imagine a liberal response to economic and cultural alienation. It is much harder to figure out the liberal response to the unwillingness to listen to facts and reason.

The majoritarian acceptance of liberal restraints has kept America from the cliff's edge of extremism. It was in the crisis of the 1930s that the liberal consensus was born. What if growing numbers of Americans no longer accept those restraints? Timothy Snyder, the Yale historian of totalitarianism, has argued that the United States now finds itself in much the same place as Germany did in 1932—a brittle state, sapped by a spirit of extremism, that might succumb in a crisis to a fascist leader. Many of the contributors to a collection titled *Can It Happen Here?* are convinced that it can, and has already begun to do so. Steven Levitsky and David Ziblatt express similar fears in *How Democracies Die*.[11]

Few Germans in 1932 even imagined fascist rule; few took Hitler seriously. For that very reason, it is tempting fate to say that it can't happen here. But liberal democracy lasted only fourteen years in Germany, and it stood on rotten foundations. Liberal parties were deeply distrustful of democracy, while mass parties repudiated liberalism. If liberalism rests ultimately not on laws and even on constitutions but on norms and expectations, then Germany never had the chance to become liberal.

I do not believe that it is 1932 in the United States, because I do not think either our institutions or our political culture are so deeply compromised. But what if the thing we fear looks more like today's Poland, where opposition newspapers can still publish and opposition legislators still speak in Parliament, but the ruling party increasingly spreads its tentacles over neutral institutions of state? Because democratic mechanisms no longer operate to counteract the ruling party's brazen majoritarianism, opponents must increasingly take to the streets to make their voices heard. If the demonstrations grow large enough, the government may begin to respond with violence, with outcomes one cannot foresee. Could that happen here? Perhaps it could.

But ex-Communist states are not the likely model for an American future. The logic of Donald Trump's plutocratic populism leads elsewhere. Extreme and growing inequality, the increasing political power of the superrich, and the ideology of entitlement among that class had laid the foundations of an oligarchy before Donald Trump won the presidency. Trump made America safe for oligarchy by fusing it with populism. One can imagine a country run in the explicit interests of the rich with the support of cultural conservatives secured through appointments to the courts, social policy, and rhetorical blasts at liberal elites. A compliant Congress eviscerates most public goods. Impromptu vigilante squads rough up the occasional reporter or protester. Immigrants fear for their safety. The poor feel increasingly desperate. Public facilities crumble. America comes increasingly to resemble a Third World plutocracy rather than one of its Western allies. Indeed, Third World plutocracies become its chief allies. This America so closely resembles our own that it requires only a modicum of imagination to conjure it into being.

CHAPTER ELEVEN

A Liberal Nationalism

As I write these words, in the late winter of 2019, the fears of 1932 redux have begun to subside, at least in the United States. That is not because Donald Trump's intentions have turned out to be less toxic to liberal democracy than expected, but rather because he has done so incompetent a job of putting those intentions into effect. Like a homeopathic doctor, if an inadvertent one, he has administered small enough doses of poison to produce a healthy reaction in the patient rather than make her sicker. The reaction has taken the form of investigative journalism that is penetrating the president's web of lies and self-dealing, activism around causes like immigration and climate change, judicial pushback on abuses of the Constitution, and of course the stinging defeat that Republicans suffered at the polls in the 2018 midterm election. It is certainly plausible, as of this writing, that Donald Trump will have dealt himself out of a new term in 2020 despite presiding over vigorous economic growth.

But that is quite different from saying that reports of liberalism's demise are premature. First, the Trump effect has proved to be homeopathic only in regard to what one might call the major organs of liberal democracy—judicial autonomy, freedom of the press, the exercise of the franchise. One cannot say the same about our democracy's soft tissue, which is to say its presiding norms—the willingness of majorities to accept the legitimacy of minorities, the sense of a shared and collective purpose, the idea of reasoned debate. Here Donald Trump has decanted into the American bloodstream a virulent poison that cannot be treated with lawsuits and elections. This sickness will be afflicting Americans for long years to come.

Second, the underlying causes are still with us. Though inequality has diminished slightly in recent years, the combination of low growth, reduced social mobility, and staggering gaps between the rich and everyone else has become the steady state of life in the United States and in much of the West. The bitter certainty that globalization is good for "them"— for people in India and China, for the rich at home—and bad for "us" has become endemic. The sense that the game is rigged, even if one doesn't know quite what the game is or how it has been manipulated, has put Donald Trump in office, electrified populist parties across Europe, and provoked the spontaneous and sometimes violent yellow vest protests that have shocked the political elite in France. Nor is there any reason to expect a reconciliation over fundamental matters of values and beliefs between those who feel they've gotten the short end of the stick and those who still invest their faith in the liberal order.

In short, the fact that the illiberal tide may have crested short of an epochal flood offers very faint reassurance about the persistence of liberalism. Prophets of its demise like Patrick Deneen may still be vindicated. The political thinker David Runciman, who does not at all share Deneen's claim that the "inner logic" of liberalism leads to inequality, uniformity, and "moral and spiritual degradation," nevertheless argues that political ideas have a life span of perhaps two hundred years, and liberalism's time is up. Yascha Mounk observes that liberalism thrived in an era of steady growth and mobility, relative demographic homogeneity, and the dominance of mainstream media. Those conditions seemed perpetual when Francis Fukuyama celebrated the end of history in 1989; now we know they are not. Liberalism may thus be living on borrowed time.[1]

Yet what are the alternatives? The most immediate ones, in the sense that one can easily imagine the polity choosing them, are a dispensation to the left, with a far more intrusive state and a far more constricted marketplace, or to the right, with a far smaller state but a far greater willingness to impose collective moral standards on private behavior. Neither of those choices would imperil liberal democracy, though both entail restrictions on behavior, whether economic or personal, that liberals reject. And lurking in the background is the scenario with which I ended the previous chapter, the plutocratic illiberalism that Donald Trump has not yet succeeded in fostering. Voters in Brazil, Italy, Poland, and Hungary, to name the most prominent examples, have already chosen some version of that future. Perhaps the fever dream will break in the United States but then settle over other countries once thought securely in the liberal camp. If we consider that prospect intolerable, we must ward off our sense of fatalism and ask how liberalism can climb out of the hole it now finds itself in.

We have seen how liberalism has adapted over two centuries as the threats to its core principles have changed. What can we find in the past that should inform our understanding of the present? What lessons are to be learned from the mistakes that liberalism has made, or from its blind spots? Among the convictions that constitute today's liberal orthodoxy, what must be defended at all costs, and what modified or even abandoned? The answer to these questions may be similar to, but will not coincide with, the questions Democratic Party officials and activists ask themselves about winning elections. Democrats may win votes by ignoring liberal principles—for example, by treating free trade as a plot against American workers. Liberals will continue to advocate principles, like defending the free-speech rights of conservative extremists, that may infuriate many Democrats. Unlike politicians, liberals must be prepared to preach to the unconverted—to seek to persuade those who resolutely refuse to listen.

We need to look back to the fierce debate between liberals and progressives that broke out in the United States a century ago. Nineteenth-century liberals like Mill and Gladstone did not see a way to harness the powers of the state to combat the social and economic ills they saw around them without doing harm to the individual autonomy that lay at the heart of liberal thought. In the United States, the Jeffersonian liberals of the Democratic Party became apologists for the unchecked economic power of a rising oligarchy. Walter Weyl captured this intellectual and political failure when he wrote that the plutocrats of his day had seized on the doctrine of laissez-faire to insist that "a poor Roumanian, consumptive widow, half-supporting her children by sewing, is a 'free agent' enjoying 'economic freedom.'" The doctrine of political freedom could not serve as the pretext for economic subjection. Yet Weyl was a classically trained economist who was quite certain that the solutions to the problems created by capitalism lay within capitalism itself: "surplus" had at last made mass prosperity possible, if only the powers of the marketplace could be harnessed for social rather than private good.[2]

Materially, we live in the world that Weyl imagined: ordinary Americans own houses, work in physically comfortable settings, enjoy access to health care and higher education and basic forms of social security. Yet in so many other ways we wear the fetters that he and Herbert Croly and their contemporaries sought to break. You would have to go back to their time, before the advent of a national income tax, to find a gulf as vast between the rich and the average citizen. Then too, as now, the plutocracy deployed its wealth to dominate the political process; thus Teddy Roosevelt spoke of "the struggle of freemen to gain and hold the right of self-government as against the special interests, who twist the methods of free government into machinery for defeating the popular will." That political dominance in turn shaped a national discourse in which the rights of capital were all too easily confused with real liberty. Today we hear that "job creators"—that is, the rich—must not be hampered by undue taxation or regulation, as if the machinery of surplus would grind to a halt if capital-gains tax rates returned to the levels at which they were set for decades. We live inside an ideology of the marketplace that casts the very idea of public goods into disrepute.[3]

The war that the progressives waged was not won until FDR fused the Jeffersonian vision with the Hamiltonian—individualism with state activism. For the next two generations, Americans understood that capitalism was a means to public prosperity rather than a supreme good in itself. But ever since the resurgence in the late 1970s of the old right-liberalism of laissez-faire, that balance has been lost; today Arlie Hochschild's Cajun subjects look to the market as that which gives and the state as that which takes, despite all that the market takes from them and all that the state gives. The worship of the marketplace has hardly been limited to the pews on the far right. The neoliberals of the 1990s insisted that growth, by itself, would lead to broad prosperity; in fact the gains went overwhelmingly to the top 10 percent, 1 percent, and 0.1 percent of the population.

The time has come to restore FDR's balance. The most reflective authors of the neoliberal doctrine have begun to entertain second thoughts. In 2016, Larry Summers, Bill Clinton's treasury secretary and then director of Obama's National Economic Council, all but adopted Teddy Roosevelt's idiom in calling for a "responsible nationalism" that would "begin from the idea that the basic responsibility of government is to maximize the welfare of its citizens, not to pursue some abstract concept of the global good."[4]

What would it mean to discard this "abstract concept" in favor of an idea of the public good? Surely it would mean that we rethink economic choices that promote the global good but cause very real harm to many Americans. The obvious example is free trade, a good for all Americans as consumers and for many Americans as shareholders of global firms, but a threat at the much more profound level of employment. Any economic policy that tries to wish away the forces that move manufacturing from high-cost to low-cost nations and regions is bound to fail. Yet no policy can survive, or should survive, if it elevates the interests of "the economy" above those of actual working people. In *The Globalization Paradox*, the economist Dani Rodrik reduces this relationship to a law: "We cannot simultaneously pursue democracy, national self-determination, and globalization." Rodrik means that democratic majorities will not accept "hyperglobalization"; they could be overridden by global government, but that would eliminate national sovereignty. "Democracies have a right to protect their social arrangements," Rodrik concludes, "and when this right clashes with the requirements of the global economy, it is the latter that should give way." Any program of reform would have to combine narrowly targeted protection with far more robust efforts than we now make to move people from legacy to growth sectors of the economy, including long-term unemployment assistance.[5]

Reclaiming a sense of the public good does not chiefly, or even primarily, entail a redistribution from global to national benefits. The true work is internal. First, liberal economists since John Kenneth Galbraith have consistently made the case for enhanced public investment in infrastructure, health care, education, and the like. Those investments have shrunk drastically as a percentage of federal government spending since Ronald Reagan launched his ill-fated assault on the federal budget. The ability to pay for them has also shrunk. The top marginal tax rate when Galbraith was writing was over 70 percent; today it is 37 percent. Capital gains are now taxed at 28 percent for short-term gains and 20 percent for assets held for more than a year; forty years ago the rate for all such gains was 35 percent. That said, the rising cost of entitlements like Social Security will require not merely an increase in the progressivity of the system but broad increases in tax revenues that will also affect the upper middle class. Liberals will have to make the case that the federal government is not the enemy of the people but the instrument they can use to advance their own well-being, an argument that American leaders have made since the era of John Quincy Adams and Henry Clay. More government does not have to mean less freedom.

Free markets produce inequality; yet unchecked, inequality probably curbs economic growth and certainly corrodes the spirit of democratic equality. Whether or not the economist Thomas Piketty is right that our historically high levels of inequality are the inevitable consequence of the gap between returns to capital and returns to labor—the difference, that is, between the value of investment and the value of work—the problem cannot be attacked unless we are prepared to use the tax system for purposes of redistribution as well as revenue. Again, we may look to Teddy Roosevelt, who asserted in his "New Nationalism" speech at Osawatomie that "the swollen fortune" poses so grave a threat to democracy that it must be curbed by a progressive income tax and inheritance tax. Indeed, the estate tax both symbolizes and enables the democratic commitment to social mobility. In a free society, Herbert Croly wrote in *The Promise of American Life*, people of talent will naturally rise to the top. But that privileged position begins to corrode social bonds when it threatens to become permanent, whether through inheritance or through the exploitation of privilege. "The essential wholeness of the community," he wrote, "depends absolutely on the ceaseless creation of a political, economic, and social aristocracy and their equally incessant replacement." That rotation in turn depends on a steeply progressive estate tax. A generation later, James Bryant Conant, the president of Harvard, took Croly's principle a step further. Writing in the *Atlantic Monthly* in 1943, Conant declared that an "American radical" would be "lusty in wielding the axe against the root of inherited privilege." Conant suggested the confiscation of all inherited property every generation. The alternative, he wrote, is the solidification of a "caste system."[6]

The fact that a reform proposed by the president of Harvard three-quarters of a century ago strikes us today as an unthinkable assault on the existing order tells us how far we have drifted from a democratic faith in equality of opportunity. Perhaps the seizure Conant had in mind does, in fact, transgress our liberal faith in the right of the individual to the fruits of his or her own labor; in any case the intended beneficiaries of Conant's radical proposal might violently oppose it as an encroachment on their own liberty. But few things separate left-liberals from right-liberals so clearly as the merits of a steeply progressive estate tax as well as income tax. And few things offer so direct an attack on unearned privilege.

Class boundaries have become increasingly rigid; one of the few ways that liberals can reach across party lines is by frankly using the language of class to speak to working-class whites who feel shut out of the globalized economy. But they will encounter a problem: when liberals talk about inequality, they are thinking of the growing gap between the 1 percent and everyone else, but the inequality that drives the anger of many working-class voters is between themselves and the people they perceive as the "liberal elite." That reflex, many liberals will rejoin, simply demonstrates the success of a forty-year-long campaign to displace resentment from its real target, the plutocracy. Liberals reject the idea they are a class whose collective interests are secured by the institutions and habits of mind they have promoted. Yet it is not only conservatives like Patrick Deneen who have anatomized the "liberalocracy." In *The Retreat of Western Liberalism*, Edward Luce, very much a defender of the liberal order, uses the term "hereditary meritocracy" to express the same idea of informal oligarchy. Luce observes that about a quarter of American children from the top 1 percent of the income scale attend an elite university, while only 0.5 percent of those from the bottom fifth do. The well-to-do can ensure the perpetuation of their educational success by paying for tutors and private guidance counselors and fancy summer programs and the like. This is precisely the situation of which Herbert Croly warned, though he imagined a very different oligarchic class. "Why wouldn't the losers be angry?" Luce asks.[7]

The hereditary meritocracy is so baked into our system, so deeply reinforced by innumerable private choices and public policies, that one can scarcely see how it could be dislodged. A steep inheritance tax would help. A tiny, but symbolically powerful, step would be the elimination of so-called legacy admissions at elite universities. Why should you have a better shot at going to Yale because your father did? In what way is the cause of diversity served by artificially increasing the number of admitted students who happen to have been born lucky? Of course, the reason why elite universities take the children of alums is to increase the loyalty of those alums, who express their satisfaction with generous gifts. Yet the only way to increase the number of slots available to new aspirants to the elite, and thus to approach Croly's ideal of the "incessant replacement" of the meritocracy, is to reduce spaces now taken up by the less meritocratically deserving. The education scholar Richard Kahlenberg has proposed that Harvard do just that. What's more, after four decades of affirmative action, it has become difficult to justify reserving for well-to-do minority students spaces that might otherwise be filled by less-well-to-do nonminorities. If liberals need to be more prepared to talk about class than they have been in the past, this is a case where discrimination by class has become more salient than discrimination by race.[8]

From the time of the Great Society, liberals have dedicated themselves to the principle of equality of opportunity. That continues to lie at the heart of the liberal commitment to civil rights, whether in matters of race, gender, or sexual preference. But the 2016 election, the Brexit referendum in England, the yellow vest demonstrations in France, all represent an angry assertion on the part of majorities, or at least on the part of groups whose marginalization is not officially recognized, that they, too, cannot seize the opportunities made available in a liberal society. For those who have not been able to assemble the human or social capital required for success in the modern world, equality of opportunity requires targeted efforts on education, job training, health care; but it should also spur the recognition that the meritocratic system that advances the collective interests of liberals has not been good for everyone and is not simply inscribed in the order of nature.

How does the liberal state need to reorganize itself in order to seriously pursue these neglected public goods? This has become a matter of serious debate. Just as progressives once tried to restrain the plutocratic Gulliver with the ropes of a "democratic collectivism," so today's self-proclaimed "socialists" want to place the state in the center of the economy. The use of this freighted term has caused a world of confusion. Socialism used to have a straightforward meaning: a socialist believed in the public ownership of the economic goods owned privately in a capitalist system. To anyone older than fifty or so, the collapse of the Soviet Union demonstrated the hollowness of the socialist promise. That clarity is a thing of the past; polls show that young Americans find socialism deeply appealing, even if they're not sure what it entails. Among contributors to *The Jacobin*, the intellectual organ of the Democratic Socialists of America, some really do favor the public ownership of the means of production, but many others, like Bernie Sanders, seek greater political control of the marketplace through tax and regulatory policy, more public investment, and a far more thoroughgoing social welfare state, including universal health care. The younger authors use the term "socialism" as a rebuke to neoliberalism rather than in its traditional doctrinal sense. (Sanders himself is more than old enough to know the received meaning.) They are prepared to talk about class as neoliberals are not, because they do not accept that what is good for the rich is good for the nonrich. In classical terminology, they are not socialists but social democrats. They would like America to look more like Sweden.

The debate among liberals needs to be, in effect, "How much more like Sweden?" Unless they really have changed their nature, Americans will not accept a paternalistic, cradle-to-grave Scandinavian welfare system. Being free to succeed, and to fail, means more to Americans than to Swedes. Both Deneen's privileged liberalocrats and Hochschild's fiercely independent oil-field workers subscribe to the doctrine of equality of opportunity rather than equality of outcome. Perhaps the best way to put it is that America does not need more socialism, but it does need more social democracy—even if that marginally reduces the economic growth rate.

A century ago, Herbert Croly called for a new nationalism, and Teddy Roosevelt adopted the phrase. What they hoped to tame was the selfish individualism that consumed their time. When Larry Summers recently picked up the term, he was thinking rather of the genuflection before global goods and globalization itself. But surely he was thinking as well of rejuvenating a term that has been corrupted with chauvinism, xenophobia, and resentment. Nationalism need not be synonymous with an exclusionary populism. In *The Promise of American Life*, Croly used the term to denote a sense of collective purpose that transcends, though hardly excludes, our individual pursuit of well-being. His hero was Abraham Lincoln, who, Croly wrote, spoke of democracy as "the spirit and principle of brotherhood." Resolute commitment to that vision persuaded Lincoln to remain magnanimous even to those who wished him dead. In his mystical depths, the president regarded the nation as a spiritual entity that existed beyond the terrible divisions of the day; by insistently conjuring up this nation of brotherhood, he helped the country survive the catastrophe of the Civil War.[9]

An affirmative nationalism addresses citizens as "we." Lincoln addressed the American people as one even when they were not one, and liberals since the New Deal have learned that the "I" of individual liberty does not preclude Lincoln's "we." Indeed, today's celebrants of laissez-faire so worship the desiring and possessing self that they scarcely know how to address Americans collectively. That is why the libertarian-plutocratic wing of the Republican Party—incarnated above all in the Koch brothers, billionaire industrialists who have spent a fortune promoting their small-government low-tax views—wins policy debates only by wildly outspending its rivals. Donald Trump, more delicately attuned to public sentiment, succeeded by addressing half the nation and persuading them that the other half was not "the people." That is populist nationalism. A liberal nationalism would decline to simply reverse the terms and marshal the other half into a resentful unit; it would seek to rediscover the ethos of the whole.

What is that collectivity? The historian Jill Lepore has written that American nationalism has always been liberal—at least until very recently—and has always been founded, as Lincoln's was, upon the equality of all citizens. That vision has been tested by the nation's diversity; liberals have always reaffirmed their faith in what Frederick Douglass called "the composite nation." Douglass predicted, "We shall spread the network of our science and civilization over all who seek their shelter, whether from Asia, Africa or the isles of the sea," and "all shall here bow to the same law, speak the same language, support the same Government, enjoy the same liberty, vibrate with the same national enthusiasm, and seek the same national ends."[10]

That plurality is the American we. But there is good reason to fear that that vision has lost its binding power. Exhibit A is Barack Obama, who introduced himself to most Americans when he gave a speech at the 2004 Democratic convention insisting that America is not "blue" or "red" but one. Acutely conscious of Lincoln's precedent and gifted as few others are with something like Lincoln's gift for summoning America's better angels, Obama as president resisted almost all entreaties to address his listeners as black rather than white, Democratic rather than

Republican. He chose to ignore the blindingly obvious evidence that Republicans in Congress would do everything in their power to make him fail. He believed that if he behaved as if Americans regarded one another above all as fellow citizens, he could help make them do so. He was wrong; the nation was far more divided at the end of his tenure than it had been at the beginning. Obama provoked bitter racial resentment not by virtue of anything he said or did but simply by virtue of being a black president. The hatred unleashed on Obama, and the wildly enthusiastic reception of Donald Trump's venomous attacks on African Americans, Arabs, and Mexicans, seem to offer all the clarity we need on the attitude of many white Americans toward people of color.

The hopes for an inclusive nationalism thus run smack into the reality of race and ethnicity. The nation seems divided between the party of racial justice, however imperfect, and the party of racial resentment. Liberals are not about to surrender their civil rights principles in order to focus exclusively on the economic issues that do not alienate white voters; nor could they if they wished to, because Black Lives Matter, #MeToo, the movement for LGBTQ rights are central to the lives and the political concerns of the base of the Democratic Party. What then? What, if anything, does the party of the composite nation have to say to people—white people—whose "deep story" tells them that they are locked in a zero-sum fight with black people and immigrants? We say that angry whites have failed to see that they share class interests with the minority members whom they most resent—which is true, though apparently not very convincing. We say that their alleged conservative values are a mask for racism, patriarchy, xenophobia, that they cannot abide the loss of their unearned privilege as white male (or female) Americans—which may also be true, but is not helpful.

It may be that nothing transcends those resentments. Alternatively, the answer may lie wholly in the realm of economic opportunity: perhaps if one could improve the life chances of non-college-educated whites, they would stop seeing their situation in zero-sum terms. If either hypothesis is true, it doesn't matter how liberals present the legitimate claims of marginalized groups. But maybe it does matter. The white nationalism that Donald Trump frankly embraces pits resentful whites against an "other" that is, variously, black, Hispanic, feminist, liberal. But otherness itself has become the mirror form of identity politics—the kind embraced on the left. When marginalized groups simply sought their place in the American sun, an all-embracing language came naturally to them. It is the very different demand for full respect for particularity that shapes the identity politics of the left. And this poses a problem that demands self-reflection.

When a white poet can be rebuked—and can issue an abject apology—for adopting, as an act of empathy, the voice of a black homeless person, as happened in the pages of *The Nation* in 2018, the thing being protected is not a set of rights but the boundaries of an identity. This habit of identity policing winds up parceling out selves into nonoverlapping categories. As Mark Lilla remarks in *The Once and Future Liberal*, it has now become commonplace to introduce an opinion with the expression "Speaking as a . . . " either to claim privilege when speaking about fellow lesbians or African Americans or differently abled persons, or to tread warily when referring to groups other than one's own. Where in this minefield of identity is the national we?[11]

A politics of identity repays exclusion with a kind of retaliatory exclusion and all but guarantees a mutual hardening of barriers. An increasingly insistent otherness licenses an increasingly insistent white nationalism. What is the endgame of this downward spiral to cultural origins? Do we abandon the ethos of *e pluribus unum* and simply wait until the moment arrives when our half can outvote theirs? We must consider the possibility that this represents a wrong turn, just as liberals certain of their rightness and righteousness made a wrong turn half a century ago when they failed to subject Great Society programs to serious scrutiny. We need to distinguish between the right to equal treatment, as women or African Americans or transgender persons, and the place each of us has in the national community. The just moral claim that members of marginalized groups hold over majorities is the right to full citizenship, not the right to define and surveil the borders of one's own collective identity.

Earlier in this chapter I proposed an act of self-recognition and self-sacrifice in which liberals acknowledge that they have been the beneficiaries of a hereditary meritocracy. Such acts also challenge our national cult of selfishness. One of the innumerable ways in which Donald Trump has corrupted American culture is by reducing all values to marketplace values. Nothing constitutes a sincerer expression of his intuitive worldview, for Trump sees all relations as transactions and money as the ultimate arbiter of success or failure. Policies are good if they make money, bad if they don't. Trump is our nation's most outstanding vulgarian, but he is also preaching to the converted. For right-liberals, the marketplace is not just an instrument but an ideology. The modern Republican Party was born out of a strange fusion of God talk and market supremacy, and so it remains: the Reverend Franklin Graham lies down with the Koch brothers. Left-liberals, of course, reject both a theological morality and an economic libertarianism. But it is not enough to say that social Darwinism is the wrong approach to the economy; it is also the wrong approach to life. That is why, despite his belief in free markets, Mill argued that economic liberty, unlike political liberty, could not be regarded as an end in itself but only as a means to prosperity. We must not make a god of the marketplace.

But we do; we live in a world of marketplace hegemony. Universities compete over their brands as fiercely as car companies do. Entrepreneurs enjoy bipartisan hero worship. Tech companies allegedly dedicated to emancipating the world through information operate with the same ruthless disregard for public good as did the industrial firms they supplanted. These are hardly immemorial American values. Conservatives once regarded the marketplace as destructive of human values, but that largely ended with the supply-side revolution. Liberal resistance crumbled in the 1990s when Democrats accepted that a competitive global marketplace would maximize value for all. Competition became a universal metaphor. Where, then, is our sanctuary from market values? Can liberalism forge an ethic of the public good that is not merely utilitarian, as Lincoln did? Perhaps this presupposes a spiritual dimension to life that is contrary to the liberal spirit of secular individualism. Yet Mill combined his unflagging commitment to autonomy with an aspiration to achieve the heights of "civilization." That word has grown hoary. Let us find a better one.

If one asks which aspect of liberalism is most threatened by today's populist backlash, the answer would not be Mill's "personal liberty," since we live in a world of unleashed speech and behavior that probably would have appalled that staid early Victorian, nor is it the economic liberalism of the free market, even if nationalists like Donald Trump and Viktor Orbán exploit widespread fears over the blind forces of globalization. What is most imperiled, in Europe as well as the United States, is the constitutional liberalism that protects each of us from all of us—the neutral institutions and neutral principles that serve as a bulwark to the tyranny of the majority.

Trump's obvious bewilderment that the president of the United States cannot make the Department of Justice, or Homeland Security, or for that matter any other agency of government, do his personal bidding shows how foreign to him are the constitutional principles designed to limit the power of any one branch, and of any one man. Though the president's challenges to the constitutional order have provoked a passionate response, the fact that he was elected and remains popular with his base demonstrates that he is scarcely the only American who regards checks and balances as a plot to frustrate the will of the majority. The president continues to enjoy the virtually unanimous support of congressional Republicans, who join him in heaping abuse on agencies like the Federal Bureau of Investigation that insist on carrying out their historic mission even when doing so runs afoul of the interests of one of the parties, or at least of its leader.

Liberals are called to protect neutral principle in the face of partisan attack. The American Civil Liberties Union almost destroyed itself in 1977 when the organization defended the right of Nazis to march in Skokie, Illinois, where many Holocaust survivors had settled. Whether or not that call was the right one, the underlying premise was that the neutral principle that all have the right to speak was sacred. The attack on neutrality today is vastly broader and deeper. Figures like former FBI head James Comey who stand up for the rule of law are vilified as partisan hacks. Nonpartisan bodies like the Congressional Budget Office are simply dismissed if they produce numbers that don't support Republican policy preferences. Science is mocked as special pleading. Jurists who return verdicts adverse to the president are "Democrat judges."

The defense of neutral principle has become the heroic battleground of contemporary liberalism; we will someday enshrine the journalists and activists and public-interest lawyers who defied the will of the president in a pantheon of the collective imagination. Yet liberals must resist the temptations of martyrdom. The deal that European leaders made with Turkey to stop the flow of refugees outraged defenders of human rights, but since an unending torrent of refugees eventually, and perhaps quickly, would have brought xenophobic populists to power, it was a necessary compromise. Similarly, it is not only morally unnecessary but morally wrong to surrender to the side that wins by breaking the rules. That is how democracies give way to fascism. Republicans won the 2000 election by playing dirtier than the Democrats. One can't help feeling that if the relentless Bill Clinton had been on the ballot that year, he would have fought, as he liked to say, until the last dog died. Perhaps he would have done things he would rather the public not know. Would it have been wrong? There is no good way out of the terrible dilemma forced on the rule-obedient by the rule violator. But acting in such a way as to yield power to rampant rule violation is plainly intolerable.

Liberals need to man the ramparts against unchecked majoritarianism. Yet they also need to avoid inflaming the inevitable tension between liberalism and majoritarianism. Both issues arise in the case of the judiciary, which the framers of the Constitution made equal and independent in order to check the branches of government more responsive to the public will. In *Federalist* 78, Alexander Hamilton cited Montesquieu to the effect that "there is no liberty, if the powers of judging be not separated from legislative and executive powers." The autonomy of the judiciary, as discussed earlier, is under direct assault by Republican-controlled legislatures at the state level and jeopardized at the federal level by the exercise of congressional fiat. Insofar as this effort succeeds, the rule of law will succumb to the rule of individuals. If judges fear punishment for overturning laws that entrench the power of the ruling party, for example through gerrymandering, then political majorities will be able to reproduce themselves by changing the rules as needed. The judiciary has already been brought to heel by the ruling parties in Hungary and Poland. It would be naive to suppose that it cannot happen here.[12]

Liberals must fight for judicial autonomy. But countermajoritarian institutions like the courts cannot permanently sustain democratic support if they are seen as protecting minorities at the expense of majorities; defending through the judiciary rights that cannot prevail in democratic debate ultimately endangers both the courts and political parties. Popular anger at the civil rights and defendants' rights decisions of the 1960s drove many traditional Democrats out of the party's ranks; more recent decisions on abortion, gay marriage, and other controversial questions of personal morality have helped fuel the culture war that rages all around us. The Democrats' dependence on the judiciary implies a Hamiltonian distrust of the public. Populists like Donald Trump can go to town on that condescension. Indeed, in *The People vs. Democracy*, Yascha Mounk writes that liberals have helped provoke the populist backlash by seeking refuge in the courts and other sanctuaries against popular opinion.[13]

The struggle to preserve the independence of the judiciary must be waged, not as a battle cry of liberals against conservatives, but as a pledge of faith in the rule of law against an intolerant populism. That is a campaign for Americans of all political stripes. But liberals should also reconsider their bias for the courts. Even the great holy war over abortion has begun to look increasingly Pyrrhic. The fact that abortion is adjudicated in the Supreme Court rather than in legislatures, state and national, has turned every Supreme Court nomination into a life-and-death battle, has vastly exacerbated national polarization, and quite possibly got Donald Trump elected president. That's a very high price to pay. Whatever their defects, legislatures are instruments of popular representation. Other countries, including heavily Catholic ones like Argentina and Ireland, have also engaged in pitched battles over abortion in recent years, but they have done so through the political process. Liberals need to be prepared to fight for their principles in statehouses. They may not have much choice in the matter, because both the Supreme Court and the federal judiciary are becoming a great deal friendlier to conservatives. Perhaps Donald Trump has done liberals a favor: by taking judicialism for the right, he has forced them to embrace the virtues of parliamentarism.

It is the very obviousness of the populist challenge to neutral institutions that accounts for the urgency and vibrancy of the response, at least in the United States. The dam is being breached; we rush over with sandbags. The slow and steady sapping of liberal norms is far more insidious and thus ultimately harder to counteract. Donald Trump has made deep and lasting inroads in our faith in one another and in the possibility of reasoning together. A polity is an imagined community—it can be conjured both into and out of being—but it takes much longer to heal than to harm. The task of an affirmative nationalism is to repair the damage that Trump and his Republican predecessors over the last generation have done, to help Americans see that, for all their differences, deep strands link them to one another. That may be the most urgent task. Yet Barack Obama tried and failed to do just that.

As if that weren't demoralizing enough, we are now confronted with the phenomenon that I described earlier as cognitive illiberalism—the loss of faith in reason, fact, and science. I don't know if there is a cure for this virus. Yet a liberal nationalism must set itself that task, for there cannot be a "we" to address absent a common faith in reason. The work of restoring that faith must come from everywhere: from tech companies that take much more seriously than they do now the job of lowering the manic temper of online discourse and weeding out the most grievous falsehoods; from universities, which must reassert their role as citadels of calm and fearless reasoning; from schools, which must replace vapid "social studies" curricula with history and civics; from media outlets that dedicate themselves to serious journalism; and from ordinary citizens who spurn internet junk food in favor of something that will test their jaws, and their convictions. Reason and science was the rallying cry of Karl Popper and Bertrand Russell, Isaiah Berlin and George Orwell. The preservation of rational discourse seems as urgent a calling today as it was in 1940.

Eighty-odd years ago, it was reasonable to believe—it was, in fact, unreasonable *not* to believe—that liberalism was dead. Stephen Spender wrote the obsequies. George Orwell was persuaded that only a society vastly more organized than the liberal ones of England and America could defeat the supremely regimented fascist state. Capitalism had proved that it could not spread prosperity widely enough to retain popular approval. But it wasn't so; as Arthur Schlesinger would write a decade later, "Experience suggests that the limited state can resolve the basic social questions which were supposed to compel a resort to the unlimited state."[14]

Liberalism flourished in the second half of the twentieth century by virtue of defeating and outlasting totalitarianism. The threat that the limited state faces today is incomparably more modest than it was then. Yet liberalism can no longer prove itself through single combat. Francis Fukuyama was wrong in imagining that the consensus would thrive in the absence of a coherent rival ideology. Liberal values are endangered today because citizens in the liberal world are losing faith in them. A crisis of faith can be overcome only at the level of faith—through the exercise of what Schlesinger called "radical nerve." Liberalism will renew itself only if enough people believe that its principles are worth fighting for.

Acknowledgments

I PROBABLY WOULD NEVER HAVE UNDERTAKEN THIS PROJECT HAD I not happened to read Edmund Fawcett's deeply thoughtful and spritely 2014 work, *Liberalism: The Life of an Idea*. This book departs in very important ways from that one, but *Liberalism* provided an inspiration and a framework for thought. I also learned from Edmund Wilson's *To the Finland Station* that you can write about an idea through the people who thought about it without diminishing the complexity of the idea.

My son and ex officio editor Alex Traub both pointed me to Wilson as a possible model and read large parts of the manuscript. My friends Leonard Groopman and Jules Coleman also read significant portions and forced me to rethink, revise, and even, alas, eliminate.

My editor, Lara Heimert, not only made it possible for me to write this book but read the final draft with her usual searching attention and forced me to reduce it to readable dimensions. My developmental editor, Roger Labrie, did not merely edit copy but demanded logic where he found it missing. My agent, Andrew Wylie, only insists on one thing: that I write about what matters to me most.

Notes

INTRODUCTION: WHY LIBERALISM MATTERS

1. Arthur Schlesinger Jr., "Liberalism in America: A Note for Europeans," in *The Politics of Hope* (Boston: Houghton Mifflin, 1963), 63.

2. Ed Pilkington, "Obama Angers Midwest Voters with Guns and Religion Remark," *Guardian*, April 14, 2008, www.theguardian.com/world/2008/apr/14/barackobama.uselections2008.

CHAPTER 1: PROTECTING THE PEOPLE FROM THEMSELVES

1. James Madison, "Federalist No. 51," in *The Federalist Papers*, ed. Isaac Kramnick (New York: Penguin Books, 1987), 321.

2. Ibid., 319–321.

3. Richard Brookhiser, *James Madison* (New York: Basic Books, 2011), 54.

4. James Madison to William Bradford, January 24, 1774, and April 1, 1774, in *Letters and Other Writings of James Madison, Fourth President of the United States*, vol. 1, *1769–1793* (Philadelphia: J. B. Lippincott, 1865), 12, 14.

5. James Madison, "Memorial and Remonstrance Against Religious Assessments," June 20, 1785, The Founders' Constitution, University of Chicago Press and the Liberty Fund, http://press-pubs.uchicago.edu/founders/documents/amendI_religions43.html.

6. Quoted in Brookhiser, *James Madison*, 41.

7. Gordon Wood, *The Creation of the American Republic, 1776–1787* (Chapel Hill: University of North Carolina Press, 1998), 16; Thomas Paine, *Common Sense* (Cambridge, MA: Belknap Press, 2010), 5.

8. James Madison to Thomas Jefferson, February 19, 1788, in *Letters*, 426.

9. Thomas Paine, *The Rights of Man* (New York: Dutton, 1951), 103.

10. James Madison to Thomas Jefferson, October 17, 1788, in *Letters*, 469.

11. Ibid., 271.

12. James Madison, "Federalist No. 10," in *The Federalist Papers*, 126.

13. Ibid., 124.

14. George Washington, "Washington's Farewell Address to the People of the United States," September 19, 1796, Senate Document No. 106-21, www .gpo.gov/fdsys/pkg/GPO-CDOC-106sdoc21/pdf/GPO-CDOC-106sdoc21 .pdf; Madison, "Federalist No. 50," in *The Federalist Papers*, 318.

15. Madison, "Federalist No. 51," in *The Federalist Papers*, 319–320.

16. John Locke, *The Second Treatise of Government and a Letter Concerning Toleration* (Mineola, NY: Dover Publications, 2002), 57; Louis Hartz, *The Liberal Tradition in America* (New York: Harcourt, Brace and Co., 1955), 5ff.

17. James Madison to James Monroe, October 5, 1786, in *Letters*, 251.

18. Wood, *The Creation of the American Republic*, 61.

19. Alexander Hamilton, "Federalist No. 8," in *The Federalist Papers*, 116.

20. Benjamin Constant, *Écrits et discours politiques* (Paris: Chez Jean-Jacques Pauvert, 1944), 76.

21. Ibid., 27.

22. Ibid., 33.

23. Ibid., 73.

24. Ibid., 44, 49.

25. Stephen Holmes, *Benjamin Constant and the Making of Modern Liberalism* (New Haven: Yale University Press, 1984), 6.

26. Ibid., 32.

27. Benjamin Constant, "The Liberty of Ancients Compared with That of Moderns (1819)," Online Library of Liberty, http://oll.libertyfund.org/titles /constant-the-liberty-of-ancients-compared-with-that-of-moderns-1819.

28. Ibid.

29. Ibid.

30. Ibid.

31. Ibid.

32. Benjamin Constant, *Principles of Politics Applicable to All Governments* (Indianapolis, IN: Liberty Fund, 2003), 19.

33. Ibid., 31, book 14, chapter 5.

34. Ibid., 325; Holmes, *Benjamin Constant*, 142.

35. François Guizot, quoted in John Stuart Mill, "Guizot's Essays and Historical Lectures," in *Dissertations and Discussions: Political, Philosophical, and Historical*, vol. 2 (Elibron Classics, 2005), 281.

36. François Guizot, "Lecture 6," in *Historical Essays and Lectures*, ed. Stanley Mellon (Chicago: University of Chicago Press, 1972), 46.

37. Alexis de Tocqueville, *Democracy in America*, vol. 1 (New York: Vintage Classics, 1990), 7, 10.

38. Ibid., 260, 263.

39. Ibid., 322.

40. Alexis de Tocqueville, "Note, 1841," in *The Tocqueville Reader: A Life in Letters and Politics*, ed. Olivier Zunz and Alan S. Kahan (Oxford: Blackwell Publishing, 2002), 282, 219.

CHAPTER 2: JOHN STUART MILL AND THE DEFENSE OF LIBERTY

1. John Stuart Mill, "On Liberty," in *On Liberty, Utilitarianism, and Other Essays*, ed. Mark Philp and Frederick Rosen (New York: Oxford University Press, 2015), 8.

2. John Stuart Mill, *Autobiography* (Boston: Houghton Mifflin, 1969), 13.

3. Jeremy Bentham, *An Introduction to the Principles of Morals and Legislation* (London: Methuen, 1982), 1–15.

4. Mill, *Autobiography*, 42.

5. Ibid.

6. Ibid., 89.

7. Ibid., 97.

8. John Stuart Mill, "The Spirit of the Age," in *Mill*, ed. Alan Ryan (New York: W. W. Norton, 1997), 3; John Stuart Mill, "Vindication of the French Revolution of 1848," *Dissertations and Discussions: Political, Philosophical, and Historical*, vol. 2 (Elibron Classics, 2005), 344.

9. John Stuart Mill, "M. de Tocqueville on Democracy in America," *Dissertations and Discussions*, vol. 2, 8, 58–59.

10. Ibid., 182.

11. John Stuart Mill, "Coleridge," in *Dissertations and Discussions*, vol. 1, 422.

12. Mill is quoted in Nicholas Capaldi, *John Stuart Mill: A Biography* (New York: Cambridge University Press, 2004), 203.

13. Mill, *On Liberty*, 105.

14. Crane Brinton, *English Political Thought in the 19th Century* (New York: Harper Torchbooks, 1962), 105.

15. Capaldi, *John Stuart Mill*, 208.

16. Ibid., 247; Mill, *On Liberty*, 3.

17. Capaldi, *John Stuart Mill*, 236.

18. Mill, *On Liberty*, 19.

19. Ibid., 37, 22, 41.

20. Ibid., 20, 27, 29, 33.

21. Ibid., 40.

22. Ibid., 58, 56.

23. Ibid., 77.

24. Ibid., 70.

25. Ibid., 68, 64.

26. Ibid., 15; John Stuart Mill, "Utilitarianism," in *On Liberty, Utilitarianism, and Other Essays*, 140.

27. Mill, *On Liberty*, 83–84.

28. Ibid., 80.

29. Ibid., 83–84.

30. Ibid., 93, 107.

31. Ibid., 103.

32. Ibid., 108.

33. Ibid., 112.

34. Eugenio Biagini, *Liberty, Retrenchment and Reform: Popular Liberalism in the Age of Gladstone, 1860–1880* (New York: Cambridge University Press, 1992), 94.

35. Ibid., 167.

36. Ibid., 174.

37. Ibid., 170.

38. E. J. Feuchtwanger, *Gladstone* (New York: St. Martin's Press, 1975), 262.

39. John Stuart Mill, *The Subjection of Women* (Cambridge, MA: MIT Press, 1970), 17, 24.

40. Ibid., 13.

CHAPTER 3: THE *NEW REPUBLIC* AND THE REFOUNDING OF AMERICAN LIBERALISM

1. Walter Weyl, "The Strikers at Lawrence," *Outlook*, 1912, Walter E. Weyl MSS, Rutgers University Libraries.

2. Ibid.

3. The Populist platform is quoted in Brian Stipelman, *That Broader Definition of Liberty: The Theory and Practice of the New Deal* (Lanham, MD: Lexington Books, 2012), 40.

4. Robert H. Wiebe, *The Search for Order, 1877–1920* (New York: Hill & Wang, 1967), 96; Stipelman, *That Broader Definition of Liberty*, 46.

5. David Forcey, *The Crossroads of Liberalism: Croly, Weyl, Lippmann, and the Progressive Era, 1900–1925* (New York: Oxford University Press, 1961), 52–88.

6. *Walter Weyl, an Appreciation*, privately printed, 1922, Walter E. Weyl MSS, Rutgers University Libraries.

7. Walter Weyl, *The New Democracy* (New York: Macmillan, 1912), 32, 49.

8. Ibid., 152.

9. Ibid., 174–175.

10. Ibid., 191, 195, 260.

11. Roosevelt is quoted in Forcey, *The Crossroads of Liberalism*, 53.

12. Herbert Croly, *The Promise of American Life* (Princeton, NJ: Princeton University Press, 2014), 35.

13. Ibid., 219.

14. Ibid., 222.

15. Ibid., 57.

16. David Levy, *Herbert Croly of the New Republic* (Princeton, NJ: Princeton University Press, 1985), 132; Theodore Roosevelt, "New Nationalism Speech," Osawatomie, Kansas, August 31, 1910, Teaching American History, http://teachingamericanhistory.org/library/document/new-nationalism-speech/.

17. John Morton Blum, *Woodrow Wilson and the Politics of Morality* (Boston: Little, Brown, 1956), 32, 40.

18. Ibid., 62.

19. Arthur S. Link, *Woodrow Wilson and the Progressive Era, 1910–1917* (New York: Harper & Bros., 1954), 79.

20. Levy, *Herbert Croly of the New Republic*, 195.

21. "Presidential Complacency," *New Republic*, November 21, 1914; "Editorial Notes," *New Republic*, January 16, 1915.

22. "Not Our War," *New Republic*, June 5, 1915.

23. "Mental Unpreparedness," *New Republic*, September 11, 1915.

24. "Youngstown," *New Republic*, January 29, 1916.

25. Francis Hackett, "Are Convicts Human?," *New Republic*, January 15, 1916; Booker T. Washington, "My View of Segregation Laws," *New Republic*, December 4, 1915.

26. Forcey, *The Crossroads of Liberalism*, 256–258.

27. "Woodrow Wilson," *New Republic*, June 24, 1916.

28. Thomas C. Leonard, *Illiberal Reformers* (Princeton, NJ: Princeton University Press, 2016).

29. "Negro Segregation in St. Louis," *New Republic*, March 18, 1916.

30. Walter Weyl, *The End of the War* (New York: Macmillan, 1918), 14.

31. Walter Weyl, "Prophet and Politician," in *Tired Radicals, and Other Papers* (New York: W. B. Huebsch, 1921), 88.

32. "Walter E. Weyl, 1873–1919," *New Republic*, November 19, 1919.

33. Charles R. Kesler, *I Am the Change: Barack Obama and the Crisis of Liberalism* (New York: Broadside Books, 2012), 110; Franklin Delano Roosevelt, "June 27, 1936: Democratic National Convention" (sound recording), Philadelphia, Pennsylvania, June 27, 1936, Miller Center, University of Virginia, https://millercenter.org/the-presidency/presidential-speeches/june-27-1936-democratic -national-convention.

34. Franklin D. Roosevelt, Commonwealth Club Address, San Francisco, California, September 23, 1932, Teaching American History, http://teaching americanhistory.org/library/document/commonwealth-club-address/.

CHAPTER 4: ISAIAH BERLIN AND THE ANTI-TOTALITARIANS

1. Isaiah Berlin, "The Pursuit of the Ideal," in *The Crooked Timber of Humanity: Chapters in the History of Ideas* (London: Pimlico, 2013), 6.

2. Ibid., 11.

3. Ibid., 16.

4. Benjamin Constant, *Écrits politiques* (Paris: Gallimard, 1997), 169.

5. Isaiah Berlin, "John Stuart Mill and the Ends of Life," in *Liberty*, ed. Henry Hardy (New York: Oxford University Press, 2002), 243.

6. Isaiah Berlin, "Alexander Herzen," in *Russian Thinkers* (New York: Penguin Books, 1986), 202.

7. Isaiah Berlin, *Freedom and Its Betrayal* (Princeton, NJ: Princeton University Press, 2002), 43–44.

8. Ibid., 53, 52.

9. Berlin, "John Stuart Mill and the Ends of Life," 234.

10. Stephen Spender, *Forward from Liberalism* (New York: Random House, 1937), 8.

11. Karl Popper, *Open Society* (Princeton, NJ: Princeton University Press, 2013), xliv, 168.

12. Ibid., 431; Bertrand Russell, "Philosophy and Politics," cited in Andrew David Irvine, "Bertrand Russell: Science and Philosophy," *Times Literary Supplement*, October 2, 2018.

13. F. A. Hayek, *The Road to Serfdom: Text and Documents* (Chicago: University of Chicago Press, 2007), 99, 108, 110.

14. Keynes and Berlin are quoted in Bruce Caldwell, introduction to *The Road to Serfdom*, 2, 23; George Orwell, "The Intellectual Revolt," in *Essays* (New York: Everyman's Library, 2002), 999–1002.

15. "Statement of Aims," Mont Pelerin Society, April 8, 1947, www .montpelerin.org/statement-of-aims.

16. Hayek, *The Road to Serfdom*, 48.

17. Karl Polanyi, *The Great Transformation* (Boston: Beacon Press, 2001), 147.

18. Ibid., 245, 228.

19. Ibid., 264.

20. George Orwell, "Spilling the Spanish Beans," in *Essays*, 71.

21. George Orwell, "Notes on the Way," in *Essays*, 254, 259.

22. George Orwell, "Literature and Totalitarianism," in *Essays*, 361–362, 364.

23. George Orwell, "The Lion and the Unicorn: Socialism and the English Genius," in *Essays*, 328, 341.

24. Michael Ignatieff, *Isaiah Berlin: A Life* (New York: Henry Holt, 1998), 197.

25. Isaiah Berlin, "Two Concepts of Liberty," in *Essays*, 168.

26. Ibid., 173.

27. Ibid., 175.

28. Ibid., 178, 172.

29. Ibid., 180.

30. Isaiah Berlin and Ramin Jehanbegloo, *Recollections of a Historian of Ideas: Conversations with Isaiah Berlin* (New York: Charles Scribner's Sons, 1991), 41.

31. Isaiah Berlin, "Pursuit of the Ideal," in *The Crooked Timber of Humanity*, 18–19.

32. George Orwell, "Looking Back on the Spanish War," in *Essays*, 439; George Orwell, "The Prevention of Literature," in *Essays*, 936.

33. George Orwell, *1984* (New York: Signet Classics, 1977), 167.

34. Ibid., 73.

CHAPTER 5: AMERICA AFTER THE WAR: LIBERALISM AS CIVIC RELIGION

1. Arthur M. Schlesinger Jr., *The Vital Center: The Politics of Freedom* (Boston: Houghton Mifflin, 1962), 153.

2. Ibid., 26, 14.

3. Ibid., 37, 115.

4. Chester Bowles, "Blueprint for a Second New Deal," in *Saving American Capitalism: A Liberal Economic Program*, ed. Seymour Edwin Harris (New York: Alfred A. Knopf, 1948), 19.

5. Carl Solberg, *Hubert Humphrey: A Biography* (New York: W. W. Norton, 1984), 114, 116.

6. Alonzo L. Hamby, *Beyond the New Deal: Harry S. Truman and American Liberalism* (New York: Columbia University Press, 1973), 203.

7. Hubert H. Humphrey and Norman Sherman, *The Education of a Public Man: My Life and Politics* (Minneapolis: University of Minnesota Press, 1991), 29.

8. Ibid., 55.

9. Humphrey and Sherman, *The Education of a Public Man*, 113; Solberg, *Hubert Humphrey*, 116.

10. Humphrey and Sherman, *The Education of a Public Man*, 46; Steven Gillon, *Politics and Vision: The ADA and American Liberalism, 1947–1985* (New York: Oxford University Press, 1987), 47.

11. Hubert Humphrey, "Speech at the Democratic National Convention," Philadelphia, July 13, 1948. The audio, but not the video, of the speech is available on YouTube: MrJohnCJ00, "Hubert Humphrey 1948 Democratic National Convention," 9:51, posted December 6, 2012, www.youtube.com/watch?v=-xQZX5ZvcnY&t=123s.

12. "The Great Decision," *New Republic*, April 7, 1917.

13. Stuart Patrick, *The Best Laid Plans: The Origins of American Multilateralism and the Dawn of the Cold War* (Lanham, MD: Rowman & Littlefield, 2009), 106.

14. G. John Ikenberry, *Liberal Leviathan* (Princeton, NJ: Princeton University Press, 2011), 119, 146.

15. George Marshall, "The Marshall Plan Speech," Harvard University, June 5, 1947, George C. Marshall Foundation, www.marshallfoundation.org/marshall/the-marshall-plan/marshall-plan-speech; George Herring, *From Colony to Superpower: U.S. Foreign Relations Since 1776* (New York: Oxford University Press, 2008), 620.

16. Arthur Schlesinger Jr., *The Politics of Hope* (Boston: Houghton Mifflin, 1963), 68; Reinhold Niebuhr, "The Sources of American Prestige," in *Major Writings on Religion and Politics* (New York: Library of America, 2015), 670.

17. George H. Nash, *The Conservative Intellectual Movement in America Since 1945* (New York: Basic Books, 1976), 58; Hartz, *The Liberal Tradition in America*, 5ff.

18. William Buckley and L. Brent Bozell, *McCarthy and His Enemies: The Record and Its Meaning* (New Rochelle, NY: Arlington House, 1970).

19. Nash, *The Conservative Intellectual Movement*, 123.

20. Schlesinger, *Politics of Hope*, 81, 93.

21. G. Calvin Mackenzie and Robert Weisbrot, *The Liberal Hour: Washington and the Politics of Change in the 1960s* (New York: Penguin, 2009), 14.

22. John Kenneth Galbraith, *The Affluent Society* (Boston: Houghton Mifflin, 1958), 60, 115.

23. Ibid., 308, 276.

24. Humphrey and Sherman, *Education of a Public Man*, 165–166.

25. Gillon, *Politics and Vision*, 132; Humphrey and Sherman, *Education of a Public Man*, 180; John F. Kennedy, "Inaugural Address," Washington, DC, January 20, 1961, Our Documents, National History Day, National Archives and Records Administration, and USA Freedom Corps, www.ourdocuments .gov/doc.php?flash=false&doc=91&page=transcript.

26. Gillon, *Politics and Vision*, 139.

27. Stephen E. Ambrose and Douglas Brinkley, *Rise to Globalism: American Foreign Policy Since 1938* (New York: Penguin, 2011), 194.

28. Solberg, *Hubert Humphrey*, 227.

29. Galbraith, *The Affluent Society*, 323.

30. Lyndon B. Johnson, "January 20, 1965: Inaugural Address" (video), Washington, DC, January 20, 1965, Miller Center, University of Virginia, https://millercenter.org/the-presidency/presidential-speeches/january-20-1965 -inaugural-address; Lyndon Johnson, "Howard University Commencement Address," Howard University, June 4, 1965, *The American Yawp Reader*, www .americanyawp.com/reader/27-the-sixties/lyndon-johnson-howard-university -commencement-address-1965.

31. Mackenzie and Weisbrot, *The Liberal Hour*, 102–103.

32. Robert Alan Goldberg, *Barry Goldwater* (New Haven, CT: Yale University Press, 1995), 49.

33. Ibid., 145; Barry Goldwater, *The Conscience of a Conservative* (Princeton, NJ: Princeton University Press, 2007), 30, 56.

34. Reinhold Niebuhr, "Goldwater Versus History," in *Major Writings*, 685.

CHAPTER 6: THE END OF HISTORY IN POSTWAR EUROPE

1. H. W. Koch, *A Constitutional History of Germany in the Nineteenth and Twentieth Centuries* (London: Longman, 1984), 64.

2. Ralf Dahrendorf, *Society and Democracy in Germany* (Garden City, NY: Anchor, 1969), 379.

3. Koch, *A Constitutional History of Germany*, 334.

4. Wolfgang J. Mommsen, *Max Weber and German Politics, 1890–1920* (Chicago: University of Chicago Press, 1984), 345; Edmund Fawcett, *Liberalism: The Life of an Idea* (Princeton, NJ: Princeton University Press, 2014), 305.

5. Steven Greer, Laurence W. Gormley, and Jo Shaw, *The European Convention on Human Rights: Achievements, Prospects and Problems* (New York: Cambridge University Press, 2006), 14.

6. European Social Charter, October 18, 1961, Turin, Italy, Council of Europe, European Treaty Series No. 35, https://rm.coe.int/168006b642.

7. Sartre is quoted in Brian C. Anderson, *Raymond Aron: The Recovery of the Political* (Lanham, MD: Rowman & Littlefield, 1997), 14.

8. Ibid., 8.

9. Bernard-Henri Lévy, *Left in Dark Times: A Stand Against the New Barbarism* (New York: Random House, 2008), 85.

10. Ibid., 58; Raymond Aron, "Solzhenitsyn and European 'Leftism,'" in *In Defense of Political Reason* (Boston: Rowman & Littlefield, 1994), 118.

11. Charter 77, January 1, 1977, "Making the History of 1989," item #628, Roy Rosenzweig Center for History and New Media, George Mason University, http://chnm.gmu.edu/1989/archive/files/declaration-of-charter-77_4346 bae392.pdf.

12. Lévy, *Left in Dark Times*, 103.

13. Milan Kundera, "A Kidnapped West or Culture Bows Out," *Granta* 11, March 1, 1984, https://granta.com/a-kidnapped-west-or-culture-bows-out/.

14. Václav Havel, "The Power of the Powerless," in Václav Havel et al., *The Power of the Powerless: Citizens Against the State in Central-Eastern Europe* (Armonk, NY: M. E. Sharp, 1985), 29–30, 40.

15. Adam Michnik, "On Resistance: A Letter from Bialoleka 1982," in *Letters from Prison and Other Essays*, trans. Maya Latynski (Berkeley: University of California Press, 1985), 88.

16. Timothy Garton Ash, *The Magic Lantern: The Revolution of '89 Witnessed in Warsaw, Budapest, Berlin, and Prague* (New York: Random House, 1999), 151.

17. Jürgen Habermas, "What Does Socialism Mean Today? The Rectifying Revolution and the Need for New Thinking on the Left," *New Left Review* 183, September/October 1990, https://newleftreview.org/I/183/jurgen-habermas-what-does-socialism-mean-today-the-rectifying-revolution-and-the-need-for-new-thinking-on-the-left.

18. Ivan T. Berend, *Europe Since 1980* (New York: Cambridge University Press, 2010), 79.

CHAPTER 7: THE GREAT SOCIETY GOES UP IN FLAMES

1. Thomas Byrne Edsall with Mary D. Edsall, *Chain Reaction: The Impact of Race, Rights, and Taxes on American Politics* (New York: W. W. Norton, 1991), 49.

2. The Port Huron Statement of the Students for a Democratic Society, June 11–15, 1962, Citizen Source, www.citizensource.com/History/20thCen /PHS.pdf.

3. Lyndon B. Johnson, "April 7, 1965: Address at Johns Hopkins University" (video), Johns Hopkins University, April 7, 1965, Miller Center, University of Virginia,https://millercenter.org/the-presidency/presidential-speeches/april-7 -1965-address-johns-hopkins-university.

4. Todd Gitlin, *The Sixties: Years of Hope, Days of Rage* (New York: Bantam Books, 1993), 184, 256, 242.

5. Edsall and Edsall, *Chain Reaction*, 59.

6. Ibid., 70.

7. Humphrey and Sherman, *Education of a Public Man*, 297.

8. Wallace is quoted in Edsall and Edsall, *Chain Reaction*, 22.

9. Edsall and Edsall, *Chain Reaction*, 5.

10. Office of Policy Planning and Research, Department of Labor, *The Negro Family: The Case for National Action*, March 1965, https://web.stanford.edu /~mrosenfe/Moynihan%27s%20The%20Negro%20Family.pdf.

11. Daniel P. Moynihan, "The Politics of Stability," in *Coping: Essays on the Practice of Government* (New York: Random House, 1973), 191.

12. Daniel P. Moynihan, "Politics as the Art of the Impossible," in *Coping*, 255.

13. Ted Van Dyk, "School Busing Didn't Work. And to Say So Isn't Racist," *Politico*, August 6, 2015, www.politico.com/magazine/story/2015/08/school -busing-civil-rights-121077.

14. Morton Kondracke and Fred Barnes, *Jack Kemp: The Bleeding-Heart Conservative Who Changed America* (New York: Sentinel, 2015), 17.

15. Geoffrey Kabaservice, *Rule and Ruin: The Downfall of Moderation and the Destruction of the Republican Party, from Eisenhower to the Tea Party* (New York: Oxford University Press, 2012), 352.

16. Bruce R. Bartlett, *Reaganomics: Supply-Side Economics in Action* (Westport, CT: Arlington House Publishers, 1981).

17. Jack Kemp, *An American Renaissance: A Strategy for the 1980s* (New York: Harper & Row, 1979), 20.

18. Kemp's speech is quoted in Bartlett, *Reaganomics*, 219.

19. Kondracke and Barnes, *Jack Kemp*, 81; David Stockman, *The Triumph of Politics: How the Reagan Revolution Failed* (New York: Harper & Row, 1986), 49.

20. Ronald Reagan, "A Time for Choosing" (speech), Los Angeles, October 27, 1964, American Rhetoric, www.americanrhetoric.com/speeches/ronald reaganatimeforchoosing.htm.

21. Michael Sean Winters, *God's Right Hand: How Jerry Falwell Made God a Republican and Baptized the American Right* (New York: HarperOne, 2012), 143.

22. Ibid., 324.

23. Irving Kristol, "Confessions of a True, Self-Confessed—Perhaps the Only—Neoconservative," in *Reflections of a Neoconservative: Looking Back, Looking Ahead* (New York: Basic Books, 1983), 75.

24. Irving Kristol, "On Corporate Capitalism in America," in *Reflections of a Neoconservative*, 212.

25. Stockman, *The Triumph of Politics*, 48.

26. Irving Kristol, "Human Nature and Social Reform," in *Reflections of a Neoconservative*, 77.

27. Thomas Piketty, *Capital in the Twenty-First Century* (Cambridge, MA: Belknap Press, 2013), 24.

28. Jackson is quoted in Edsall and Edsall, *Chain Reaction*, 207.

29. William Galston and Elaine Ciulla Kamarck, *The Politics of Evasion: Democrats and the Presidency*, Progressive Policy Institute, September 1989, www .progressivepolicy.org/wp-content/uploads/2013/03/Politics_of_Evasion.pdf.

30. David Mills, "Sister Souljah's Call to Arms," *Washington Post*, May 13, 1992, www.washingtonpost.com/archive/lifestyle/1992/05/13/sister-souljahs-call -to-arms/643d5634-e622-43ad-ba7d-811f8f5bfe5d.

31. Bill Clinton, *My Life* (New York: Vintage, 2005), 411.

32. Steven Levitsky and Daniel Ziblatt, *How Democracies Die* (New York: Crown, 2018), 102.

33. Dan Balz and Ronald Brownstein, *Storming the Gates: Protest Politics and the Republican Revival* (Boston: Little, Brown, 1996), 321.

34. Steven Gillon, *The Pact: Bill Clinton, Newt Gingrich, and the Rivalry That Defined a Generation* (New York: Oxford University Press, 2008), 36–37; Newt Gingrich, *Window of Opportunity* (New York: Tom Doherty Associates, 1984), 6, 11.

35. Newt Gingrich, *To Renew America* (New York: HarperCollins, 1995), 8.

36. Clinton, *My Life*, 601.

37. Gillon, *The Pact*, 207.

38. Jeffrey Toobin, *Too Close to Call: The Thirty-Six-Day Battle to Decide the 2000 Election* (New York: Random House, 2001), 7.

39. George W. Bush, State of the Union Address, January 29, 2002, White House Archives, https://georgewbush-whitehouse.archives.gov/news/releases /2002/01/20020129-11.html.

40. Gary C. Jacobson, *A Divider, Not a Uniter: George W. Bush and the American People* (New York: Pearson Longman, 2006), 5.

41. Barack Obama, *The Audacity of Hope* (New York: Crown, 2006), 36, 37; "Illinois Sen. Barack Obama's Speech," Associated Press, February 10, 2007, www.washingtonpost.com/wp-dyn/content/article/2007/02/10/AR2007021000879.html.

42. Barack Obama, "Barack Obama's Keynote Address at the 2004 Democratic National Convention," Boston, Massachusetts, July 27, 2004, *PBS NewsHour*, PBS, www.pbs.org/newshour/show/barack-obamas-keynote-address-at-the-2004-democratic-national-convention.

43. Glenn Kessler, "When Did McConnell Say He Wanted to Make Obama a 'One-Term' President?," *Washington Post*, September 25, 2012, www.washingtonpost.com/blogs/fact-checker/post/when-did-mcconnell-say-he-wanted-to-make-obama-a-one-term-president/2012/09/24/79fd5cd8-0696-11e2-afff-d6c7f20a83bf_blog.html.

44. Jack Cashill, *"You Lie!": The Evasions, Omissions, Fabrications, Frauds, and Outright Falsehoods of Barack Obama* (New York: Broadside Books, 2014), 47; Will Bunch, *The Backlash: Right-Wing Radicals, Hi-Def Hucksters, and Paranoid Politics in the Age of Obama* (New York: HarperCollins, 2010), 55.

45. Bunch, *The Backlash*, 55.

46. James Traub, "The Right Against the Law," *Democracy: A Journal of Ideas*, fall 2018, no. 50, https://democracyjournal.org/magazine/50/the-right-against-the-law/.

CHAPTER 8: EUROPE IN THE GRIP OF NATIONALISM

1. "Double-Take: Poland's Top Leaders Are Twins," Associated Press, July 10, 2006, www.nbcnews.com/id/13800932/ns/world_news-europe/t/double-take-polands-top-leaders-are-twins/#.XMNdLS-ZP5Y.

2. Viktor Orbán, "Speech at the Bálványos Free Summer University and Youth Camp," Băile Tușnad, Romania, July 26, 2014, *Budapest Beacon*, https://budapest beacon.com/full-text-of-viktor-orbans-speech-at-baile-tusnad-tusnadfurdo-of-26-july-2014/.

3. The source for this quotation has been taken down from the AEI website.

4. Marlise Simons, "Rotterdam Journal: Proudly Gay, and Marching the Dutch to the Right," *New York Times*, March 12, 2002, www.nytimes.com/2002/03/22/world/rotterdam-journal-proudly-gay-and-marching-the-dutch-to-the-right.html.

5. Bruno Waterfield, "Ban Koran Like Mein Kampf, Says Dutch MP," *The Telegraph*, August 9, 2007, www.telegraph.co.uk/news/worldnews/1559877/Ban

-Koran-like-Mein-Kampf-says-Dutch-MP.html; Wilders speech at Koblenz, January 22, 2017, at www.youtube.com/watch?v=_uXsn_QGY2g&feature =youtu.be&fbclid=IwAR2s0xWNC8Zjp3bw_PTyxTHeRBL3J_NWWuJVaj EdlOJjK58jVuymuMpOzCI.

6. See Christopher Caldwell, *Reflections on the Revolution in Europe: Immigration, Islam and the West* (New York: Doubleday, 2009) for extensive analysis of poll findings as well as the broader question of the integration of Islam in Europe.

7. Shadi Hamid, *Islamic Exceptionalism: How the Struggle over Islam Is Reshaping the World* (New York: St. Martin's Press, 2016), 244.

8. Cas Mudde and Cristóbal Rovira Kaltwasser, *Populism: A Very Short Introduction* (New York: Oxford University Press, 2017).

9. The discussion of Sweden here draws on reporting I did for *Foreign Policy*, previously published in "The Death of the Most Generous Nation on Earth," *Foreign Policy*, February 10, 2016, https://foreignpolicy.com/2016/02/10 /the-death-of-the-most-generous-nation-on-earth-sweden-syria-refugee-europe.

10. Steven Erlanger, "Migration in Europe Is Slowing, but the Political Issue Is as Toxic as Ever," *New York Times*, June 22, 2018, www.nytimes.com/2018/06/22 /world/europe/migration-europe-merkel-seehofer-germany.html.

CHAPTER 9: THE POPULIST PLUTOCRAT

1. James Traub, "Trumpologies," *New York Times Magazine*, September 12, 2004, www.nytimes.com/2004/09/12/magazine/trumpologies.html.

2. Donald Trump, "Presidential Announcement Speech," New York, June 16, 2015, *Time*, http://time.com/3923128/donald-trump-announcement-speech/; Ted Cruz, "Speech at Liberty University," Lynchburg, Virginia, March 23, 2015, *Washington Post*, www.washingtonpost.com/politics/transcript-ted-cruzs-speech -at-liberty-university/2015/03/23/41c4011a-d168-11e4-a62f-ee745911a4ff _story.html.

3. Jan-Werner Müller, *What Is Populism?* (Philadelphia: University of Pennsylvania Press, 2016), 21.

4. Arthur Schlesinger Jr., "Liberalism in America: A Note for Europeans," in *The Politics of Hope* (Boston: Houghton Mifflin, 1963), 63.

5. "Transcript: Read the Full Text of the Primetime Republican Debate," *Time*, August 11, 2015, http://time.com/3988276/republican-debate-primetime -transcript-full-text/; Donald Trump, "Speech at Las Vegas, Nevada, Rally" (video), Las Vegas, Nevada, October 8, 2015, Shallow Nation, www

.shallownation.com/2015/10/05/video-donald-trump-speech-at-las-vegas
-nevada-rally-oct-8-2015/.

6. Trump, "Presidential Announcement Speech."

7. Yascha Mounk, *The People vs. Democracy: Why Our Freedom Is in Danger and How to Save It* (Cambridge, MA: Harvard University Press, 2018), 35.

CHAPTER 10: WHY DID ONE-HALF OF AMERICA CHOOSE ILLIBERAL DEMOCRACY?

1. Edward Luce, *The Retreat of Western Liberalism* (New York: Atlantic Monthly Press, 2017), 31–35.

2. Anne Case and Angus Deaton, "Mortality and Morbidity in the 21st Century," *Brookings Papers on Economic Activity*, Spring 2017, www.brookings .edu/wp-content/uploads/2017/08/casetextsp17bpea.pdf.

3. Max Ehrenfreund, "A Majority of Millennials Now Reject Capitalism, Poll Shows," *Washington Post*, April 26, 2016, www.washingtonpost.com/news /wonk/wp/2016/04/26/a-majority-of-millennials-now-reject-capitalism-poll-shows/.

4. Arlie Hochschild, *Strangers in Their Own Land: Anger and Mourning on the American Right* (New York: The New Press, 2016), 92.

5. Ibid., 14.

6. Ibid., 138–139.

7. Patrick Deneen, *Why Liberalism Failed* (New Haven, CT: Yale University Press, 2018), 24–34.

8. Ed Pilkington, "Obama Angers Midwest Voters with Guns and Religion Remark," *Guardian*, April 14, 2008, www.theguardian.com/world/2008/apr/14 /barackobama.uselections2008.

9. "Americans' Views on the Media" (press release), Ipsos Public Affairs, August 7, 2018, www.ipsos.com/en-us/news-polls/americans-views-media-2018-08-07; Anthony Brooks, "Trump Labels News Media 'Enemy of the American People,'" *On Point*, WBUR, Boston, July 31, 2018, www.wbur.org/onpoint/2018/07/31 /trump-labels-news-media-enemy-of-the-american-people.

10. Jason Schwartz, "Fox News Hosts Ramp Up 'Deep State' Conspiracies," *Politico*, January 26, 2018, www.politico.com/story/2018/01/26/fox-news -deep-state-conspiracies-372856.

11. Timothy Snyder, *On Tyranny: Twenty Lessons from the Twentieth Century* (New York: Tim Duggan Books, 2017); Timothy Snyder, *The Road to Unfreedom: Russia, Europe, America* (New York: Tim Duggan Books, 2018); Steven Levitsky and Daniel Ziblatt, *How Democracies Die* (New York: Crown, 2018).

CHAPTER 11: A LIBERAL NATIONALISM

1. David Runciman, *How Democracy Ends* (New York: Basic Books, 2018), 24.

2. Walter Weyl, *The New Democracy* (New York: Macmillan, 1912), 152.

3. Theodore Roosevelt, "New Nationalism Speech," Osawatomie, Kansas, August 31, 1910, Teaching American History, http://teachingamericanhistory .org/library/document/new-nationalism-speech/.

4. Summers is quoted in Edward Luce, *The Retreat of Western Liberalism* (New York: Atlantic Monthly Press, 2017), 71.

5. Dani Rodrik, *The Globalization Paradox* (New York: W. W. Norton, 2011), xvii.

6. James B. Conant, "Wanted: American Radicals," *Atlantic Monthly*, May 1943, www.theatlantic.com/past/docs/issues/95sep/ets/radical.htm.

7. Luce, *The Retreat of Western Liberalism*, 44–45.

8. Anemona Hartocollis, "What Would Happen if Harvard Stopped Considering Race in Admissions?," *New York Times*, October 23, 2018, www.nytimes .com/2018/10/23/us/harvard-admissions-race.html.

9. Herbert Croly, *The Promise of American Life* (Princeton, NJ: Princeton University Press, 2014), 95.

10. Jill Lepore, "A New Americanism," *Foreign Affairs*, March/April 2019, www.foreignaffairs.com/articles/united-states/2019-02-05/new-americanism -nationalism-jill-lepore.

11. Mark Lilla, *The Once and Future Liberal: After Identity Politics* (New York: HarperCollins, 2017), 90.

12. Alexander Hamilton, "Federalist No. 78," in *The Federalist Papers*, ed. Isaac Kramnick (New York: Penguin Books, 1987), 437.

13. Yascha Mounk, *The People vs. Democracy: Why Our Freedom Is in Danger and How to Save It* (Cambridge, MA: Harvard University Press, 2018), 53–98.

14. Arthur M. Schlesinger Jr., *The Vital Center: The Politics of Freedom* (Boston: Houghton Mifflin, 1962), 153.

Index

JAMES TRAUB has spent the last forty years as a journalist for America's leading publications, including the *New Yorker* and the *New York Times Magazine*. He now teaches foreign policy and intellectual history at New York University and at NYU Abu Dhabi, and is a columnist and contributor at *Foreign Policy*. He is the author of six previous books on foreign and domestic affairs, including *John Quincy Adams: Militant Spirit*. He lives in New York City.